THE BOOK OF REVELATION IN A POST-CHRISTIAN WORLD:

Yesterday's Message for Today's Culture

By J. Rodney Taylor

Other Books by Dr. J. Rodney Taylor

So You Want to Build a House: How to Be a Self-Contractor

Countdown to Midnight **A Novel**

The Signs of the Christ: A New Perspective on the Gospel of John **Textbook Edition**

The Signs of the Christ: Study Guide

The Signs of the Christ: Teacher's Guide

The Dead Sea Scrolls and the Gospel of Matthew

The Anatomy of Major Gifts: Seeking Gifts from the Super Wealthy

THE BOOK OF REVELATION IN A POST-CHRISTIAN WORLD: YESTERDAY'S MESSAGE FOR TODAY'S CULTURE

ISBN: 9798540342322

Cover Design by Craig Granger, Las Vegas, Nevada

Printed in the United States of America.

U. S. Printing History
First Edition: 2021

Published by Iron Horse Publishing
Franklin, Tennessee

IRON HORSE PUBLISHING

DEDICATION

For her encouragement and companionship, I dedicate this book to Patty, my wife of more than sixty years. To the members of the former Sanctuary Bible Class of First Baptist Church, Pensacola, Florida, and especially to John Holder, who met the Master face to face in November 2005, I also offer a special word of dedication.

ENDORSEMENTS

I love the Bible but would never elevate myself as a trained theologian. It's obvious Rodney Taylor loves the Word just as I do, and I am pleased that he has provided these insights on Jesus Christ's revelation to the Apostle John. At this point in my life I'm like the custodian when asked by seminary students, "What? After centuries of disagreement over the Book of Revelation, you have it all figured out?" He replied, "I do. Jesus wins!" Thank you, Rodney, for shining light on this marvelous book of Scripture.

Kay DeKalb Smith
Singer, Speaker, Humorist
Nashville, Tennessee

It has been said that the book of Revelation is the book that people in the church most want to hear preached, because they don't know what it means. It has also been said that Revelation is the book of the Bible that most preachers don't want to preach, because they don't know what it means either! This is exactly the reason I'm grateful that my friend and fellow church member Rodney Taylor has poured his heart into this volume, as it will help both people and preachers alike grasp the power and perspective of the Book of Revelation. Written with the skill of a scholar and the heart of a Bible teacher, *The Book of Revelation in a Post-Christian World* is clear, accessible, and powerful. In challenging times, the church needs not to fear the message of Revelation but rather be encouraged and strengthened by its central truth: *The kingdom of this world has now become the kingdom of our Lord and of his Christ and he will reign forever and ever!*

Jay Strother
South Region Lead Pastor
Brentwood Baptist Church
Brentwood, Tennessee

Several years ago, I preached through the Seven Signs of Jesus from the book of John. I learned Rodney Taylor had written a book on the Signs. I got it and quickly devoured it. His thoughtful work helped me greatly in my study and preaching. He has done it again with the book of Revelation. If you are an academic, you will appreciate Rodney's scholarship. If you are someone simply wanting to understand the Bible better, you will enjoy the way he is down to earth. In short, if you are looking for a book to help you better understand and apply one of the Bible's most interesting books, Rodney Taylor's work will benefit you tremendously.

Matt Pearson, Teaching Pastor
Church at West Franklin
Franklin, Tennessee

My Dad, who pastored until age 83, is a great Bible student and understands the book of Revelation quite well. I have sat under preaching and learned from some of the best preachers in America. All those people have seminary educations. To say that Revelation is an easy book to understand is inaccurate, but the way my friend J. Rodney Taylor – also seminary-educated – has broken down this complex book makes it possible for anyone to comprehend. And it's not just the teachings of God, revealed to John, that are to be understood in this fine work. The timeliness of this glimpse into Rodney's mind and the realization that Revelation is as fresh in 2021 as it was when it was written more than 1,900 years ago will be a key takeaway from anyone who invests the time to uncover what I believe is a God-ordained exposition of the Bible's final book. Whether you stand before a congregation or read for your own edification, *The Book of Revelation in a Post-Christian World* should be in your library.

Dennis K. Morgan
Franklin, Tennessee

There's nothing like a late-night discussion on theology, and if you can get into the Book of Revelation, so much the better! This is why I'm so excited my friend, Rodney Taylor, has released his new book on Revelation. Getting this book is like sitting down with an old friend to talk about something that really matters. Get your coffee. Grab your pen to write in the margins. Probably like me, you'll disagree some and agree even more, but through it all, you'll come away celebrating the glory and wonder that is The Revelation of John.

Dr. Mike Glenn, Senior Pastor
Brentwood Baptist Church
Brentwood, Tennessee

The *Book of Revelation in a Post Christian World: Yesterday's Message for Today's Culture* compares and contrasts the apocalyptic imagery of the Book of Revelation to today's Post-Christian America. A unique feature of this work is that it surveys the historical events that illuminate the context of the Revelation and then makes application to our Post-Christian context. Dr. Taylor's friendly style of writing allows for a clear following and understanding concerning methods of interpretation and theological views employed to exegete the Book of Revelation, thus allowing the readers to grapple with confidence the difficult imagery recorded in the Book of Revelation. This book will be of immense value to theological students, pastors and laity who seek to understand and apply the Book of Revelation in a Post-Christian context.

Professor Doctor Godfrey Harold
Principal/CEO
Cape Town Baptist Seminary
Cape Town, South Africa

It is good to know that in the period of time in which we're living today that, at the end of it all, "Jesus wins!" Rodney Taylor's book on Revelation makes it clear that we have the hope of a great future ahead of us when we need the reminder the most. We are often afraid of the Book of Revelation because we don't know what it all means. How thankful I am for the encouragement and teaching that is brought to us from this book, and in a concise and clear way, so that we can take Rodney's teachings and apply them to our own lives. His sections on the applications to the Post-Christian world are especially helpful and spirit-filled. Rodney Taylor says it best himself when he tells us this Book of Revelation is "Yesterday's Message for Today's Culture." It is timely. It is needed today.

Alex-Zsolt
Musicianary
Nashville, Tennessee

The biblical Book of Revelation was inspired by God and is the only Book in the Canon of Scripture with a blessing pronounced on the reader (Revelation 1:3). As I began reading Rodney's book, my eyes were immediately opened to his heart and what Proverbs 23:7 says, "For as a man thinks in his heart, so is he." Reading this book helped me to see inside the author's heart. I saw a writer that loves and honors the Word of God. I saw a man that today would be considered a prophet. His passion and love for truth are obvious. His plea for his readers to remember that, "TODAY IS THE DAY OF SALVATION" is repeated many times. Even as we live in truly what I believe are the last days, the author's passion is for those who have not trusted Christ for eternal life to do so while they can. The author's prophetic warning is also evident for those who have been caught up in religion to forsake their own ways and trust in Jesus Christ for their salvation. The book recognizes the works of darkness and how Satan has blinded many church leaders and attenders from knowing without any doubt that they have eternal life. John, the writer of Revelation was an Apostle who emphasized knowing Jesus Christ personally and wrote in his Gospel what it meant to be a true follower of Jesus Christ. A true follower is one who is committed to loving and obeying the Word of God and as an evidence of God in one's life, loves others. In John 20: 30-31, John says he wrote these things (chapters 1-20) so we may believe that Jesus Christ is the Son of God. In I John 1:4 John says, "And these things I have written that your joy may be full." Eternity is too long not to be confident in your salvation.

The Book of Revelation was written to show us the hope we have in Christ and how the end of the story plays out. We have hope! As I read Rodney's book about the end times, I was immediately reminded of what the LORD said to the prophet Joel (1:2), "Has anything like this ever happened in your days, or in the days of your fathers?" The end of time is closer today than ever before, and I believe what the LORD said to Joel is as relevant to us in this post-Christian world as it was in Joel's days. TODAY IS THE DAY OF SALVATION!

Having read Rodney's book, my heart is made to rejoice in the hope we have through Christ Jesus. Truly the Holy Spirit that inspired John to write what he saw wanted us to remember there is an end; and for those who have found THE DAY OF SALVATION, it closes with a great celebration of praising our LORD for His unspeakable gift. Christ wins and Satan loses. Thanks for committing your time and life to such a worthy book!

Monty Lankford
Healthcare Executive/Political Strategist
Franklin, Tennessee

So very informative and helps a layman like me understand it.

Buddy Hyatt
Musician/Producer
Nashville, Tennessee

Many people have a hunger to know more about the future redemptive plans of God yet often struggle to make sense of the imagery and complex symbolism within the Book of Revelation. That's why I'm appreciative that Dr. Taylor has written a book that is both easy to understand and compels the reader to engage in further personal study and reflection about these timely scriptures. There have always been varying interpretations of these end-time events by pastors, theologians, laymen, etc. So, I'm grateful that Dr. Taylor promotes unity and provides clarity by emphasizing the urgent priority we should all have to consistently share the gospel with our lost and searching world. His encouragement to apply biblical truths from the book of Revelation practically will equip future generations of Christ-followers to confidently navigate a post-Christian context.

Aaron Bryant, Pastor
The Church at Avenue South
Nashville, Tennessee

TABLE OF CONTENTS

CHAPTER TITLE **PAGE**

CHAPTER TITLE	PAGE

ACKNOWLEDGMENTS

This book is the result of many years of studying the Book of Revelation. As a student at Southeastern Baptist Theological Seminary, I was privileged to work with one of the great New Testament scholars of the twentieth century, Dr. Edward A. McDowell. As his graduate assistant, he and I often engaged in theological discussions—high order stuff. But he was a man that acknowledged and appreciated the value of mentally and spiritually exercising one's theological thought processes. I could never match wits with his intellectual prowess or his knowledge of the New Testament. Nevertheless, it was always an uplifting experience.

Dr. McDowell was probably the greatest influence on my theological life. He helped me to understand the Gospel of John in a way that no other person has ever directed me. It remains, to this day, my most favorite book in the entire Bible.

Among the greatest influences he had on my life was to help me understand the Book of Revelation. As one of the most recognized authorities on Revelation, Dr. McDowell had earlier authored *The Meaning and Message of the Book of Revelation*. After having read this work, he and I would often meet and "discuss." I did not always agree with him, but he was inevitably wonderful in complimenting me on the depth of my thinking and even acknowledged that I could be right on occasion. Admittedly, this book will reflect the incredible influence he exerted on my theology of the Book of Revelation.

References to Ray Summer's book, *Worthy is the Lamb*, have also influenced me in many ways. A true Southern Baptist theologian of the past, his book on Revelation is a dynamic and living interpretation of this most misunderstood book. I am indebted to him for opening vistas of understanding to me about Revelation that I have hitherto not known.

A final source of both inspiration and thought is a series of sermons by Dr. John Bisagno, pastor of the First Baptist Church of Houston, Texas. In 1979-1980 Dr. Bisagno preached a series of fifty-two sermons on the Book of Revelation. In his characteristic, booming voice, he laid out Scripture and interpretation which, to this day, is recognized as one of the great sermon series of all time. I came to know John personally and told him how much I admired this series and hoped to use it one day as a basis for a book on Revelation. He not only approved but encouraged me to write such a book. I have, therefore, been inspired and influenced by this man and his incredible sermon series and have used it as a major resource for this book. I am indebted to this man of God, who is today abiding with his Heavenly Father.

This book is written in an effort to provide the layman with a perspective on the Book of Revelation that can be understood. It is, in part, a transcription of a series of lectures that I delivered at the First Baptist Church of Pensacola, Florida, in May 1984. Members of the class offered encouragement to me to put my ideas in a book, and several friends have supported that encouragement over the years, including Dr. Bisagno.

The book offers insight into Revelation that is also helpful to living in today's post-Christian world. It is not an attempt to provide a deep, detailed theological treatise or commentary on this marvelous book, rather it is simply one man's spiritual journey through the Apocalypse. Much of the interpretation of the text is based upon linguistic analysis and its impact on one's understanding of complex themes. Its goal is not only to help the reader comprehend the theological implications of what was written but also to provide strength in times of spiritual crisis.

As in The Revelation, this book is written both to inform and to encourage. It is my hope and prayer that these writings will offer you confidence in your daily walk with God, will provide strength in times of spiritual chaos and offer a hope that is both present and eternal.

INTRODUCTION

The Book of Revelation is considered by many people to be a rather bizarre literary work, a mystery not easily revealed. Thus, it is often misconstrued or misunderstood. To comprehend it properly, one must recognize the historical milieu in which it was written. Acknowledging this historical background against which Revelation was written provides a beginning point for unraveling the mystery.

Revelation was written during a time of extreme physical and spiritual crisis. Its purpose was to help first century Christians deal with the specific troubles and tribulations that arose out of this crisis. It was also written to offer these believers support and encouragement along their spiritual journey. As with all of us who face crises in our lives—whether physical, material, social or spiritual—a little positive reinforcement that says, "all will be well," goes a long way toward providing the necessary strength to traverse the "valley of the shadow of death" or persevere in the face of disabling difficulty.

Let me emphasize, parenthetically, that this book is called THE Revelation. It is not the Book of Revelations but rather a single revelation from God to John the Apostle. The original title is the Αποκάλυψις Ἰωάννου, (*Apokalupsis Iōannou),* which is translated as "The Apocalypse (or Revelation) of John." Αποκάλυψις (*Apokalupsis*), used 19 times in the New Testament, means an "unveiling, uncovering." As a verb it is used 26 times in the New Testament and means to "reveal" or "make known." So, this Revelation of John is an unveiling of a very special message. It is, of course, not the Revelation of John but "The Revelation of Jesus Christ" given to John through an angel. It should always be referenced in the singular as the "Book of the Revelation."

Revelation is a part of a classification of writings that is referred to as apocalyptic literature, that is, its nature or character is solely eschatological. The term "eschatology" is derived from two Greek words, ἔσχατος, (*eschatos)* and λόγος, (*logos)* which, when combined, literally means "the study of last things" or "the study of events that lead up to the second coming of Christ." It refers generally to the end time, the time when Jesus will return to earth, the millennial period, the tribulation and ultimately the end of the earth as we know it. The use of the term ἔσχατος (*eschatos*) or any of its

English derivatives refers to the second coming of Jesus and the end of time.

Revelation is, therefore, a book of eschatology. Its coded message not only provided encouragement to the Christians who were experiencing extreme persecution, but it also became the means through which God conveyed, under the inspiration of the Holy Spirit and through the pen of John, how events would transpire in the end time. It is not a book of wild predictions or forecasts; it is not a worldly book; it is a spiritual one with an intentional message designed to inform the Christians of the first century that all will eventually be well, and to permit us, centuries later, a momentary prophetic glimpse of the events of the end time.

The message of the Book of Revelation was spoken by the Holy Spirit in a given historical setting, and it provides encouragement to modern Christians in whatever circumstance they may find themselves, revealing expectations with respect to the second coming of Christ. The lessons learned, then, are that (1) the Holy Spirit does not contradict Himself, (2) He is in control and (3) we are a part of that latter history of which the Book of Revelation speaks. The message that the Holy Spirit gave to these first century Christians is as valid for us in the twenty-first century as it was for them.

In June 2007 then Senator Barack Obama said, "Whatever we once were, we are no longer a Christian nation." At a 2009 press conference in Turkey as President of the United States, he re-emphasized his statement from 2007 by stating: "I've said before that one of the great strengths of the United States is – although as I mentioned we have a very large Christian population – we do not consider ourselves a Christian nation." With the advancement of the New World Order and the New Age movement, America has increasingly shifted from a Christian, constructive and confident perspective on life and society to a non-Christian, destructive and depressing attitude toward existence and culture. And while the world has never been considered to be pre-dominantly Christian, many of the principles laid down and lived and espoused by Jesus have been the foundation upon which many countries have based their laws and social traditions. Yet, like America, cultural change has led to devaluing these principles and traditions. It is these changes in our world, and especially my beloved America, that motivated me to write this book. So, throughout the book, the reader will encounter sections designed to apply the truths of The Revelation to these trends in our modern culture, both present and future.

Before we delve too deeply into the actual text of the Book of Revelation, an understanding of one important piece of background information is essential to even a perfunctory comprehension of its meaning and message. By any measure, Revelation is a mysterious book, so it is vital to recognize and acknowledge the purpose for which it was written, the background against which it was written and the method and character in which it was written. I have, therefore, written this book for the average reader who may or may not be a believer. While it is a bit scholarly in its approach, it is written in a form that proclaims a truly evangelical message. Both its purpose and its writing style offer a simple, easy-to-understand learning experience of a complicated, enigmatic and often misunderstood and misinterpreted book. It is my hope that, in this book, I have presented a clear and unambiguous view of the Book of Revelation that both interested layman and enquiring scholar can understand and appreciate. Furthermore, I pray that the gravity and transparency of the message is such as to cause a non-believer to re-think his/her spiritual condition and to profess faith in the One whose truth is revealed in this book.

Above all, remember that the message of Revelation is more important than the symbols contained in it. Because the real message of this marvelous book is to reveal who Jesus Christ is, then focus on the message. TODAY TRULY IS THE DAY OF SALVATION!

PROLOGUE

Before we take a deep dive into the meaning and message of the Book of Revelation, let's first explore the meaning of the context in which Revelation is being applied in this book—namely, post-Christianity. By understanding this context, we should be better able to observe any parallels between the message of Revelation and events in history or even experiences and occurrences in today's world.

We all know that we serve an omniscient God, a God who has designed a plan for His creation and who knows how that creation will respond to Him. He also designed a plan for our redemption, knowing that we would fall into the trap of sin and require a redeemer. In the same way, He designed a plan for sending that Redeemer as well as a strategy for disseminating the Gospel of that Redeemer.

Probably no better time in history could have been selected by our Heavenly Father to initiate the spread of the Gospel than the first and second centuries AD. From the time of Jesus' ascension, the disciples and the early church lived in a time and place perfectly prepared to receive the Gospel.

In AD 27 Caesar Augustus ascended the throne of Rome, having overthrown efforts by Marc Antony and Marcus Amelius Lepidus to gain control of Rome. For the next 200 years, a relative peace and a sense of stability characterized the Roman Empire. This period has come to be known as the *Pax Romana* or "Roman Peace." During this time, the Empire offered protection for and even governed the provinces with a light hand, allowing them to enact their own laws. It was a time of relative calm, tranquility and harmony—the ideal setting for the spread of the Good News of the Gospel of Jesus Christ and His church.

During the *Pax Romana*, the disciples shared their experiences with the Lord, and following Pentecost, the church was born. Because the Roman Empire did not bring down its heavy hand on the citizenry as it had in times past, the church strengthened, a missionary movement was launched, and the message of the Gospel spread like wildfire. Soon whole cultures were influenced, and, in AD 380, Roman emperor Theodocius decreed Christianity to be the state religion.

From that point until today, many nations and cultures have been heavily influenced by Christianity. Europe and the United States, especially, have recognized rights and enacted laws based upon the principles of Christianity. English common law was comprehensively inspired by the Bible as was many Western legal traditions. As the colonies of newly settled America established rules by which to live and laws to govern such rules, biblical principles, especially from the Mosaic Law, were employed as a background against which such laws could be created.

In the emergence of the American form, numerous differing religions joined the American experiment. With individual rights in mind, tolerance of dissenting views invested the culture with a mixture of ideas, with Christianity being the major inspiration. However, as time has progressed, the major influence on its political system, laws and culture has reverted to a mostly secular perspective. Evidence of such reversion can be observed in the decrease of empiricism and the increasing pressure of separatists, advocates for secularism and rationalists in matter of law and culture. Such evidence signals the declining influence of Christianity in an increasingly secular age.

A post-Christian world can be viewed by the replacement of a Christian worldview by such alternative worldviews as nationalism, secularism, environmentalism and even atheism. New Age movements, courses of life guided by roots from eastern ideologies and religions and one's individually defined *élan vital* have all been substituted for Christian principles espoused by Jesus and employed as a guide for developing the most powerful and successful culture in the history of the world.

The event that is considered to be the formative event for post-Christianity is the removal of prayer from the public schools in 1962. Other contributing factors include increasing tendencies toward evil, misrepresentation and ethical lapses of so many of our governmental official and escalating attacks on individual rights and collective culture. The desire, on the part of our governmental representatives as well as departmental leadership, for personal power and wealth has resulted in a level of moral decay never before experienced. Families are collapsing, schools are rewriting history to suit a specific agenda, relativity has become the norm, including with respect to the truth, and God is being evicted from every aspect of society. It is this kind of world in which we are called to be salt and light.

In a world where sex has become the common topic of discussion in the media, in a world where the name of Jesus is spoken as an exclamation, in a world where selfishness is best defined by our "selfies," in a world where lying by governmental officials has become the order of the day, in a world that is simply becoming increasingly evil, we are urged to preach the Gospel with an even greater motivation and intensity. So, it is this kind of world I seek to apply the message of The Revelation.

CHAPTER 1
CHARACTER OF APOCALYPTIC LANGUAGE AND LITERATURE

The Book of Revelation is first and foremost an apocalyptic book. Apocalyptic language is, by its very nature, vague and mysterious. In order to interpret the Apocalypse meaningfully, knowledge of the characteristics of apocalyptic literature is essential.

It has been generally recognized that two books written in apocalyptic language have been included in the canon of Scripture. And while there are fragments or remnants of other works that are apocalyptic in nature, none is written entirely in apocalyptic form. Besides Revelation, the other major apocalyptic book in the Bible is the Old Testament Book of Daniel.

Since the very word "apocalyptic" comes from the Greek ἀποκάλυψις (*apokalupsis*) which means "an unveiling," "a revealing," "a revelation," then apocalyptic literature is believed by many to have been written in a mysterious "code" which the Christians of the first century would likely have recognized and understood. It is generally characterized by basic features that no other literature possesses, and so stands in stark contrast to other types of literature of its day. As you understand these characteristics, you will see how the author weaves them into his message throughout the Book of Revelation. Many other scholars repudiate any codification in the book.

FIRST CHARACTERISTIC OF APOCALYPTIC LANGUAGE AND LITERATURE

One characteristic of apocalyptic literature is that it is always written in a particular setting and against a specific background in history. This means that actual historical events are employed to convey the writer's meaning. Generally, some kind of critical historical condition exists with which the apocalyptic message can be associated. The language and the message are not some isolated theological gobbledygook, but rather they have a specific historical setting to which they relate. Understanding the historical situation in which the author writes, then, provides help in ascertaining a correct interpretation of the words that are written in a specific apocalyptic message. Conversely, to take no notice of the historical circumstances is to ignore the key ingredient in the recipe for interpreting apocalyptic literature. Understanding the history of the times lays the very foundation for interpreting apocalyptic language.

APPLICATION TO OUR POST-CHRISTIAN WORLD

The post-Christian world is not so different from the world to which John wrote the Book of Revelation. First, our world, especially the political and economic universe in which we live, provides a complicated and intense background that often leads to actions and events that can be interpreted only against that known background. For example, a thousand years from now, when humans will be traveling, perhaps, in vehicles powered by hydrogen, atomic fuel rods, or some other futuristic form of locomotion, an unidentified archaeologist might unearth a twenty-first century hybrid automobile and wonder, "what kind of machine could this be"? By learning about the economic conditions of the world during the early twenty-first century, he will understand that this is a passenger-carrying vehicle commonly used during that time period and uniquely designed because of a perceived growing shortage of fossil fuel. By recognizing the historical setting in which that vehicle was designed and fabricated, the archaeologist can begin to unravel that mystery. So, too, Revelation can best be interpreted against the historical backdrop during which it was written. TODAY IS THE DAY OF SALVATION!

SECOND CHARACTERISTIC OF APOCALYPTIC LANGUAGE AND LITERATURE

A second characteristic is that the authors of apocalyptic literature generally do not identify themselves, that is to say, they use a pseudonym or false name. They would often write in the name of some great man of the past or even a famous personage of the present. Anonymity offered the writers the security of knowing that they could expect no backlash from powerful political adversaries or influential ecclesiastical authorities. They needed only to write down their visions, personally accepting no acclaim for them.

On the one hand, no consensus exists among scholars that the prophet Daniel wrote the book that bears his name. Many, however, hypothesize that it was likely written by someone else who used the name of the prophet because he was a well-known figure. On the other hand, John used his real name because he believed that, by attaching his name to the book, it would have a greater significance for and impact upon the people. People would tend to read the book and believe its words. He was little concerned about his own individual fame. He was little concerned with what personal gain would result from writing this covert yet puzzling treatise. He was far more concerned that the sole object of his writing be service to God and the well-being of his beloved fellow believers.

Inspired by God and by the visions he saw, John departed from the typical pseudonymous approach. Rather, he willingly offered his name as the author of The Revelation.

APPLICATION TO OUR POST-CHRISTIAN WORLD

Who of us living in these post-Christian times has not read a book authored by someone who wrote under a pseudonym? Consider these rather famous nineteenth and twentieth century writers whose given names are certainly not as well-known as their pen names: O'Henry, whose real name was William Sidney Porter or Mark Twain whose real name was Samuel Clemens or perhaps the most famous of all, Dr. Seuss whose real name was Theodore Geisel. As in the ancient apocalyptic writings so in our post-Christian world, the use of pseudonyms is not unique or unknown.

Today as then, however, the purpose of writing under a pseudonym remains generally unchanged. Writers often use pen names either to avoid fame or to preclude any threats that might result from the writings. John sought no fame, and the message of his book certainly produced a threat, but he was confident in God's protection and wrote under his actual name anyway. TODAY IS THE DAY OF SALVATION!

THIRD CHARACTERISTIC OF APOCALYPTIC LANGUAGE AND LITERATURE

A third characteristic of apocalyptic literature is the use of visions as a means of presenting the message. Recall the Book of Daniel and the marvelous visions interpreted by the prophet. In chapter 4, for example, notice how Daniel describes the vision of the great tree and ultimately interprets that vision for King Nebuchadnezzar. In chapter 7, Daniel portrays in vivid detail the vision of the four beasts; or in chapter 8, Daniel describes the vision of the ram and the he goat and offers an interpretation.

As in Daniel, so it is in the Book of Revelation that we read in meticulous detail how John employed visions to explain and convey specific information to the reader. The method was often used by prophets in their writings throughout the Old Testament (Ezekiel 1:1; 1:4f; 37:1f; Isaiah 1:1f; 21:2f). It was also employed by prophets who did not write books of the Old Testament but rather spoke prophecies (2 Samuel 7:4, 17; Genesis 15:1). However, in purely apocalyptic prose, visions were elevated to a quality of expression found in no other biblical writings. It was the chief method of expressing truth as the writer knew it.

Apocalyptic visions occur both in heaven and on earth. The figures comprising these visions include such heavenly personages as angels who actually oversee the revelation of the message to the one who experienced these visions.

Did the authors really encounter these visions or were they simply the results of the Seer's wild imagination? Could the visions simply have been a literary tool to convey a particular message to a particular people? We do not really know. Some scholars believe that the apocalyptic writers, for example the author of the Book of Revelation, in fact did physically hear and see God's message as revealed through the Holy Spirit; then out of his own background, out of the social, political, and economic conditions that surrounded him, and out of his own literary experience, he wrote his apocalypse. He created the images, he fashioned the revelation, employing both his experience and his imagination. But he employed these visions to portray a purpose and to convey a truth that had been revealed to him by the Holy Spirit.

Many divergent opinions exist in the theological world concerning whether the writer of Revelation introduced his own personal bias into the book. The form used by John in presenting the message of the Book of Revelation is of far less significance than the truths about which he was writing. After all, like any book in the Bible, The Revelation of John is a faith affirmation, and the value of that affirmation for one's faith is of far greater value than the form applied in either receiving or revealing that truth or any personal belief system implied. Such is the key to understanding this complex and often mysterious book.

APPLICATION TO OUR POST-CHRISTIAN WORLD

Our day is really no different from that of John, the Apocalyptist. Often modern-day "visionaries" appear in television programs or in accounts of murders and missing persons in the newspaper. They may claim to see the general location of a person, living or dead, or they hear the voices of loved ones who have already died, so it is not uncommon for psychics to be employed by police departments to assist in locating a body or a person. John's experiences as the Seer of Revelation place him among many who have encountered similar visions and testified to their truth. John, however, saw ultimate truth. He saw a God, high and lifted up, who saw the sufferings of his people and wept. Unlike the modern psychic, John saw and heard from the God of the universe who delivered a message of comfort and peace to his people through the Seer. TODAY IS THE DAY OF SALVATION!

FOURTH CHARACTERISTIC OF APOCALYPTIC LANGUAGE AND LITERATURE

Unique to the Book of Revelation is another fundamental characteristic of apocalyptic writings, its use of prediction. Probably better described as forth-telling, apocalyptic language typically was employed during very dark days, during times of uncertainty and bleak expectations. Not concerned with the details of the future, writers did not attempt specifically to forecast future occurrences or the results of these occurrences but simply wrote with broad strokes the nature of future events and their impact on the faithful. This written form offered readers an encouraging word in the midst of threatening and gloomy circumstances.

Understanding and acknowledging this predictive element is the key to interpreting this marvelous book rightly. It is at this very point that so many in today's world are lured into the trap of unsound doctrine. When one is so caught up with identifying current events with the message of Revelation, misinterpretation inevitably will occur. Are there signs and events in today's world to which the message of Revelation points. Of course. But all too often such efforts are simply an attempt to legitimize one's own theological position. However, to ascribe the events of Revelation to events occurring today without considering when it was written is to deny the historical setting out of which the book emerged. Its predictive element offers a general futurist view, a common forth telling which deals with the wide-ranging nature of the events of the future. But to spend precious time trying to legitimize the message of Revelation by matching its words with current events dismisses its purpose, namely evangelization and the spread of the Gospel.

The apocalyptic writer looked and saw evil all around him; he saw chaos and confusion; he witnessed the persecution of his friends and acquaintances; he daily observed disruption, disorder and disturbance. Yet his visions revealed a future of glory, triumph and, for modern man, freedom in the midst of a world characterized by moral decay, spiritual emptiness and widespread corruption. Apocalyptic literature offered an encouraging word that the future would be brighter, offered a hope for a better day and offered a word from God that "this too shall pass."

APPLICATION TO OUR POST-CHRISTIAN WORLD

In our post-Christian world, religions or cults often arise with a "unique foreknowledge" of the end of the world. Unlike these religions and cults, Revelation was not written to provide a specific timetable of events to which we can point and say "Oh, we have ten years to go before the end comes." Remember the words of Paul in 1 Thessalonians 5:1-2: "About the times and the seasons: Brothers, you do not need anything to be written to you. For you yourselves know very well that the Day of the Lord will come just like a thief in the night." Or consider the words of Jesus Himself when, in Matthew 24:35-36, He said: "Heaven and earth will pass away, but My words will never pass away. Now concerning that day and hour no one knows—neither the angels of heaven, nor the Son—except the Father only." So, while there is a distinctive predictive element in the Revelation, it is not intended to force us to the mountaintops to "await the Day of the Lord." TODAY IS THE DAY OF SALVATION!

FIFTH CHARACTERISTIC OF APOCALYPTIC LANGUAGE AND LITERATURE

Likely the most recognizable and baffling characteristic is the use of symbols in apocalyptic language. Many people who may not be theologically trained in the language and historical setting of

Revelation encounter difficulty in understanding its message because of the symbolism. Confusing and distorted interpretations abound because of the symbolism employed in the book. Often the idea of the symbols has been misrepresented to the point where the book's fundamental meaning has been lost. The symbol has **become** the meaning. Not true! The symbol is not the meaning, rather it is the meaning that underlies the symbol, that is far more important than the symbol itself. Uniquely, the writer of Revelation "was faced with the task of seeing the invisible, painting the unpaintable, and expressing the inexpressible."[1] He accomplished that formidable task through the use of symbols.

In order to deliver a message that would be understood by its intended readers, writers of this type of literature developed a complicated system of often confusing symbols and metaphorical expressions that were employed to communicate religious and spiritual ideas. The apocalyptic writer found himself responsible for making what he saw in his visions sufficiently clear to those who read them. The symbols have a meaning for those who recognize them and are familiar with the lingo. But for those who are not familiar with the language and who do not understand the symbols, the writings of apocalyptic are nothing more than the muddy, disconnected thoughts of a confused mind. This is not to say that there are not church-affiliated men and women who understand the symbolism and yet still have a murky and sometimes ambiguous understanding of what has been written. But also, not to be discounted is the fact that not a few interpreters of apocalyptic literature in general, and Revelation in particular, promulgate an ill-conceived belief system out of a selfish desire for some type of personal gain. Understanding the symbols will help one to avoid being drawn into a misguided belief system.

Remember, the writer is employing these symbols as a method of communicating his thoughts based upon his visions and the inspiration of the Spirit. The symbols are often arbitrary, and sometimes the use of these symbols is not even natural, but they are included to serve a purpose nonetheless.

One of the principal symbols employed in apocalyptic and especially in the Book of Revelation is the ancient system of numerology, the use of numbers. Understand, however, that numbers are not a uniquely biblical idea. They emerge from a long history and were used principally when they could add a measure of discernment for the reader. The symbol of the numbers found their basis in

Hebrew numerology, sometimes called the Gematria; it was common among the Hebrews and other ancient peoples. They were often used to represent ideas, thoughts, or even specific words.

Used so commonly, their concepts often were more easily communicated than by a series of words or sentences. The symbols became a kind of ancient shorthand.

Numbers symbolized ideas. For example, the number one expressed the idea of unity or wholeness. Fairly simple, isn't it? And it made sense. Independent existence, the number one. One stands alone. It was sometimes used in place of the indefinite article in the Hebrew language and might have been used to identify a non-specific individual such as "someone" or "anyone." Some commentators believe that it also represented God and his lordship as expressed in the *Shema*, the biblical entreaty, "The Lord our God, the Lord is One." (Deuteronomy 6:4)

The number two was a much stronger number; it was more effective than one. Two came to stand for one plus the strengthening of one, a confirmation of strength or a doubling of whatever object or character to which it might refer. (Note the two cherubim on the top of the Ark of the Covenant in Exodus 25:18f; the reference to a two-edged sword in Proverbs 5:4 and Hebrews 4:12; the testimony of two required to corroborate and strengthen truth.) Two could also stand for doubling whatever characteristic to which it might be applied. It was one better than one. It was two, and two represented strength.

The number three represented divinity or divine perfection. Consider examples of its divine symbolism in the Bible: Jonah in the belly of the whale for three days; Jesus, one of three crucified; Jesus in the tomb for three days; the Trinity, The Father, Son and Holy Spirit. What a number!

The number four represented the world, but more specifically an earthly representation of what ancient man thought of the physical world around him. For example, there are the four cardinal directions of the earth, north, south, east and west; the proverbial four winds; the four seasons; the four corners of the earth; and the four chambers of the human heart. In the Bible the fourth commandment is the first of the commandments to refer to the earth; the fourth clause of the Lord's Prayer is the first phrase in that prayer to refer to the earth. It would seem natural, therefore, that here in Revelation the four living creatures appear, representing the four classifications of animal life and the four horsemen who symbolize destructive forces in the world.

The number four referred to all that surrounded man, the natural world in which man lived. Four was a cosmic number, and it included the known universe.

The number seven symbolized fullness, maturity, completeness, some even say spiritual perfection. The number seven was considered to be a perfect number because it combined the divine number three with the earthly number four.

One interesting perspective on the use of the number seven is that of John Bisagno. He suggests that the period between Adam and Abraham was estimated to be 2,000 years; the time between Abraham and Jesus was 2,000 years; the period between Jesus and today is 2,000 years. Finally, there is to be a 1,000-year (millennial) reign of Jesus which will bring all of time to its completed end, all adding up to 7,000 years. The perfect plan of God.

Six was a fascinating number. Being one short of spiritual perfection, it possessed a very sinister meaning; it represented man and human weakness, the evils of Satan and the manifestation of sin. If seven was the number for divine perfection or completeness, the number six stood for evil because it fell just short of that perfection. No surprise. Six represented the runner who, in spite of intense effort, falls just short of the finish line; it snatched defeat from the jaws of victory; it spelled catastrophe.

It was also quite a powerful number. Representing Evil, it described Satan and his power, a power that matches that of God Himself. Read accounts of those who have personally experienced the power of Satan, and you will discover that Satan has immense power in this world. Evil exercises great power, and vigilance is essential lest we be overcome by Evil. Even though we dedicate ourselves to God, and we wish God to be the chief influence in our lives, even though we want God to be our God, we must be watchful.

Numerical multiples were ancillary but very important in the system of numerology. These multiples occur in many of the higher numbers found in the Book of Revelation. For example, seventy was a very sacred number. When Jesus was asked, "How many times does one forgive?" what did he say? "Seventy times seven." He used the word "seventy." How did he select that specific number? It is actually a multiple of seven, the number for spiritual perfection, times ten, the number representing human completeness. The two numbers together provided intense strength to each other. Jesus used the number seventy as a sacred number. Its combination of divine completeness and human completeness resulted in ultimacy or eternity.

The symbolism of this example means that the mature Christian forgives as many times as that Christian is wronged. Forgive forever, never hold a grudge, and never number the times that one forgives another.

While the number one thousand does not often appear, it is an important number because it represented ultimate completeness. A combination of ten (the number for divine completeness) times ten times ten, it symbolized completeness raised to the Nth degree.

As with all apocalyptic literature, Revelation contains a wealth of metaphorical language. From beasts to weapons and birds to the precious stones described in the wall of the New Jerusalem, all serve a single purpose. The symbols, the numbers and the metaphorical language are employed by the writer to convey to his readers the ultimate victory of Good over Evil.

APPLICATION TO OUR POST-CHRISTIAN WORLD

Not unlike John's world, people of the post-Christian era employ the use of symbols both reverently and irreverently. Who of you does not observe a bald eagle and think of the strength of our nation? Or who of you does not avoid the number 13? How often have you found a high rise building that has a floor number thirteen? Even some trademarks have become synonymous with the product to which that trademark is connected. For example, have you ever heard someone say, "I have my Kodak with me to take pictures?" Or "Put that in the Frigidaire." These are trade names that became synonymous with the camera and the refrigerator. So, the post-Christian world should not be afraid to read the Book of Revelation and recognize the value of symbols as a way of conveying truth.

Rather, the over-arching question for modern interpreters is, How can we understand these symbols and be confident of their meaning? The answer to this question lies in two sources, Jesus and the Scriptures. In parts of Revelation, Jesus will speak and offer an explanation of events and circumstances. After all, this is "the revelation of Jesus Christ that God gave Him." And since it is His prophecy, who better to explain it?

The second source is Scripture. The best interpretations of Scripture, especially the mysteries of Scripture, are best explained with other Scripture. Revelation is no different. By referring to other books of the Bible as well as texts in Revelation itself, some mysterious parts of Revelation can be explained. Further, the Bible throughout, including the Book of Revelation, abounds with interpretations of symbols and figurative language. In short, the Bible is its own best interpreter. We can trust the words of 1 Peter 1:20-21 to offer confidence in our interpretation when we rely on other Scripture, "He was chosen from the foundation of the world but was revealed at the end of times for you who through Him are believers in God, who raised Him from the dead and gave Him glory, so that your faith and hope are in God." TODAY IS THE DAY OF SALVATION!

SIXTH CHARACTERISTIC OF APOCALYPTIC LANGUAGE AND LITERATURE

Finally, apocalyptic literature is characterized by the use of high drama, and it is most effectively put to use by John in Revelation. The figures or symbols used by the Seer serve to convey the dramatic story of the power struggle between the dominion of God and Good over Satan and Evil. The high drama employed by the Seer adds an element of clarity in fulfilling the writer's purpose. These impressions are made even more vivid by his use of weird, grotesque and larger-than-life symbols. They are exaggerated but exaggerated for dramatic effect.

Let me make clear here that, although I consider Revelation as prophecy yet unfulfilled, we must weigh these characteristics when we interpret this book. Otherwise, it becomes such a mystery that we are overwhelmed and give up. And many people do! Each of these characteristics contributes to understanding this work. John wrote what he saw, and what he saw simply may have been a "type" of what actually will take place. By writing in symbols, he does not diminish the message.

APPLICATION TO OUR POST-CHRISTIAN WORLD

High drama. Our world is filled with it. No television set can be turned on without seeing evidence of drama, either fictionalized or in real time. Drama has a way of highlighting truth, fashioning truth and eliciting a response. John's use of drama should not go unnoticed by those of us in the post-Christian era. TODAY IS THE DAY OF SALVATION!

MILLENNIALISM

One of the most important theological doctrines emerging from the Book of Revelation is that of millennialism. The idea of a millennial kingdom dates back to the third century BCE. Evidence can be found in such inter-biblical books as 1 Enoch, 2 Enoch and Jubilees. It seems natural that the idea of a millennial kingdom would be a natural interpretation of the Book of Revelation.

Controversial, and with a myriad of interpretations, millennialism generally is the belief that there will be a period of a thousand years during which Christ will reign in peace with his saints on the earth. This belief finds its origin in Revelation 20:4: "Then I saw thrones, and people seated on them who were given authority to judge. I also saw the people who had been beheaded because of their testimony about Jesus and because of God's word, who had not worshiped the beast or his image, and who had not accepted the mark on their foreheads or their hands. They came to life and reigned with the Messiah for 1,000 years."

The time in which this millennial period occurs depends entirely upon one's interpretation of the book and millennial view. Literally interpreted, the thousand years is an actual event that will occur in the last days. If not viewed literally, these words are considered to be figurative or symbolic only. Both views accept the prospect of the thousand-year reign of Christ, but the difference lies in whether the years are a foretelling of actual events to come or simply a picture of the supremacy of Christ.

Among the millennialists, three groups are distinctly identifiable, and each has its own set of basic beliefs. While the common ingredient is the thousand years, each approaches the thousand years completely differently.

POST-MILLENNIALISM

Postmillennialism, which is historically the most recently asserted idea, is an eschatological view that focuses on the progressive goodness of man and the expansive impact of Christianity on the world. Systematized by Daniel Whitby (1638-1725), an Armenian priest in the Church of England and later a Unitarian, it supposes that we are actually living now in the "Millennium" and that, during this indefinitely long period of time, Christians are responsible for expanding the Kingdom of God in the world through

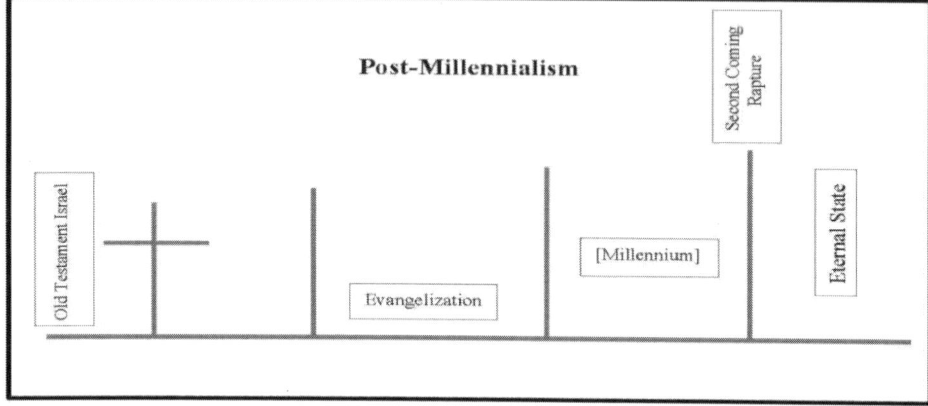

the preaching of the Gospel and the saving work of the Holy Spirit in the hearts of individuals.

Postmillennialists believe that the world will become increasingly good and, as more people are won to the Lord, the Millennium will become a progressively rising golden age of spiritual vibrancy with enriched social, economic, political and cultural life. The world will eventually enjoy a state of righteousness, reconciliation and reasonableness never before seen. Only after this state has been reached will Christ return. And upon Christ's return the Rapture will occur and Eternity begins.

Post-millennialism assumes that the thousand years mentioned in Revelation 20:1-6 refers to a figurative period of time. The "Millennium" will be a time when Christ will rule through the church. Best described as an optimist's view of the Millennium, Post-Millennialism adopts the position that by preaching the Gospel, through missionary work and through education, the world will eventually be won to Christ and a wonderful period of peace and prosperity will be experienced after which the Lord Jesus will come personally for a final Judgment, when both good and evil will be judged and the end of the world will occur. As a result, Christ will see the fulfillment of all that He sought for the earth and, satisfied with the state of man, Jesus will say to His angels, "Glory, Hallelujah. It's time for Me to return." Christ will then come back to earth to reclaim what belongs to Him. It is an evolutionary view, a view of continuous progress in which Satan's forces are gradually defeated in their attempt to subjugate the world—the classic "good will win over evil" story.

Post-millennialists hold that the thousand years are solely figurative, i.e., they may be only a brief time or a protracted span of time. Whether brief or extended, the Millennium will comprise a figurative thousand years. After this period of time, all of God's people will be taken to live with Him.

Since Christ will not come until after the Millennium, then the Lord will not reign during the Millennium. The reign of Christ will occur only after the thousand years, hence, "post-millennialism." Since the turn of the 20th century, as the world has exhibited ever increasing evil tendencies, this view has fallen into some disrepute. Today, many who have espoused this notion have shifted their position to A-Millennialism.

PRE-MILLENNIALISM

The literal interpreter of Revelation will also be a pre-millennialist. Pre-Millennialism views these verses of the thousand years as an actual time period during which Jesus will reign on the earth at His Second Coming. Generally considered to be an opposing view to Post-Millennialism, it is the belief that the Lord Jesus Christ will come literally and bodily prior to the Millennium. All of the covenants made with Israel literally will be fulfilled, and He will set up His kingdom and reign from the throne of David out of a rebuilt city of Jerusalem. Pre-Millennialism considers the end times as being initiated with the Rapture of the church subsequent to the Christian era followed by the seven-year Tribulation period. The central issue in this and all the other views is whether or not the Scriptures will be fulfilled literally or figuratively (symbolically).

At the beginning of the Tribulation, Christ will come *for* His saints and gather them to Him. After seven years in Paradise, Christ will then come *with* His saints, He will be enthroned in Jerusalem and the Millennium will commence. Christ and His saints reign for a thousand years on the earth during a Golden Age of peace and prosperity.

Once the thousand years is complete, Christ, the Son, will turn the Kingdom over to His Father, at which point it will merge with the eternal Kingdom of God the Father. Then will come the Great White

Throne Judgment and Eternity begins. The predominant concept of Pre-Millennialism is that Christ will appear personally **before** the millennial period; He will usher it in, and He will reign over the earth during the earth during this time.

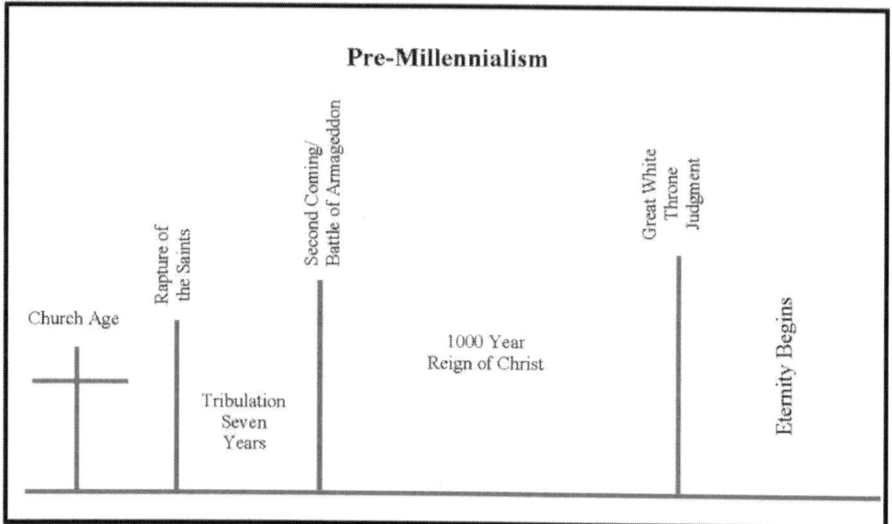

Pre-Millennialism also advocates a good and evil element much like Post-Millennialism. However, the pre-millennialist believes that, instead of the goodness of man prompting Jesus to return, the opposite is true. The world is expected to become progressively more evil, increasingly more sinister, and the Kingdom age cannot begin until Christ returns to destroy those who have led the world in its downward spiral. Jesus rescues His children from a future in which evil triumphs over good during the Tribulation. The second coming becomes a rescue mission for believers who no longer must endure the overwhelming evil that exists in the world.

The early Christians most certainly must have been pre-millennialists. In Acts 1:6 Luke writes that the disciples questioned Jesus about the coming Kingdom. Understanding their anxiety over a Kingdom about which He had spoken so often, he answered, "It is not for you to know times or periods that the Father has set by His own authority." Whether that time is tomorrow or ten thousand years from now, Christ will return, He will rapture believers and He will reign with His saints for a thousand years before rendering ultimate judgment and eternity begins.

A-MILLENNIALISM

A third view of the thousand years is A-Millennialism. Its name is derived from two Latin words, "a," pronounced "ah," meaning none or nothing and *mille*, meaning thousand. First suggested by Augustine, he had been heavily influenced by Clement of Alexandria. Clement and his students tended to see the Scriptures as strictly spiritual in nature and so spiritualized the Book of Revelation to the extent that A-Millennialism became the accepted point of view. Early Reformers like Calvin and Luther looked to Augustine for guidance in their theological thinking and adopted A-Millennialism. Thus, the concept flourished, especially during the early days of the Reformation period.

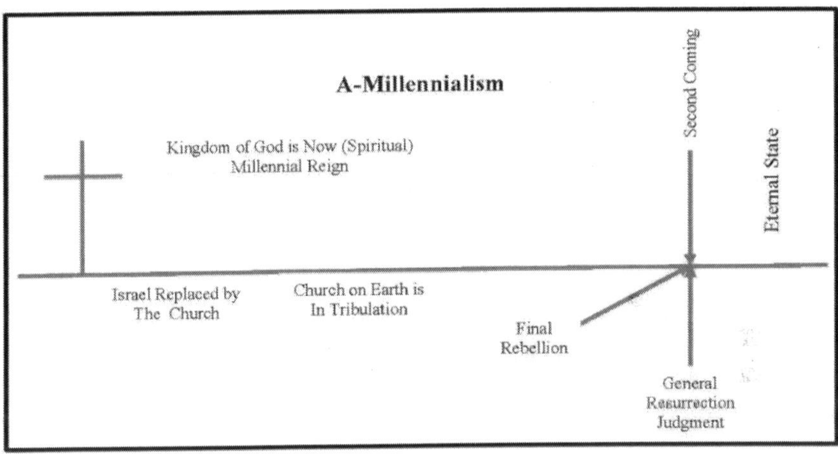

A-Millennialism denies that there will be a literal thousand-year reign of Christ on the earth. The words of Revelation 20 are strictly symbolic and are not intended to be viewed literally. Essentially, we are today, in the Millennium and have been since the destruction of Jerusalem. The Millennium will end when Christ returns in final judgment, at which point He will establish His reign.

In summary, we can expect no more Millennium than is being experienced today. Eternity will begin immediately upon the Second Coming of Christ which will occur simultaneously with the General Resurrection of the saints and the Final Judgment of man. Once these events have happened, Eternity begins.

Since it is so important to an understanding of each of these views, let me pause here to share a word about the Rapture. The word

"Rapture" does not appear in the Bible. It is a Latin word derived from the Greek word ἁρπάζω (*harpadzō*), meaning to "seize," "snatch" or "carry away by force." It is the kind of event that comes without warning.

The Rapture occurs prior to the Tribulation. The scene of chapters 4 and 5 is inarguably in heaven. It is only as chapter 6 begins that the Tribulation is introduced. So, it seems fitting that God would keep His word from 3:10 by taking His saints out of the world before the terrifying events of the Tribulation.

With respect to the Rapture, the church is not mentioned in the remainder of the Book of Revelation after chapter 3. Could it be because the church is not present? I believe so. There are numerous references to the church in chapters 1-3 yet none in chapters 4-18. Rather, these chapters refer to Israel, not the church. The church age, the season of the Gentiles, is past, and the Tribulation period begins the seventieth week of Daniel and God's dealings with the house of Israel.

You may ask, But what about the Scripture in Matthew 24:29-31? Jesus' message here appears to be quite plain. He said: "Immediately after the tribulation of those days: The sun will be darkened, and the moon will not shed its light; the stars will fall from the sky, and the celestial powers will be shaken. Then the sign of the Son of Man will appear in the sky, and then all peoples of the earth will mourn; and they will see the Son of Man coming on the clouds of heaven with power and great glory. He will send out His angels with a loud trumpet, and they will gather His elect from the four winds, from one end of the sky to the other."

While Jesus' message might be self-evident, note some key differences in Scripture. While the sound of the trumpet and the calling of His elect are vital components to the Rapture, verse 31 does not seem to agree with other Scripture. For example, in 1 Thessalonians 4 Paul writes that the Lord will descend "from heaven with a shout, with the archangel's voice, and with the trumpet of God." Here in Matthew we hear the trumpet but no archangel. We know that, in the Rapture, Christ will snatch us up to "meet Him in the air." Here it is angels who do the "gathering." There is no being caught up in the air. Rather it is a gathering from the four winds or what the ancients identified as the four corners of the earth.

Scripture seems to confirm the Rapture as a sudden removal of God's saints from the earth. It comes during a time of peace as Paul wrote in 1 Thessalonians 5:3. At the sound of the trumpet, Christ will call us home, and the church age ends.

As we progress through the book, you will become more and more aware of the importance of the end times. While the Second Coming and Judgment are not to be feared by the Christian, all can rest assured that eternity is drawing nigh. We may not know the day or the hour, but God has issued the warning throughout Scripture that life on this earth is not eternal. As you study this marvelous work, may God open your eyes to the need to be proactive in sharing the Gospel with others not as fire insurance for the future but for a rewarding relationship with the One who offers you eternal life with Him.

APPLICATION TO OUR POST-CHRISTIAN WORLD

While our post-Christian world is generally suspicious of any idea of a spiritual nature, the words of Jesus and the message of the Book of Revelation are, nonetheless, clear and faithful. Christ will return to the earth to reclaim the title deed to His creation. He will call home those who have dared to declare Him as Lord and Saviour. The Book of Revelation is simply a chronicle of the prophecy which shall be fulfilled when the Father decides to dispatch Jesus back to the earth. His coming will be sudden, and those who mock Christians for being "old-fashioned," stodgy, close-minded, fundamentalist, zealous, judgmental, hypocritical and anti-everything will find themselves on the short end of the stick in eternity. Reprobate minds, unrepentant hearts and shameless cynics will experience both suffering on earth and extreme suffering in eternity.

Can you measure eternity? Impossible! For example, if you start counting the grains of sand on earth and count until you have counted every single grain of sand, then eternity will have just begun. Even though this example does not truly really parallel eternity, it offers, in human terms, a perspective on eternity. What a long time to suffer! And it never ceases. Post-Christian earth will do well to hear and to heed the message of Jesus to repent and believe. TODAY IS THE DAY OF SALVATION!

CHAPTER 2
BACKGROUND TO REVELATION

The Book of Revelation is the sixty-sixth book of the Bible. And there is good reason for that placement. All throughout the Scripture, from the beginning to the end, God's plan is revealed. From the בְּרֵאשִׁית (*berêšît*), "in the beginning" of Genesis 1:1 to the Ἡ χάρις τοῦ κυρίου Ἰησοῦ μετὰ πάντων (*Hē charis tou kuriou Yēsou meta pantōn*), "The grace of the Lord Jesus be with all" of Revelation 22:21, the redemptive plan of God unfolds. Therefore, at the very beginning in Genesis, yea, even before He created the universe, God also initiated the *eschatos*, the end. From Roman numeral one and the commencement of His plan to infinity and its consummation, God charted the course of redemption, and the Book of Revelation is but the crowning glory of that plan. It is placed last for a reason, and that reason offers insight into the climax of time, earth and all that is in or on the earth.

But the pressing questions are, How does one understand such a complex and puzzling story? How can one draw out of its pages practical wisdom for daily living? What does its message mean in today's post-Christian world? This book will attempt to address these very real questions.

KEYS TO UNDERSTANDING

Revelation can be understood only in the context of the form in which it was written. You might wish to re-read chapter one of this book to fully grasp the nature of apocalyptic literature and its role in the ancient world. Here I would like to add five keys that, I believe, unlock the mystery of Revelation.[2]

PURPOSE OF THE REVELATION

The first key is the purpose of the Revelation. While John the Apostle is given credit for authoring the Book of Revelation, the book is not about John, nor is it John's message. It is not about the seven churches, not about the Tribulation, not about judgment, not about the kingdom or eternity or even the end of time. Rather, it is about Jesus Christ in all His consummate glory (19:10). To this point in Scripture, the story of redemption has focused on the humiliation and propitiation of Jesus, but now, in this one book, the glory of Jesus is revealed—a restored glory as written in John 17:5—a glory that outshines time and eternity. Jesus relinquished everything in order that He might become sin for us. He longed for that glory, but He didn't even know when or if He would get His glory back. The Book of Revelation then, is a picture of how Jesus obtains that restored glory.

THE IDENTITY OF THE AUTHOR

The second key to unlocking the secrets of The Revelation is the identification and orientation of the author. Unlike traditional apocalyptic literature, the author makes no effort to conceal his identity by using a pseudonym. While apocalyptic writers generally employed pseudonyms, John did not seek to hide his identity. He identifies himself as John, but which John?

Tradition holds that the writer of Revelation was John, the son of Zebedee, one of the twelve. Testimony of the Church Fathers is heavily on the side of this view. Justin the Martyr, in his *Dialogue Against Trypho*, Irenaeus, Clement of Alexandria, Tertullian, Origen and the *Muratanian Canon* all attest to John the Apostle as its author. The author was doubtless a Palestinian Jew because the book is strongly colored by Hebrew thought and language, numerology and symbolism. Apparently, the author thought in Hebrew and Aramaic and then mentally translated, writing his translated thoughts into Greek.

Another reason for considering John the Apostle as the writer is that there is a strong bond of kinship and similar ideas between the Gospel of John and the Apocalypse of John, leading one to believe that John the Apostle was the author of Revelation. Some of these thoughts include fundamental concepts of God, Christ, redemption and sin. In Revelation, these ideas are clothed in apocalyptic language, but although less symbolically presented, these ideas also appear in the Gospel of John just as clearly as they do here in the Apocalypse.

Yet another theory is that the author might have been John, the pastor of the Church at Ephesus. Known as John the Elder, he was mentioned by Church Fathers, Eusebius and Papias, in their writings. If John the Elder is the author of Revelation, he is likely the author of the Second and Third Epistles of John because the author of these letters specifically identifies himself as The Elder. However, he likely would not have been the author of the First Epistle of John because the First Epistle is so close in character, language and ideology to the Gospel of John. John the Apostle is generally accepted to have written the Gospel and the First Epistle.

There is yet another possibility that the author could have been another John that was well-known to the churches of Asia but not well-known to us. John the Apostle was the father of the Ephesian school, and the author of Revelation could have been one of his students. Such a student would have known the Apostle, would have been familiar with his writings, would have been conversant with his ideas and therefore could have clearly communicated them. He would have been an heir of the Johannine thinking and spirit of John the Apostle and his school.

The abundance of evidence, however, lies with John the Apostle. John, the Forerunner, had known Jesus, and he would have possessed a unique perspective on Jesus' teachings. His fervent beliefs regarding Jesus and his second coming make John the Apostle the most likely author of this wonderful and compelling book. This message, then, has come down to us from the Father: God gave the glorious message to the Lord Jesus Christ; the Lord gave it to the angels; and angels gave it to John.

When John wrote The Revelation, he was not sitting in a palace on the banks of the Mediterranean. He was not ensconced in an apartment provided by the emperor. He was a prisoner, exiled to the Island of Patmos, about thirty-five miles from Sicily. Patmos was a penal colony reserved for both political and civilian criminals. It was a forced labor camp where the prisoners spent their days breaking rocks, digging caves and struggling to survive. John was there because he had refused to offer a sacrifice to the emperor. He had remained faithful to his God and to his Lord Jesus Christ. He was now paying the penalty. It is under these circumstances that John experienced the vision and found the inspiration to pen these words. However, it was only because John was too popular to execute and too powerful to ignore[3] that he found himself exiled to Patmos.

THE READER

The reader of The Book of Revelation presents a third key to unlocking its secrets. Verse 3 gives a hint about the reader. John acknowledges that anyone who reads or hears the words of this prophecy and keeps these words is blessed. Within its own text, the "reader" becomes anyone who reads or hears the prophecy and keeps it. It is a prophecy designed to change lives, to encourage one to holy living and to offer support in troubled times.

Revelation is not for the theological bystander who enjoys history, language and culture, but it is intended to present Jesus Christ in such a way as to kindle a holy fire inside the heart of the reader or hearer. Revelation is not for the faint of heart. The consummation of time is not a happy time for those who do not have a relationship with Christ. It will be a time of tribulation, heartbreak, suffering. John is writing to encourage his readers to stay strong in the Lord, continue to declare His glory because, in the end, everything will come under the control of Jesus Christ.

APPLICATION TO OUR POST-CHRISTIAN WORLD

If the message of The Book of Revelation is meant for anyone who reads it, then its message is meant for all of us. If you are a Christian, its message is one of comfort and joy, knowing that Christ and His kingdom will be victorious in the end. If you are not a Christian, then you should read the message of the Book with caution, recognizing that an unrepentant spirit and an impenitent heart grieves Jesus and, because He is a loving God who keeps His word, He will avenge all Christians by releasing His divine anger on all who unashamedly refuse to acknowledge Him. TODAY IS THE DAY OF SALVATION!

THE RECIPIENTS

In verse 4, John lists the recipients of this letter—"the seven churches in Asia." Immediately notice the number of churches. Based upon the analysis of chapter 1, this would represent completeness. That is, the message of this Book to these churches comprises a complete plan for complete redemption.

There were, at the time, seven principal, identifiable, geographically locatable, New Testament churches that represented the condition of all churches for all time. The Book of Revelation was written specifically and originally to these churches. It was to be copied and circulated in tangible and transportable form among the churches. Their characteristics epitomize the negative issues and positive influences of both the New Testament churches and churches today.

APPLICATION TO OUR POST-CHRISTIAN WORLD

Today, throughout the world, an example of each of these churches can be found. Whether it is a church that has lost its initial fervor for the Lord, whether it is a church influenced heavily by the New Age movement, New World Order or modern culture, whether it is a lukewarm church that has all of the trappings of an alive church but is dead at its heart, whether it is a church that tolerates sin and allows false teaching—no matter what the church looks like, it will be found among the churches to which The Book of Revelation is written. TODAY IS THE DAY OF SALVATION!

THE RESOURCE

What is the source of this letter? Where did it come from? Three sources are immediately identifiable. The text offers a hint as to the first source. In 1:4 John writes: "Grace and peace to you from the one who is, who was, and who is to come." But to whom do these words refer? Who is the author of "grace" and "peace"? None other than God the Father. This book does not derive its message, its ideas, its inspiration from John or from an angel or from some itinerant preacher in the wilderness. It is from God Himself.

The second source is described in 1:4b: "from the seven spirits before his throne." To whom does this refer? Does it refer to the Holy Spirit? Yes! Then are there seven Holy Spirits? Of course not. Seven represents the Holy Spirit in all its fullness as illustrated in the Old Testament. Consider Isaiah 11 in which the prophet suggests the character of the awaited Messiah. The first characteristic, shown in verse 2, is the "Spirit of the Lord" which is none other than the Holy Spirit. Then verse 2 describes other characteristics of the Spirit personified in the: "Spirit of wisdom," "Spirit of understanding," "Spirit of counsel," "Spirit of strength," "Spirit of knowledge," and "Spirit of fear of the Lord." Seven kinds of spirits, indicating fullness, completeness. But does that mean that there are seven spirits? No! It is one Holy Spirit, complete in every way. God will not give us a source for the Revelation that is incomplete. There is one Spirit who is characterized in Isaiah in all of His fullness. THE Holy Spirit, manifested in all His attributes.

The third source is Jesus Christ Himself, "the faithful witness, the firstborn from the dead, and the ruler of the kings of the earth." Let's look at each of these.

1. Jesus is a witness to the Father. He is a faithful witness to the truth of the Father, so much so that if you have seen Jesus you have seen the Father. In John 14:9, Jesus said, "The one who has seen Me has seen the father."

2. Of all those who have been raised from the dead, Jesus is the foremost, the preeminent one. He is first in priority to all others who have been raised.[4]

3. Jesus is chief over the rulers of the earth. He is King of Kings and Lord of Lords. In Psalm 22:28, He is "king of the Nations"; in Psalm 24:7, He is the "King of glory"; in Matthew 27:29, He is the "King of the Jews"; in John 12:13, He is the "King of Israel"; in 1 Timothy 1:17, He is the "King eternal, immortal, invisible"; in Revelation 15:3, He is "King of saints" (KJV); in Revelation 19:16, He is "King of Kings."

With these keys comes a greater insight into the message of the Book of Revelation. It is not simply a book of antiquity with no application for today. In fact, it is as current as today's news. Take to heart the message of this book, and you will find your life more satisfying and complete. You will find less worry and strife in your life, and you will understand the urgency of being a faithful witness for Christ.

DATE OF AUTHORSHIP

Before considering the various methods of interpretation of Revelation, let us discuss the dating of the book. A major reason for doing so is that one's interpretive method may be based solely upon what is determined to be the time in which the treatise may have been authored.

There is a fair degree of unanimity among biblical scholars with respect to the time during which Revelation was written. Based upon first century history, the book was probably written during the reign of the Emperor Domitian, who ruled from AD 81 until AD 96. Domitian actually followed in the footsteps of the notorious Emperor Nero.

Since we know that John, the Beloved Disciple, is the author of The Revelation, it might be helpful to know the dates during which he lived. The son of Zebedee and the brother of James, he is believed to have been born around AD 6. An apostle of Jesus, he was at the foot of the cross when Jesus was crucified, and it was to him that Jesus directed His words, "Here is your mother." Tradition holds that John ultimately settled in Ephesus where he cared for Mary until her death, purported to have been around AD 48.[5]

John lived to sometime beyond AD 98, perhaps AD 100 or 101. Tradition, largely promoted in the second century by Tertullian, declares that the Roman ruler of that time, Domitian, wished to kill John by placing him in a vat of boiling oil. Standing in the oil, John emerged unhurt, angering Domitian to the point of exiling John to the Island of Patmos. There he received the Revelation from God and committed it to writing.

Scholars are consistently divided on the date of this writing. One school of thought,[6] for example, argues for a date during the reign of Nero. While Nero persecuted Christians severely, his reason for doing so was not their refusal to worship him as God. Other scholars believe the book to have been written during the latter part of the reign of Vespasian. The main issue with this position is that Vespasian did not persecute the Christian community at all.

Domitian, who reigned from AD 81 to AD 96, was the cruelest of the cruel rulers. Alleged to have slain his own brother, Domitian put to death members of his own senate, confiscating their homes and estates and having their families slaughtered. He demanded that he be addressed as "Lord and God" and commanded that he be worshipped as such.

Since this consideration is so crucial to the dating of The Revelation, let's take a little closer look at these arguments. If Nero was an evil sovereign, Domitian was far worse. The Hollywood film, *Quo Vadis*, depicts quite graphically the diabolical persecution of Christians by Nero. Remember how he fiddled while the city of Rome was destroyed in a fiery conflagration set by his own soldiers in order to lay blame on the Christians? Yet as evil as Nero might have been, Domitian's gruesome persecution of Christians was far worse and far more extensive. So, there are several reasons for rejecting the Neronian date and considering a later date.

First, while Nero celebrated the persecution of Christians, the persecution described in the Revelation was considerably more extensive than that suffered by the Christians under Nero. It was worse, significantly worse. Under Nero Christians suffered and died generally in the city of Rome only, and the persecution was somewhat localized. There is no evidence that the Neronian persecution extended out from Rome into the provinces of the Roman Empire. History tell us that the persecution described in Revelation had extended its ghastly tentacles deep into the provinces.[7] The writings to the seven churches offer one indication. All of these churches were far outside the local area of Rome. Then Revelation 2:13 refers to the church at Pergamum and its faithfulness. One of their loyal number, Antipas, had suffered martyrdom under Domitian, lending strength to the idea that the persecution had extended far beyond the bounds of the city of Rome. Both of these arguments seem to support a later writing.

Domitian demanded that he be referred to as "Lord and God," and those who refused to address him as such often faced his wrath.[8] While the first general persecution of Christians occurred under the rule of Nero, the first persecution of Christians resulting from royal policy extensions into the provinces occurred under the reign of Domitian. History testifies to these events as having occurred during the latter part of his reign or approximately AD 90-96.

Going beyond the reign of Domitian to that of Nerva or Trajan, the emperors who followed him, history witnesses that they did not continue to persecute the Christians. A date later than AD 96 does not appear to stand the test of historical scrutiny. A date prior to AD 81 is generally rejected because of the character and extensiveness of the persecution described in Revelation. Prior to that date the persecution of Christians occurred, but that persecution was not nearly as systemic and horrific as afterward.

Another reason to reject the Neronian date can be found in 13:3 where John describes the beast. One of the heads of the beast—this beast had seven heads—is said to have suffered a fatal wound which apparently had healed. The description of this beast was commonly considered to be a reference to Nero. It was based upon a myth about Nero that spread like gossip.

This myth concerning Nero, both as a person and as an emperor, had circulated throughout the Empire. This myth declared that he had died, been resurrected and would eventually lead an army back to Rome and take the reins of the Empire once more. Although the author of the Book of Revelation does not give any credence to this myth, Revelation 13:3 fairly confirms the writer's knowledge of the tale since he referred to it symbolically. The use of this myth of Nero's resurrection by the author would lead us to believe that The Revelation certainly was not written during Nero's lifetime, because the myth did not arise until after his death.

Evidence offered in the descriptions of the seven churches offers yet another reason to reject an earlier date of authorship. It suggests that these institutions had been around a sufficient length of time to permit the once enthusiastic Christians to become somewhat lethargic in their devotion to Christ. Also, these churches had allowed the intrusion of heresies such as Gnosticism to displace the spiritual eagerness of these first century Christians. They had certainly existed long enough to allow the cooling of the initial ardor of these people. Paul's writings offer examples of how the early Christians had dealt with heresies that had seemed all too frequently to infiltrate their churches. In order for the heresies to get a foothold, the churches would have needed to be there long enough for them to have lost that initial energy so characteristic of new Christians. They would have allowed these heresies and other religious influences, especially the Gnostic heresy and the Judaizers, to gain access to the churches. Based upon this characteristic of these churches, the Neronian date is further rejected.

External evidence such as early church history also supports a date later than the Neronian reign. The writings of the Church Fathers, among them Ireneaus, Clement of Alexandria and Origen, date the writing of the Book of Revelation during Domitian's reign. Although men like the early Church Fathers are not the ultimate source for absolute proof, they are so much closer historically to the actual happenings, so their words and observations should be weighty.

The persecution instituted under Domitian, at least the most severe activity, came during the latter part of his reign. Based on both internal and external evidence, the writing of the Book of Revelation can best be dated during the reign of Domitian, perhaps AD 92 to AD 95.

As with so many other rulers that history has seen come and go, Domitian insisted that he be worshipped as a divine being. The

Revelation was written to encourage Christians who were subject to this policy of Domitian to resist and endure. It declared that victory would be theirs. To hear such endearing words was difficult, especially during the days when Domitian was burning the crucified bodies of Christians to light the highways of his kingdom. To hear that victory was near was likely a hollow promise to those who suffered painfully under the grotesque and maniacal persecution that Domitian perpetrated on those early Christians. But even as we read in the twenty-first century about the persecution of Christians in many countries, Revelation offered then and offers today reassurance that God's victory over evil is ultimate.

Emperor worship was not new. Nero had demanded it; all of the Caesars demanded it. But Domitian raised emperor worship to heights never achieved up until that time. He took some type of gloomy and cynical pleasure in the shouts that greeted him on arrival when he would come before the people at the amphitheaters. Κύριος Καῖσαρ (*Kurios Kaesar*), "you are Lord, Lord Caesar, god Caesar."

But in those crowds there mingled Christians who would not bow to Caesar, who refused to join in the shouts of *Kurios Kaesar*. Instead, they would shout Κύριος Χριστός (*Kurios Christos*), "Lord Christ" or Κύριος Ἰησοῦς (*Kurios Yesus)*, "Lord Jesus." In Asia, where they were proud to be a part of the Holy Roman Empire, Christians resisted this emperor-god idea. Resistance was met with arrest and persecution and oftentimes death for these Christians as well.

As the persecution gained momentum, it caught in its wake one of the leaders of the Asian churches. But instead of being killed, God protected Him, and he was banished to the Island of Patmos, located off the coast of Asia. There he could ponder, listen and meditate on the meaning of the conflict of his brethren between the Roman state and his beloved church. He remembered those who were dying; he remembered those who were being arrested; he remembered those who were suffering. He saw this conflict in its religious, its historical and its cosmic significance. He understood what it meant to the time in which he lived and what it would mean to the world after he was gone. His willingness to listen to the Holy Spirit, his awareness of the times in which he lived and his discernment of the message that God conveyed to him are keys to the greatness, importance and relevance of the Book of Revelation.

John brooded over the vast implications of the current happenings in the Holy Roman Empire. He fell into a kind of ecstasy, and he came under the inspiration of the Holy Spirit who revealed to him the visions of God, the visions that were written in his book. Thank God for these visions.

This Seer of Patmos recognized in his visions the irreconcilable nature of this rising conflict between the Roman Empire and Christianity—symbolic of the conflict between Good and Evil. They could not exist side by side. In the meantime, Christians were dying in the conflict, others would suffer and lose their lives because of their loyalties to God's Gospel. In this context, John addressed this impassioned letter to the seven churches of Asia. It was doubtless intended to be circulated to and read by all the churches of Asia, not just these seven, and perhaps the churches of the entire Holy Roman Empire even beyond those in Asia. The letter was circulated in an effort to help Christians answer the challenge of the Caesars. The cry was not to be *Kurios Kaesar*, it was to be *Kurios Christos*, "Lord Christ." The book's message was one of encouragement, hope and ultimate victory for those who remained loyal to Christ.

Another reason for accepting this period as the dating of The Revelation is the condition of the churches at that time. Once established, now the churches had experienced several generations of leadership. The heat of their founding fervor appears to have cooled a bit, and the heresies that were expanding—namely, the Nicolaitans and the Gnostics—were influencing those remaining in the church. The churches were in such decline that they did not "test the spirits" but often accepted their heretical teachings without question, or adapted those principles to the teachings of Scripture, thereby weakening the truth of the Gospel.

In addressing the issue of date, Irenaeus, the great second century church father, wrote: "For that (speaking of the apocalyptic revelation) was seen not a very long time since but almost in our own day, toward the end of Domitian's reign."[9] So it is the conclusion of this author that the Apocalyptist, having been unsuccessfully killed by Domitian, was exiled to the Island of Patmos where he experienced the spirit of God and penned, around AD 95 or 96, with spiritual inspiration, the words describing his vision from God.

METHODS OF INTERPRETATION

One's understanding of The Revelation hinges primarily on the method applied to interpret its words and symbols. It is, after all, apocalyptic in nature, and as mentioned in the earlier chapter, apocalyptic literature employs symbols to communicate a specific message. Each symbol possesses explicit meaning inspired by the Holy Spirit to reveal a particular thought or point. Unlike the idea held by some people that the book is sort of an adventure book or a biblical version of Harry Potter, it is designed to deliver a message of encouragement to Christians living at the time it was written and a prophetic word to us today with respect to the ultimate victory of good over evil, of Christ over Satan.

The first consideration in interpreting Revelation is one's position on whether it is history or apocalyptic. Whichever side of this debate you take will determine, in part, the kind of interpretive method you will employ. If history, you will see it as fulfilled or allegorical. If apocalyptic, you will view it as futuristic, prophetic and as yet unfulfilled.

For insight on the second coming of Christ, it might be helpful to study Old Testament prophecies about the first coming of Jesus. In the apocalyptic Old Testament book of Zechariah, the prophet writes, "Look, your king is coming to you; He is righteous and victorious, humble and riding on a donkey, on a colt, the foal of a donkey" (Zechariah 9:9). For the historical interpreter, the donkey would be unlikely; it simply is a sign of humility. But, alas, look at Matthew 21:1-9 for the fulfillment of prophecy. Jesus, the Messiah, entered Jerusalem on a donkey, just as Zechariah had prophesied. No symbolizing the act, no spiritualizing of the scene, just Jesus riding atop a literal donkey. When we view Revelation, the literal interpretation is often the most sensible.

I like to think that, when God inspired John to write The Revelation, He did not wish to miscommunicate with or confuse us. And while the book employs symbols to convey its message at times, God intends that these symbols have meaning, meaning that can be discerned by language, context and historical setting. God does not communicate in conundrums; He says what He means and means what He says.

With these ideas in mind, let's focus attention on the four principal views or methods of interpretation: Idealist, Preterist, Historicist, and Futurist.

IDEALIST (PHILOSOPHY OF HISTORY)

The Idealist method appears to have been introduced by the ancient church father, Origen (AD 184-AD 253). It was later amplified and made popular by Augustine. In this method of interpreting The Revelation the happenings of the story are not connected to any definitive historical event. It is considered to be a generic description of the continuing struggle between good and evil, God and Satan. It is an interpretation characterized by a philosophy of history that acknowledges no specific historical fulfillment of prophecy. It is A-Millennial in its position of the thousand-year reign of Christ and has been the position taken by the Roman Catholic church as well as some mainline Protestant denominations. This position is what Lance Ralston calls a "grab bag position."[10] Merrill Tenney states in this interpretation, "the Apocalypse may thus mean anything or nothing according to the whim of the interpreter."[11]

HISTORICIST (CONTINUOUS-HISTORICAL)

In opposition to the Idealist method of interpretation so common in Roman Catholicism, this view of Revelation began with Joachim of Flores (1145-1202), Abbot of the monastery at San Giovanni in Fiore, Italy. It reached its greatest popularity during the Protestant Reformation primarily through its identification of the pope and the papacy with the beasts of Revelation 13. Martin Luther and John Calvin espoused its tenets. Other scholars who have held this view include John Wycliffe, John Knox, John Wesley, Jonathan Edwards, George Whitfield and Charles H. Spurgeon.

This view of Revelation holds that the book covers the entire history of the world from the resurrection of Christ to His Second Coming or the time of the interpreter. The symbols would correspond to specific events in history. Based upon the apostasy of the Roman Catholic church, it is a view that results primarily in speculation and especially subjectivity. That is, one is disposed to interpret the text through the context of the period in which he lives rather than employing traditional hermeneutical principles. Thus, the interpreter is required to reinterpret and reapply its message to each new event or series of events. Furthermore, this method of interpretation does not take into account any significance for or application to those of the first century who happened to be John's specific audience.

PRETERIST

Although some Preterists would say that this method of interpretation was introduced by the Apocalyptist himself, most assign the founding of the Preterist school to Luis de Alcazar (1554-1613), Jesuit Father serving the Palace Theological Society in Seville, Spain. Derived from the Latin *preter*, which means "past" or "what is past," Preterism views Revelation as being fulfilled completely in the past, over a short period of time with the destruction of the Temple in Jerusalem in AD 70 by the Romans. It is an A-Millennial position meaning that there will be no thousand-year reign but, rather, the Millennium is simply the writer's way of expressing an extended period of time when the church becomes increasingly stronger and will win over evil. In a sense it is a view that the world will get better and better so that the Lord must come to claim His own.

The Preterist interpretation typically limits John's apocalyptic theology, believing it to be an allegory of what he experienced of Christian persecution by the Romans, and thus he prophesies concerning the ultimate fall of Rome and the victory of Christ. Since it is limited to John's experience, it would, of necessity, have been fulfilled with the fall of Jerusalem.

Crucial to this view is the date of the authorship of Revelation. Obviously, if the book were written at the end of Domitian's reign as emperor of Rome or around AD 96, this view of interpretation would be incomplete, since it presupposes that the Temple and Jerusalem were still in existence, and Revelation is a prophecy of their downfall and destruction. However, if it is actually from a period that pre-dates the fall of Jerusalem and the destruction of the Temple, then Preterism at least has history upon which to base its assumptions.

Not only does Preterism base its view on the date of authorship, but it also leans on its interpretation of Revelation 1:1, "The revelation of Jesus Christ that God gave Him to show His slaves what quickly must take place." The word translated "quickly" here is the Greek word τάχει, *tachei*, from the root word τάχος, *tachos*, meaning "speed," "quickness" or "haste." However, in context, it can also mean "soon" or "in a short time" even though no definitive example can be found of this translation in the New Testament. The Preterists base their view on the translation of this word to mean "soon" or "shortly" and that it refers to events that happened between the resurrection of Christ and the fall of Jerusalem and the destruction of the Temple. Thus, it would have already been fulfilled in history.

This view was held deeply by my seminary major professor, Dr. Edward A. McDowell, and he wrote about it in his book, *The Meaning and Message of the Book of Revelation*. He and I had many a discussion about these interpretations.

FUTURIST

The Futurist view of interpretation recognizes the book as being a prophecy regarding apocalyptic times or the end of days and has yet to be fulfilled. This view would also interpret the Olivet Discourse as being fulfilled in the future as well.

The Futurist is typically a Pre-Millennialist who believes that the world will become ever more sinful until Christ has had enough and returns to claim His world for Himself and His followers as His own. But before Jesus returns, there will be a seven-year period of Tribulation during which horrible disasters and tragic catastrophes will occur in a literal fulfillment of the scroll, trumpet and bowl judgments.

This view generally accepts a literal approach to interpreting Revelation but only to explain the original sense in keeping with the normal, customary usage of its language. The rules of grammar are applied, remaining consistent with the historical background and the context of the writing. It is important to note that a literal approach does not preclude the figurative or symbolic language that is so common in Revelation. It is just more important to consider the context of the literature when interpreting signs and symbols. Figurative or symbolic language does not validate an allegorical conclusion.

As with the Preterist method, this view depends heavily upon the date of the authorship of Revelation to support its principles. Believed to have been written while John was exiled on Patmos by Domitian, its date is trusted to be around AD 96.

One major argument in favor of this view is the letters to the seven churches. What is described by John does not appear to reflect the fervor, excitement and intensity of the early churches. Rather,

John seems to be describing the conditions of second-or third-generation churches that had lapsed into lethargy and did not experience the enthusiasm of the first generation. Furthermore, if John had written Revelation in AD 65, it would have overlapped with Paul's letters to the church at Ephesus and to Timothy. But Paul makes no mention of either the loss of first love or the threat of the Nicolaitans.[12]

John also wrote to the church at Smyrna. In AD 65, the church at Smyrna did not exist during Paul's ministry. Also, Laodicea, reprimanded for being lukewarm in Revelation is commended three times by Paul in Colossians. And since history tells us that Laodicea, along with Colossae and Hieropolis, was ravaged by an earthquake in AD 60, the city would have been in ruins and unlikely in the state described by John.

CONCLUSION

As we approach The Revelation, we must keep in mind the various methods of interpretation. My firm belief is in the Futurist method, and I will employ the Futurist approach to the book combined with elements of the Preterist view. I believe the message of Revelation was encouraging to the first century Christians because it gave them confidence that the cause of Christ would ultimately win over evil. But I also believe that God would not go to all the trouble to offer these visions and deliver this message of encouragement and victory without having them apply to His return. Elsewhere in the Bible, God has assured believers that He will return, and the Book of Revelation is a more detailed account of how His return and the end of the age will occur. It is my firm conviction, therefore, that the primary purpose of the book is eschatological in nature, designed to enlighten Christians of all ages of the ultimate victory of God over Satan and the future judgment that God will bring on evil and the unrepentant.

CHAPTER 3
THE INTRODUCTION AND COMMAND
1:1-20

Chapter one is, for the most part, an eloquently scripted introduction to the message that is to follow. Lacking in apocalyptic depth, it serves as a greeting by John who then offers a description of the setting of the vision followed by a preliminary account of the vision itself.

John begins by making it clear that this revelation is not his revelation but that of Jesus Christ. John is only the messenger, the amanuensis, the writer. The message is that of God the Father, who gave it to Jesus Christ, who communicated it to the angel and on to John. John claims no authority in the message; he only serves as the conduit through whom the message is delivered.

Notice that God not only conveyed the revelation through His angel, but He also "signified" it. This is a throw-back by John to his Gospel in which he outlined seven signs that Jesus, the man, was Christ the Son of God and Messiah. The word here rendered "signify" is the Greek σημαίνω (*sēmainō*), which is the verb form of σημεῖον (*sēmeion*), "sign." It is the same word John employs in his Gospel when he describes the seven "signs" of the Messiah. Here Jesus, through His angel, shows by symbol and certifies by sign the truth of the revelation and its significance to and importance for the persecuted church.

Blessings (v. 3) are also reserved for those who receive the message and take it to heart. The word "blessed" is the same word used by the Psalmist (1:1) as well as by Jesus in the Beatitudes. It becomes the first of seven occurrences of "blessed" here in Revelation.[13]

The salutation of Revelation clearly discloses from whom this letter originates. It is none other than the Triune God, the Eternal One "who is, who was, and who is coming." God, who is the great Creator, who is supreme in and over all that exists, who is sovereign and majestic—this God has taken time out from His heavenly appointment to offer a message of hope and comfort to His people. He is joined by the Holy Spirit, described here as the "seven spirits."[14] And finally from Jesus Himself who is "the faithful witness, the firstborn from the dead and the ruler of the kings of the earth." He is not only One who keeps His word as a witness, but He is also the first among many who have experienced resurrection. He is also Lord over all earthly royalty and potentates and will later be described as "King of Kings and Lord of Lords" (Revelation 19:16). He it is that extends "grace" and "peace"—grace for our sins, and peace for our hearts.

John is so moved by the spirit of his experience that he breaks into a doxology, praising God and shouting, "To Him who loves us and has set us free. . ." Here John juxtaposes the present tense with the aorist tense. Jesus loves us (present tense) and continues to love us and has set us free (aorist tense) once and for all with nothing else necessary to effectuate our salvation. These words offer the absolute assurance of the eternal lordship of Jesus Christ in all His eternal love and redemptive character.

With praise still on his lips, John echoes the words of Daniel to present Christ as the exalted Son of Man, the One who sits at the right hand (favored) of the Father waiting to return in glory and power. Hear the words of Daniel 7:13: "I saw One like a son of man coming with the clouds of heaven." These words resound through the voice of Jesus when asked by the High Priest if He were the "Messiah, the Son of the Blessed One" (Mark 14:61). Jesus answered, "I am, and all of you will see the Son of Man seated at the right hand of the Power and coming with the clouds of heaven." John acclaims Him as the Suffering One described in Zechariah 12:10-14 who, through His sacrificial death on the cross is given the position of power with the Father. By way of this assertion, "Jesus identifies himself as the great Danielic Son of man."[15]

John offers the most fitting description of God found in Scripture: "I am the Alpha and the Omega," the beginning and end of everything, almighty beyond our ability to comprehend. I am the eternal One who is, who always has been and who forever will be. And His coming is assured through His words.

Verse 9 begins a dramatic soliloquy in which John describes "the *redeeming* lamb, who dominates the action of this book."[16] Acknowledging who he is and the reason for being on Patmos was part of his personal testimony. He had been faithful to his mission and loyal to his Christ, and it had cost him dearly—separation from friends and fellow-believers. You can almost hear him say, "Take heart; this is temporary; our Lord shall return in glory. Let me tell you the story of what I saw personally." Then, after identifying himself with other believers ("brothers"), after declaring his partnership with them in tribulation and after promising endurance in waiting for the coming kingdom, the actual vision encountered by John begins to unfold for us in all its dramatic form.

John writes that the spirit came to him on the Lord's day. The word translated "Lord's" presents an interesting dilemma for interpreters. By simply reading the English, one does not comprehend the nuance that the sentence presents. "Lord's" here is grammatically an adjective of possession meaning belonging to the Lord. While some scholars believe that it refers to the "Day of the Lord" of the future,[17] the context would seem to argue for understanding the word as referring to a day of worship. But could John have been referring to the Sabbath Day? After all, biblically speaking, Sunday had not yet been firmly established as a day of worship. Only when Justin Martyr wrote about it in the second century[18] was Sunday believed to have become the traditional day of worship. However, we do know from Acts 20:7 that the first century Christians initiated the tradition even though it was not officially established.

Since John would have been familiar with the early practice of worship on the first day of the week, I believe that he is referring here to a day when he would have gathered with fellow believers to worship the Almighty Father in Christ. Today, he will worship Him in majesty and glory because he gains a glimpse, albeit a small one, into what God plans for the future.

"Write on a scroll," Jesus said. What was to be revealed would be too terrible, too complex, too weighty to simply commit to memory. There must be a permanent record; it must be written down for all time and eternity.

The letters were to go to the seven churches of Asia Minor. The churches to which the letters were addressed represent the major regions where Christian churches had been established and flourished. While a separate letter was addressed to each church, the intent was that all of the letters be circulated to all the churches of the Empire and beyond where churches had been established. Each of the churches addressed represented a "type" of congregation, those faithful and those not so faithful.

John begins to describe the vision of none other than the risen and transcendent Christ. John turns to behold a Christ who has assumed the characteristics of Jehovah in His mighty power and resplendent glory. He witnessed with his eyes and heard Jesus with his own ears, the triumphant Lord Christ, with a voice like a trumpet, a voice that projected wisdom, knowledge and authority, a voice to be heard and heeded. That voice revealed John's mission.

John sees this great "ancient of days" standing among seven golden lampstands. In antiquity a lampstand was a small gold, pottery or metal cup filled with oil and from which a small wick extended. Its sole purpose was to give light. Using this imagery, the lampstands are seen as the seven churches, the light of the world to which the letters are addressed, with Jesus standing in the middle of them. The light from these lampstands is reminiscent of the words of Christ in the Sermon on the Mount: "No one lights a lamp and puts it under a basket, but rather on a lampstand, and it gives light for all who are in the house" (Matthew 5:15). They are not THE light but, like the moon and its relation to the sun, they get their light from Christ and share that light with the world.

This Christ, who is giving His orders to John, has appeared before. Familiar with the Scripture, John remembers, then shares, the qualities of Jehovah God, the "ancient of days" as foreshadowed in the visions of Daniel in 7:9-14 and 10:5-6. Notice the similarity of the pictures. Here John illustrates the invincible Christ as "dressed in a long robe and with a gold sash wrapped around His chest" (verse 13), signifying both His priestly and His royal roles.[19] In the Danielic passages, the Ancient of Days is also described in symbolic terms demonstrating His glory, His holiness, His authority and His power.

His physical appearance is further described in verse 14: "His head and hair were white like wool—white as snow," symbolic of his wisdom and holiness. It is a physical depiction resounding the words of Daniel 7:9. John further adds, "His eyes like a fiery flame," all-knowing, penetrating and perceptive, a phrase that could have been taken directly from Daniel 10:6. They are eyes that see all our essence and refine like gold. And His "feet were like fine bronze as it is fired in a furnace," describing one whose strength can conquer nations or unseen enemies who seek to undermine the power of the Almighty. And since feet are always signs of judgment, He comes in judgment with superiority and authority. He declares words of judgment that have the power and sound of a mighty waterfall, not to be misinterpreted.

John observes the majesty of Christ in both reassurance and judgment. That majesty is pictured in "His face was shining like the sun at midday," shining at its brightest. The risen and majestic Christ held in his right hand the seven stars. The right hand had, for centuries represented deliverance and protection.[20] It was the hand of strength and skill and often was used in conjunction with a personification of God to illustrate His protection. Even in the New Testament, at meals, the right hand was a favored position. Here Christ gives assurance of his protection to the stars of the churches.

Who are the stars? These seven stars are the "angels" or the pastors of these seven churches. When reference is made in Revelation to the seven stars or the seven angels, it always refers to the pastors of the churches represented as the seven lampstands.

But the same Christ who would protect the pastors, will assuredly rain down judgment upon the sinful works of man. The "sharp double-edged sword" protruding from His mouth represents God's judgment on unrepentant man. It is not a small sword but a large one designed to behead a criminal. It is a sword of Divine Judgment—judgment that cuts both ways delivering the ultimate penalty for ultimate sin.

Like Daniel in 10:15-19, John is overwhelmed by this vision of the Risen Christ. He falls to the ground in fear, but Christ assures him "don't be afraid." The linguistic construction of this phrase indicates an ongoing action that is forbidden to continue. It is an admonition from the one who is "the First and the Last."[21]

Christ speaks words of reassurance, words of a holy, righteous, all-knowing, all-powerful God who is not only the beginning of all things but also the end of all things; His rule will prevail; His purpose will be victorious. That God of victory stands amidst the churches holding their fate in his hands and determining their destiny by the very words of His mouth. He is the eternal, divine locksmith who can open the doors of death and Hades, doors which no one can open or shut without His approval. He is the Judge; He proclaims sentence, a sentence for which no appeal is available.

"Therefore write." Christ commands John to write down the vision, pen a description of conditions as they really are and inscribe the events that are to come. These words of Christ are not optional but imperative; John has no choice in the matter. Furthermore, "write" is in the aorist tense, indicating a completed action. It is viewed as a single, collective whole, a one-point-in-time action.

Now John has received his commission. He is Christ's recorder, Christ's scribe, to write "what you have seen" (the visions and symbols), "what is" (the events, situations and settings of John's time in history), and "what will take place after this" (prophecies relating to the future). The One speaking is none other than the risen Christ, the Redeemer and the One who holds the keys to all that is, including "death and Hades." He it is who charges John to write about the struggle and the victory to come. He it is who declares victory even before the battle has begun. He is the Lamb of God, redeeming the world, powerful and almighty. He is truly "King of Kings and Lord of Lords."

APPLICATION TO OUR POST-CHRISTIAN WORLD

Our post-Christian world today is characterized chiefly by planned obsolescence. Whether we purchase an automobile, a refrigerator or a television set, it has been designed to become obsolete. Take, for example, the Iphone. Apple Corporation releases a new version of the Iphone almost every year. Does that mean that the phone I purchased last year is worn out, broken or unusable? No! It is a means to encourage a gullible and naïve population to buy the latest and best. Or take an automobile. Have you ever had your car break down shortly after the expiration of the warranty? I've had several. After all, they are generally designed to operate for so many miles before breaking down, and that break down usually occurs immediately after the expiration of the warranty.

Praise God, what we read in The Revelation is permanent. The words are those of a God who was, is and always shall be. He needs no new model to present. He will never deteriorate to the point of uselessness, and those whose accept His salvation shall never worry about losing or wearing out that salvation. Unlike the day in which we live where material possessions and even life are temporary and transitory, He is the Alpha and Omega, the beginning and the end, and His kingdom shall never fade or disappear. He shall sit on the throne forever.

He has given us this wonderful book to encourage us in whatever circumstance we may find ourselves. We may not know the date or time of His return, but we do have the assurance that He **will** return. But what if your friend tells you, "I don't believe in God, I don't believe in a hereafter or any return of your Jesus"? An excellent response I once heard from a wise old preacher is worth repeating: Would you rather run the risk of being right and returning to the dust from which you came with no existence hereafter or would you rather find that you are wrong, Jesus' words were true and spend your eternity in a place of torment? Is life worth the gamble? TODAY IS THE DAY OF SALVATION!

CHAPTER 4
THE LETTERS TO THE SEVEN CHURCHES
2:1-3:22

Probably the best-known passages in Revelation, the letters to the seven churches serve as a fitting introduction to the message that is to follow. These chapters describe the state of the churches in Asia Minor at the time of the book's writing. By understanding the churches, one can better understand the range of issues encountered by the emerging church of the first century. The characteristics of these churches offered John a canvas upon which to paint a picture of encouragement that appears throughout Revelation.

The number of the recipient churches is not accidental. Recall that the number seven in Hebrew numerology represents fulfillment, completeness and inclusiveness. Because the messages of the letters are complete, the letter addressed to each church is destined for all the churches and as a composite, all of the letters are destined for each church. Accordingly, the Book of Revelation is not intended to be directed to or solely read by the seven churches to which it was addressed, but its encouragement was to be shared among all of the churches in Asia Minor. For example, the letter to the church at Ephesus was intended to provide a message not only to the Ephesians but also, because of the timeless nature of the letter, would and should be available for reading by all the churches.

A glance at a map of the times reveals that the seven churches to which the letters are addressed were located in western Asia Minor (present-day Turkey), accessible by way of the Aegean Sea and along the ancient trade routes between the West and the East. For a variety of reasons, whether trade, military or political, these cities became major cultural hubs, casting a vast net of influence over the geographical area in which they were situated. The arrangement of the route of the letters is intentional because it forms a circle on the map so that the deliverer of the letters would simply pass through each town in the order of direction, making his way to the churches most efficiently and then returning to the original church.

The letters to these seven churches are letters to actual churches, actual congregations that worshipped in each of these urban centers. Some scholars suggest that the letters were proposed separately by the author and inserted by him into the remaining portion of his work at a later time, perhaps after the main part of the book was actually completed. Without doubt, John simply wrote what he was being told by the spirit. Nevertheless, on one side of this coin his formula for the letters is so precise, and the remainder of Revelation speaks so directly to the issues of these churches that it seems plausible, even likely that he added these letters after the message of the book was completed. On the other side of this coin, John may have written exactly what Christ, through His Spirit, communicated. After all, the detailed form in which the letters were written could be a reflection of the wisdom of our Lord. In either case, the letters offer hope for those churches and for us today.

The letters shed significant light on the author's purpose and the manner in which he approached the problem that confronted him, namely awakening these churches to the seriousness of the impending crisis that he envisioned. The author is offering prophecies of the coming age in these letters, but he is also writing letters that serve to relate the entire book to an actual historical situation. The letters are authentic; they are real; they are based upon the background of the crisis that was facing the churches, namely that Domitian was demanding that he be worshipped as a god.

Other scholars interpret the letters to be somewhat more revelatory in nature. This view questions that the letters were intended for actual churches but rather construes that the letters to the seven churches serve to provide a revelation of Jesus Christ. John actually saw supernaturally, he actually heard supernaturally, everything he wrote in this book, including what he wrote to these seven churches. These scholars believe that the letters were not intended for first century Christians at all and were not to be interpreted within the current historical context. They can only be understood over time in the milieu of each passing day. Therefore, they are not intended for a specific church or a specific group of churches. Rather the Book of Revelation and the letters to the seven churches are characteristic of the age to come. They are to be interpreted, therefore, in light of the development of events as they occur throughout the world. While this is an interesting interpretation of Revelation, it does not fit with the entirety of the book.

The message is clear; the reason Christ chose the number seven is unmistakable. These letters are for all people, for all time. This means all of us, everybody. After all, sooner or later you and I will either be one of these seven churches or a member of one or all of them.

FORMAT OF THE LETTERS

John employs a distinctive format as he unfolds these letters to the seven churches. In so doing, all of the letters are framed identically. Each letter illustrates the threats to the first century church—suffering and compromise. In keeping with the symbolism of the book, John includes seven elements in his format. Thus, each letter is to be read as complete in time. Like a photograph depicts a single point in time, so each letter represents the condition of each church at that particular point in history.

1. The first element of the format is a greeting comprised of two constituent parts. The first part identifies the recipient of the letter, namely, the angel of the church or the pastor. In cases where the church, perhaps, does not have a pastor at the time, the angel represents some corporate spiritual life that uniquely identified the congregation.

The second part of the greeting declares the title of the One delivering the message. The source of the writing is from Jesus Christ revealed in the seven attributes of his exalted and glorified presence written in chapter one of Revelation. Each letter, except that of Philadelphia, identifies one of these seven characteristics.

2. The second part of the format is praise. Remember the advice often heard that, before offering criticism, make sure you first say something good. Except in the case of the church at Laodicea, there is praise for good works and for faithfulness. In the case of Laodicea Christ has no good word, no approval.

3. The third element comprises blame relating to sin. It is present in all of the letters except those to the churches at Smyrna and at Philadelphia.

4. The fourth element is counsel, and it appears in all of them. In each refrain Christ counsels them to be spiritually strong and encourages them to do what is needed to make them more godly, removing anything that hinders their single-hearted devotion to Jesus Christ.

5. The fifth element is a warning included in all of the letters except Smyrna and Philadelphia. Since there is not an accusation to those churches, there would necessarily be no warning to them.

6. The sixth element is a promised reward. Christ promises a blessing to all those who have an ear to hear, who gird themselves with knowledge, who want to know more and who listen to the words of God as He speaks to them.

7. Each letter concludes with a seven-fold refrain. The words at the close of each letter are a call to the unsaved. They are also an appeal to the people of the church who are not, in spirit, a part of the church. It is a command to listen carefully to the words of the Risen Lord simply because they resound with truth. This refrain is a warning that symbol over substance will not be tolerated, and God will hold all accountable, especially those who claim to be of the household of faith but, in fact, are not. It is a prophetic application of the letters to the seven churches, and it sounds a clarion call to the church to fulfill its historic role not only in those ancient times but also during the subsequent centuries from the time of the early church to today.

As we learn about each church, I will follow a specific outline as much as possible so that distinguishing characteristics can be revealed, and comparisons made among the churches. The commentary on each letter will begin with a historical description of the city in which the church is located. That will be followed by what we know about the church itself, its history and the character of its people. These two sections will then lead us into the seven elements of the formula and a commentary for each church.

Remember, as you read these letters and as you travel on life's highway, sooner or later, you will, perhaps, find yourself a member of or associated with each one of these churches. Sooner or later, what Paul wrote to Ephesus, what he wrote to Thyatira, what he wrote to Philadelphia will be a letter to the church of which you are a member. Along your journey with Christ, eventually, one of these letters will be a letter to you.

EPHESUS, 2:1-7

Ah, the church at Ephesus! Such an energetic and uncompromising congregation. The city of Ephesus was a magnificent city founded by Androclos, the son of the King of Athens. The fourth largest city in Asia, it comprised a major port city, known for its trade and commerce. At the terminus in Ephesus were four main roads, so Ephesus became the marketplace of Asia. In addition to being an ideal place through which false teachers passed, Ignatius described it as the "highway for martyrs."[22]

The city was an architectural wonder, known for its Temple of Artemis, considered one of the seven wonders of the ancient world, the Library of Celsus, and its theatre, which was capable of holding 25,000 spectators. This open-air theater was used initially for drama, but during later Roman times gladiatorial combats were also held on its stage. The city had one of the most advanced aqueduct systems in the ancient world, with multiple watercourses of various sizes to supply different areas of the city.

Ephesus was not the official capital but was recognized as being "the first city" and was granted status by the Romans as a free city. This meant that Ephesus was self-governed, a status given by a king or emperor, who ultimately supervised the city's affairs through his curator. Such free cities also possessed the right to issue civic coinage bearing the name of the city.

The church at Ephesus had been founded by Paul during his third missionary journey. It had been a vibrant church, full of missionary zeal, on fire for God. It was a well-grounded church, but now it had become a cold church, indifferent and accommodating to the world.

TITLE.—To the Ephesians Jesus describes Himself as "the One who holds the seven stars in His right hand and who walks among the seven gold lampstands," a characterization from 1:13 and 1:16. This salutation to the church reveals that Jesus knows what is happening within the church because He is there, He stands among them. Jesus did not operate on hearsay, rather, He knew what was happening in the church because He walked among them.

PRAISE.—The Ephesians were a people who rendered a valuable service with pain and perseverance. Jesus refers to their "works," a reference to efforts considered to be more purposeful and gritty than mere toil. It is hard work, sweaty work, the kind of work one performs when one labors relentlessly and ends the day with achiness and fatigue. The work of the Ephesians was an effort that produced results at the cost of pain, severe discomfort and, perhaps, even personal tragedy.

Along with their determination, the Ephesians were patient. Patience, here, means to bear up under a heavy load; sticking to the job at hand even when that job becomes difficult and seemingly impossible. In the everyday grind they maintained a sense of doggedness that produced real results. They seemed to enjoy working for God in the midst of persecution.

They had been steadfast in resisting those who promulgated evil within the church. They resisted the legalists who insisted on keeping the Law as a part of their obedience. They resisted the mavericks who insisted that self-indulgence was acceptable and encouraged licentiousness. They took a strong doctrinal stand by testing the people who claimed to be teachers and apostles and missionaries, i.e., the Nicolaitans, and they found them to be false and so rejected them. And while they were generous to a fault, they did not allow the beggars and "hangers on" to deplete their resources. This church loved the Lord Jesus and hated sin, and it did not become burdened in the work of the Lord.

BLAME.—Notice Christ's accusation against the Ephesians. He says: "But I have this against you, you have abandoned the love you had at first." What love? Nothing less than the *agapē* love that had been preached to these early Christians by Paul and John. The church had forsaken the zeal of that Christ-like love that had so typified their initial life as Christians. They had lost their enthusiasm for Christ, that initial fervor that defined them as a people of God.

By this time in history, the city of Ephesus was in decline. Commerce had waned, and the city no longer boasted about its culture and accomplishments. As the city sank deeper into the depths of deterioration, so the church became increasingly interested in worldly matters, and the passion of the church began to suffer. In this letter Christ implores them to be a church that is characterized by the same excitement that they possessed when they first heard about Jesus and became followers of The Way.

COUNSEL.—In verse 5, Christ offers both guidance and warning. "Remember then how far you have fallen; repent, and do the works you did at first. Otherwise, I will come to you and remove your lampstand…" What is the lampstand? Remember, it is the church. Christ counsels the church at Ephesus to "remember, repent and return."[23] Remember your joy at the first; remember from whence you have fallen; remember what motivated you. Remember the power and zeal of that first experience of *agapē* love that motivated you to love Christ and strive ceaselessly and joyfully on His behalf.

Repent from putting form over feeling. Their service was motivated by self-aggrandizement. Reverse your course, Jesus says, as He urges them to forget self and to turn again to a life of love. Return to the way it began—serving Christ out of a heart solely motivated by love. The consequences for the unrepentant church will be the refusal of Christ to acknowledge them. They will lose their influence, their ministers and their witness.

WARNING.—Jesus warns the Ephesians that refusal to repent and return to Him will result in the death of the church. History confirms that, even with the rapid decline of the city of Ephesus, the church at Ephesus actually died before the city perished. The lampstand was, indeed, removed.

REFRAIN.—John closes with a seven-fold amen which he repeats at the close of each letter. "Anyone who has an ear should listen to what the Spirit says to the churches." These words are directed at those who may be members of a church but not members of the kingdom. They come to church but are not genuinely born again. In short, they are lost church members. The warning is against spiritual apathy. In modern language He would say, "Now listen up; hear what I have to say." He is not referring simply to the few words that follow, but He is referring to the entire message of the letter to the church.

PROMISED REWARD.—As a part of the refrain of this letter Jesus offers a promise to the faithful—"I will give the victor the right to eat from the tree of life, which is in God's Paradise." Christ offers an eternal rest to those who persevere in the faith. "Victor" here is a form of the word νικάω (*nikaō*) meaning "to conquer," "be victorious," "to overcome." It is the same word used in 1 John 5:5 and is distinctive to the writings of John. He defines the overcomer, the victor in the First Epistle, "And who is the one who conquers the world but the one who believes that Jesus is the Son of God."

The reward for the believer is to partake of the "tree of life." John takes us back to the Garden of Eden. Two trees representing life and death grew in the Garden. The "tree of the knowledge of good and evil" represented death, a fall from grace, a loss of immortality. The "tree of life" represented life, being, eternal existence. The "tree of life" in the Garden of Eden has now been "transplanted"[24] into the midst of heaven and, as John writes in 22:2, it now lines both sides of the main boulevard of heaven. This life-giving tree, embodied in

Christ, offers happiness and holiness not in a Paradise on earth but in heaven where unending spiritual nourishment is provided. The Ephesians are simply asked to live a victorious life here and now.

APPLICATION TO OUR POST-CHRISTIAN WORLD

Do you know of any churches that have "died," that, though once they were vibrant, evangelistic and mission-minded congregations, nevertheless died from a loss of life-giving fervor? I could name several from my own experience.

The Ephesians were not unlike so many Christians who populate the modern church. Many Christians have grown weary in the work of the Lord. Remember those early days of your faith? You were probably on fire for the Lord and could not wait to share His love with others. Do you still have that same fire today? You can never go overboard for Christ. Never! You can never be too fervent for the Lord. Maintain that fervor; maintain that love that you exhibited when you first came into a relationship with Christ.

If I could pray long enough, if I knew that I could get on my knees and pray without ceasing for twenty-four hours a day for seven days a week and believe that God would move today's church out of its apathetic state, Lord knows I would spend my time doing just that. I truly feel concerned that so many Christians simply go about church out of habit, or because it is expected of them or even for social and business reasons. God urges us to return to our first love, confirm our holiness and live as victorious children of His in a world that desperately needs a Saviour. TODAY IS THE DAY OF SALVATION!

SMYRNA 2:8-11

The city of Smyrna is one of the oldest cities in the world. Today known as Izmir, it was once known as the "crown city of Asia." Its name actually means "myrrh," the spice or ointment used both as an anesthetic and in embalming. It is the same myrrh brought as a gift to the baby Jesus (Matthew 2:11) and offered to Him, mixed with wine, at His crucifixion (Mark 15:23).

Because of its intense loyalty to Rome, Smyrna became one of the six free Roman cities of the Empire, experiencing a kind of independence and limited self-governance. The region around the city was fertile and productive, and a major connecting road through Asia Minor found its depot there.

Religion, too, was important to the city. It became a center for worship of the Caesars, and several pagan temples were located in Smyrna. Satan's onslaught of the Christians began with the Jews of the region who were inordinately hostile to the Christians of Smyrna.

Wc know nothing about the beginnings of the church at Smyrna. Since it lay only thirty-five miles north of Ephesus, it could have been a mission from that church. One of its early pastors was Polycarp who served this church for 60 years before being burned at the stake in AD 155.

The church at Smyrna was not a wealthy church, but due to the faithfulness of its members, it suffered great tribulation, not the least of which was instituted by the Jews. But the church grew and prospered in spite of the persecution, and, as a result, Jesus had only good words to say about this church.

TITLE.—Here Jesus declares another of His attributes from chapter one. "The First and the Last, the One who was dead and came to life, says."[25] Jesus also reminds them that He is the Alpha and Omega, the first and last letters of the Greek alphabet, pointing toward His all-encompassing authority and control. He tells them that He knows their suffering because He endured in His Father's mission as they are to endure in their holy mission.

But praise God, we serve a living Redeemer. Our Saviour died, was physically resurrected and returned to abide with His Father until His expected return. Unlike other "gods," Jcsus is alivc. Buddha is dead and gone; Confucius is dead and gone; Mohammed is dead and gone; ancestors are dead and gone; but our blessed Saviour, our immutable Saviour, our invincible Saviour is very much alive, and He has a word for Smyrna and for us.

PRAISE.—The church at Smyrna was a poverty-stricken church; these were poor people. They had lost all of their material possessions as a result of Emperor Domitian's dislike for and extreme persecution of Christians. Their poverty was devastatingly obvious because the Jewish community possessed such overwhelming wealth. These people were not just poor, they were πτωχεία (*ptōcheia*) which means to be destitute. They were the poorest of the poor, yet Christ says, "You are rich." They were rich in faith, truth and all of the spiritual graces that genuinely mattered. They recognized that true wealth derives from a development of personal character, not possession of material "stuff."

As the center of Roman worship, it became one's patriotic duty to come to the altar of Rome, burn incense, give money and declare "Caesar is Lord." They refused. As a result of their refusal to bow the knee to Caesar, they were considered to be unpatriotic. Many lost jobs and friends and were ostracized from Roman society. They would only proclaim "Jesus Christ is Lord." Faithful and persevering only begin to describe this wonderful church.

WARNING.—Christ warns them of the coming storm of misery and enticement to renounce Christianity. Some of the Jews who had been persecuted along with these Christians had compromised and had escaped the tyranny of the Roman emperor and the seizure of their property. These same Jews frequently "slandered" the Christians or informed on them to Roman authorities, resulting in their arrest and harsh punishment. Hostility towards these Jews caused John to describe them in such a derogatory manner. Christ says, "I know the slander of those who say they are Jews and are not, but are a synagogue of Satan." These Jews are among those about whom Paul wrote in Romans 9. Not all Jews are real Jews, he wrote, and Satan has used them to "snitch" on dedicated and consecrated Christians who suffered harshly as a result.

As the True Israel, the Smyrna Christian community bore courageously the *affliction* forced upon them by the Jews of Smyrna. What a commendation to these people, who, in spite of their poverty and in spite of the suffering that many of them had already borne because of the Jews, Christ commends them for their perseverance.

"Don't be afraid of what you are about to suffer. Look, the Devil is about to throw some of you into prison to test you, and you will have affliction for 10 days." Notice the numbers now as we proceed. While the prophetic interpreter will declare that there is literal significance in these numbers, the number ten should not be taken literally but rather symbolizes complete or excessive tribulation that is to occur in the end times. The message is clear. The fate of some Smyrna Christians may be imprisonment or death, so they are admonished to remain faithful.

PROMISED REWARD.—Christ makes a promise to these people. "Be faithful until death, and I will give you the crown of life." How poetic that John writes a reward that parallels the very moniker of the city itself. Known as the "crown city of Asia," Jesus offers to these persevering Christians a "crown of life." He tells them, "Don't worry, even in the face of death, because your faithfulness offers the gift of eternal life." They shall not be hurt by the second death; they shall not suffer the torments of Hell or any kind of eternal punishment. On the one hand, the unbeliever who dies experiences yet another kind of death that is far more painful than physical death; on the other hand, the believer who dies will be given a crown of life. He finds eternal life, the quality of which cannot be matched on earth or described in human terms.

To the church at Smyrna Christ promises, as he does to all of us who suffer and are faithful, "Be faithful until death, and I will give you the crown of life." And God never goes back on his word.

APPLICATION TO OUR POST-CHRISTIAN WORLD

Could this be a foreshadowing of history to come for us in post-Christian America? Could we be on the brink of the kind of persecution that so many other Christians have suffered across the ages? If so, is the Christian community prepared for it? And what about you, personally? How will you endure?

Skeptics will certainly declare that this is an absurd conclusion, but observing the direction of modern America, it is the only logical conclusion based upon a faith affirmation. Our nation has forgotten its Christian roots, lost its moral compass and is quickly becoming a modern Sodom and Gomorrah. Our hedonistic society revels in its advanced state of thinking and "open-mindedness." But such broad-mindedness has only led to wide-spread ridicule of today's church, declaring it old-fashioned and out-of-date. Frankly, I would rather be a bit less progressive and selective than to be so open-minded that, like a garbage can, everything and anything can be deposited. God desires that we obey Him, live by His rules, which are compassionate and generous, and serve Him unselfishly. Do these ideas apply to 21st century America? TODAY IS THE DAY OF SALVATION!

PERGAMUM 2:12-17

Pergamum was one of the great cities in the region of Mysia. The root word for its name is the Greek verb γαμέω (*gameō*) which means "to marry." It was a city of immense wealth, and the people bragged about its fortunes within the health and arts industries. It is said to have boasted of an immense library, second only to that at Alexandria. Today it lies buried beneath the modern city of Bergama.

Pergamum was a very religious city with temples located in both the Upper Acropolis as well as the Lower Acropolis. Its most famed temple was likely the Sanctuary of Asclepius at the foot of the Acropolis. Dedicated to Asclepius, the god of medicine, medical ceremonies were conducted there from the second millennium BCE. From as far back as the eighth century BCE, it was a center for the worship of Apollo.

Pergamum was also recognized and embraced for its dedication to emperor worship. As early as 29 BCE, a temple to Emperor Augustus was constructed by the provincial synod. Other temples were later constructed to honor Trajan and Severus, making Pergamum the epicenter of the imperial cult.

Being the headquarters of the imperial cult, Pergamum was also the location of the Concilia, the spiritual Supreme Court, and as such served to control all kinds of activities that occurred in the state religion of that day. The members of the Concilia were unrelenting when it came to the enforcement of emperor worship, especially under Domitian, who insisted upon it. It may very well have been that the Concilia Court was responsible for banishing John to the Isle of Patmos. Nevertheless, there is little doubt that the Concilia saw to the seizure of material possessions from the Christians whenever they refused to serve in the Roman army or refused to bow down to the "gods" of the Romans. It is little wonder that the Christians in Pergamum suffered cruelly, as they were first in line for the dispensing of the persecution of this imperial cult empowered with the authority of the emperors and supported by the full strength of the Roman army.

Like the congregation at Smyrna, the church at Pergamum possesses a blank beginning. How it started and who initially pastored it are unknown to us. Perhaps it occurred during Paul's three-year ministry at Ephesus; possibly Paul could have sent church members from Ephesus to Pergamum to establish a ministry there. We do know that it likely had no apostolic ministry with no dynamic leadership or solid doctrinal teaching. As a result, it developed into a church heavily influenced by the Nicolaitans and the Balaamites, both of whom taught a doctrine of worldliness. By being so heavily inspired by these Satanic doctrines, the church became "married" to the world. In fact, the word "dwell" in verse 13 is the Greek κατοικέω (*katoikeō*), meaning "to dwell," "to settle in," "establish" (permanently, as though married). Pergamum became a worldly church settled into a worldly city and married to the ways of the world.

TITLE.—The city of Pergamum was, above all other cities of Asia Minor, loyal to Rome. The church at Pergamum had unusual opportunities to witness, minister, share and suffer. To the church at Pergamum Christ writes, "The One who has the sharp, double-edged sword says." What a reminder from 1:16 that the Supreme One has the power to cut both ways, to both protect and judge. And that Supreme One is Jesus Christ.

Two swords are often described in the New Testament: a small shanked sword which was a part of a soldier's offensive arsenal of personal weapons and implements; and a large sword carried by soldiers to decapitate the enemy. The sword that is mentioned here by John is an implement used to separate head from body. It represents the fact that there were problems in the church from which the church must be separated. This sword is the Word of God as written in Ephesians 6:17. The two edges represent first the separation of belief from unbelief (Hebrews 4:11-12), the preaching of that Word that brings man to a recognition of his lost condition. By acknowledging his faith in God, the new convert is then cut off from unbelief. The second edge of the sword is used by Jesus for the unbelieving world which refuses to concede its sinful ways and cuts it off from salvation. These who disavow Jesus' offer of salvation will be cut off from God in judgment. The power of the sword can separate one from unbelief or salvation. The choice is yours.

PRAISE.—Notice both a commendation and a complaint. Christ's words likely refer to the promise to shield the Pergamum Christians from the persecution and martyrdom being inflicted upon them and yet to bring judgment upon false teachers and those who, in the name of Christ, prefer to commit evil deeds.

The commendation: "I know where you live—where Satan's throne is!" These words refer to the loyalty of the city and to the altar dedicated to the emperor. They were, in every way, "living in the capital city of hell."[26]

"And you are holding on to My name and did not deny your faith in Me, even in the days of Antipas, My faithful witness, who was killed among you, where Satan lives." The Antipas to whom He refers was a member of the Pergamum church—perhaps even the pastor of the church—who suffered severely during the time of Herod Antipas and who was martyred as a result of his faithfulness. Jesus knew the fire through which many of them had gone. He had personal experience. It is through John that Christ acknowledges and commends the church at Pergamum for the fidelity of many of its members to Christ under extreme difficulty.

BLAME.—But Christ has no small complaint against this church. "But I have a few things against you. You have some there who hold to the teaching of Balaam. . . You also have those who hold to the teaching of the Nicolaitans." Who were these Balaamites? What do you remember about Baalam?[27] Recall with me the confrontation of the prophets of Baal with Elijah on Mount Hebron. They offered sacrifice, called on Baal to come down and rain fire on their altar, even cut themselves with lances. Nothing happened.

Elijah then calls down the power of God, and God answers with fire and consumes not only the sacrifice and the water but also everything around it. Elijah was fearful because all of the prophets of Baal were killed. Christ employs this Old Testament experience to reveal that some people in this church at Pergamum were holding fast to the threads of Balaam, the fundamental belief of which was to sacrifice spiritual integrity in order to acquire measurable gain and personal success. Some at Pergamum were content with the status of Christianity among them as long as they could realize some material gain from being a part of the congregation.

The Nicolaitans were a hedonistic and selfish pagan group that lived life with impunity. They appear to have originated with Nicolaus, one of the six deacons appointed in Acts 6:5. Nicolaus had apparently been converted from a pagan religion to Judaism and then ultimately to Christianity. But his theology seemingly degenerated, and he possessed considerable influence in the church at Pergamum. That theology advocated heretical living such as eating animals that had been sacrificed to idols; he also encouraged sacred prostitution. This combination of doctrinal compromise taught by the Balaamite Christians and the lifestyle compromise advocated by the Nicolaitan Christians resulted in a deadly combination that was intolerable to Christ.

WARNING.—Christ warns them to repent of this attitude of indulgence and acceptance of sin that was present in their church. Not to repent is to bring down the wrath of the Lord by fighting against them. He will employ the sword, the Word of God, and rally forth as the conquering Christ to do battle against those in the church who, although they profess the name of Christ, are in reality, pawns of Roman imperial power and enemies of Christ. He simply says, "take action to eliminate the evil, or I will eliminate the evil for you." You have a choice.

PROMISED REWARD.—Verse 17 opens with a refrain, followed by the promise of a reward, "I will give the victor some of the hidden manna. I will also give him a white stone, and on the stone a new name is inscribed that no one knows except the one who receives it." To those who are faithful, Christ offers spiritual food not unlike that of the Israelites—free, life-sustaining—spiritual nourishment that is foreign to the world. Christ offers to believers the same promise He made with Israel, "I will sustain you; I will give you what you need to live."

Pergamum was also a center for mining white stone, so the reference to the "white stone" emphasizes its uniqueness to those in this church. Whether that stone was marble, limestone or alabaster, we are not told. Because the stone would be engraved, we would know it to be a malleable stone. Ray Summers offers four uses for an engraved stone in antiquity: (1) given to a man who had been tried and acquitted; (2) given to a man freed from slavery and made a citizen; (3) given to the winner of a race or contest; and (4) given to a warrior for victory over the enemy.[28]

While all of these practices are plausible, and perhaps factual, one other common custom included wearing a white amulet or colorful adornment with an inscription of the name of one's pagan god. But Christ promises that the white stone will bear a "new name," **Christ**; it is a symbol of victory—a symbol of freedom—freedom from slavery and freedom from the penalty of sin. The inscription of Christ's name provides protection, guaranteed and unwavering, for loyalty to Christ. I will make you like a victor; I will make you like a freed slave; I will protect you.

The letter to the church at Pergamum is a letter that comes down twenty-one centuries to declare unashamedly, "Christians, when you overcome, I will sustain, I will protect, and a new name written on your life is the name of Christ. Wear it with life-giving confidence."

APPLICATION TO OUR POST-CHRISTIAN WORLD

Does the church at Pergamum sound familiar? Sound modern? Are there people in our churches today who are willing to compromise faith in order to maintain the social and material status to which they are accustomed? Are there people in your church who believe that the church is just a social order? Are there people in the Christian community today who attend church in order to connect with someone with whom they might do business? Recently, on a Sunday morning, a man who owes me some money approached me to discuss the situation. I appreciated his concern, but I told him there were enough hours in the week, and I made it a practice never to talk business with anybody at church. The church is not a place to discuss business, not a fraternal order. It is a place to exercise one's commitment to the Christ who commends faithfulness and who offers protection from sin.

The 21st century church is faced with similar challenges to that of Pergamum with respect to false teachings. All around us are the influences of the New World Order, New Age culture, "progressive thinking" and materialism. Today it is vital that the church maintain a consistency in the fundamental tenets of the Scriptures and be careful to vet those who are given the responsibility to teach. Notwithstanding personal interpretation, the primacy of scriptural faith must be maintained.

Today's church is already under fire from all corners. Its theology has been disparaged as being too restrictive; its moral perspective has been criticized for being too closed-minded; its liturgy has been decried as being either too formal or too informal. Numerous leaders in the Christian faith have, over the years, caused considerable harm to and brought disgrace upon the faith by their moral lapses of judgment and/or selfish, materialistic attitudes. The message for the church at Pergamum is, indeed, as relevant to today's church as it was when John penned these words. TODAY IS THE DAY OF SALVATION!

THYATIRA 2:18-29

Although Thyatira was considered to be an insignificant city located in Asia Minor, it was a very important trading center and headquarters for a number of trade guilds. Its most well-known product of the day was purple dye extracted from the madder root and the merchandise associated with purple dye, such as cloth. Although it was a city of little importance, a major Roman highway did run through it. The city also served as an outpost for the military defense of Pergamum, located northwest of the city. Probably best associated with the city, Lydia, a friend of Paul and Silas (Acts 16:14-15), a seller of purple, was a native daughter of Thyatira.

The church at Thyatira suffered from much the same heresy as the church at Pergamum except that it was considerably more entrenched. If Pergamum was bad, then Thyatira was ten times worse. Perhaps this is why Christ wrote the longest of these seven letters to the church at Thyatira.

We know nothing about the founding of this church. Some scholars suggest that, during Paul's ministry at Ephesus, a student or students of his or even several of his converts may have founded the church at Thyatira. It seems more likely, however, that Paul started this church in the home of Lydia whose house adequately accommodated the congregation. But absent strong leadership, the church soon experienced weakness and a naïveté concerning pagan deception.

TITLE.—Introducing Himself with words of judgment from 1:14-15, Jesus Christ declares, "Write to the angel of the church in Thyatira: The Son of God, the one whose eyes are like a fiery flame and whose feet are like fine bronze." Hear the words of the God who speaks with unchallenged power and authority! Hear the words of the God who sees all and knows all, an all-knowing God whose eyes can pierce even the densest of hardened hearts and can observe one's most intimate thoughts. Hear the words of the God, the "Son of Man," who came as humankind to be a part of the earthly condition! Hear the words of the God who will exercise judgment and bring wrath on those who reject Him! He is steadfast and strong, and He judges with perfect wisdom. He is the God who will have the final say in all that was, is or ever shall be.

PRAISE.—He says in the acclamation, "I know your works—your love, faithfulness, service, and endurance. Your last works are greater than the first." What a church! Notice the merits of these Christians that Christ acknowledges and commends. (1) He knows their "works," ἔργα (*erga*), representing deeds that exhibit consistent allegiance and skills committed to God. (2) He acknowledges the root—the foundation—of their works, their "love," ἀγάπην (*agapēn*), a self-sacrificing love and concern both for fellow Christians and the Kingdom. (3) He speaks of their "faith," πίστιν (*pistin*), their loyalty to their religious beliefs which gave birth to all other spiritual qualities. (4) He references their "service," διακονίαν (*diakonian*) to others as a servant/minister whose lives are pictured here as active love. They seek not to be served but to give themselves away by being willing to sacrifice and to be inconvenienced. (5) He knows of their "patience," ὑπομονήν (*hupomonēn*), their steadfastness, their ability to be resolute in the face of toil and suffering. John concludes this introductory section by offering Christ's commendation for the significant advancement in their efforts over the years.

BLAME.—But Christ also has a complaint against them. He says, "You tolerate the woman Jezebel." Have you ever known anyone named Jezebel? There is a peculiar aspect about names. Certain names in the Bible are commonly used. People today may be named Paul or Timothy or Matthew or Mark or Luke or John or Ruth or Sarah or Eunice or Rachael. One can often find folks with the names of those who are good; such would be common. But there are also names you will not find. Have you ever known of a boy named Judas? Or a girl named Jezebel? The parallel seems obvious here. One does not typically find people named after those who, historically, are connected with evil.

This church was permitting a woman who was guilty of heresy to hold a prominent place in the church and to wield significant influence. "Jezebel"—probably not her real name but simply a moniker and also the name of Ahab's pagan queen—may have been assigned to her because of her actions. She was obviously a woman of great influence in the church. Nevertheless, she was advancing misleading ideas from the Gnostics and encouraging Nicolaitan-type immoral conduct among the brethren. Like the Jezebel of the Old Testament, she was the epitome of wickedness, leading the Christians into all kinds of immorality and spiritual degradation, encouraging them to break their vows with God.

It is important to note here that the church itself was not specifically guilty of heresy; rather, the woman was guilty. But the church tacitly tolerated this woman in their midst, thus silently accepting the heresy she promoted. Some scholars have speculated that she may have even been the pastor's wife. But whether she was the pastor's wife or simply a "type" for the Jezebel of the Old Testament, this one fact is evident—she was a corrupt woman who led people astray in collusion with Satan. She needed discipline!

Discipline. A long-lost biblical admonition to maintain the moral and spiritual integrity of a church. If you have ever read the minutes from some of the churches in the nineteenth century, especially southern protestant churches around the time of the Civil War or shortly thereafter, you will know to what I am referring. In 1969 *The Quarterly Review* published an article that I wrote about church life during the early days of Reconstruction. The project required extensive research in readings from old church minutes. I discovered that, once the Civil War had concluded, Alabama Baptist churches started allowing black people to attend their churches. And church discipline became a fairly wide-spread practice during that era. Members—both white and black—were expelled from churches because of their unacceptable behavior, i.e., public drunkenness or gossiping or sexual immorality. It became a common practice.

During the summer of 1960, I worked as a Southern Baptist youth missionary in what was then considered to be a pioneer home missions area for Baptists, the state of Indiana. While serving there in a church of perhaps 100 members or fewer, one of its members had been arrested for public drunkenness, and news of the arrest had appeared in the newspaper. On the following Wednesday evening the church gathered for the purpose of "disciplining" this member for bringing harm on the name of the church and the Lord Jesus Christ.

Now I can almost hear you say, "Oh, we wouldn't do that." Well, perhaps we should; after all, it **is** biblical. In this case, the man in question appeared before the congregation, and with tears in his eyes, apologized profusely to that congregation for the ill he had brought on the church. He asked God's forgiveness as well as that of the congregation. But the aftermath was what set this service apart. Following the service, the man was welcomed back into the fellowship, restored and accepted. What an amazing sight!

Here Christ admonishes a church that has become so apathetic and unconcerned about sin within that it has permitted people like Jezebel to take places of leadership where they can wield influence and, without penalty, allowed them to lead Christians astray. But her life of corruption would be short-lived. While Christ gave her an opportunity to repent, she refused, rather desiring to persist in her sin. Accordingly, Christ assures that her punishment will be equal to her sin. Those who follow her will endure "great tribulation," including suffering and pain; her children, those who continue to accept her teachings and follow her lifestyle, will be killed. Christ promises to give to each one "according to your works."

WARNING.—The warning is to Jezebel and her followers. She may be evil to the core, but Jesus is giving her a chance to repent. Even those who insist on being faithful to her, continuing to believe as she believes and to act as immorally as she acts will experience tribulation. These statements can also be interpreted as prophecy so that those who are faithful to Jesus will never know the tribulation to come. Jesus acknowledges that the faithful minority who are presently experiencing tribulation and persecution will not bear the burden; just "keep on keeping on," says Jesus. But those who remain loyal to Jezebel in collusion with Satan will one day experience a kind of tribulation unparalleled in human history.

PROMISED REWARD.—Christ made a promise to the church at Thyatira in verses 26-27, rising to a crescendo in verse 28. "The one who is victorious and keeps My works to the end: I will give him authority over the nations—**and he will shepherd them with an iron scepter; he will shatter them like pottery**—just as I have received this from My Father. I will also give him the morning star." To those who overcome, Christ promises that he will "not put any other burden on you." They will find themselves completely absolved as Christians as a witness to those who dare to persecute them. The "rod of iron" represents the rule and authority of the Messiah who will reign with His persecuted faithful for a thousand years. Then He promises to the victorious the "*morning star.*"

What is the morning star? The morning star represents the "greatness and glory of the Christ."[29] Thyatira may have been a church that did not have everything going its way, but those who were not duped by the influence of this evil woman and her followers offered light in the darkness. The morning star that Christ will give is the guidance and direction needed most in the dark hour of trial, troubles and tribulation that will soon beset them.

APPLICATION TO OUR POST-CHRISTIAN WORLD

Can your church live up to the standards of Thyatira? The five virtues mentioned in these verses comprise a formula for faithfulness. How many does your church fulfill?

How much of the world has eased its way into your fellowship? Does your church ignore the personal lives of its leaders at the expense of the church's character in the community? Observe the numbers in today's churches. Generally, half or less of a church's membership regularly attends its services. Even fewer are actively involved in its ministry opportunities. And yet, if the offerings are being maintained and operations are going smoothly, then all is well. Or is it?

No! All is NOT well. Christ clearly admonishes the church to clean house of those who are living a Jezebel kind of existence inside—they are not who they say they are. Jezebel was not necessarily teaching a Bible study class. Rather she was out in the work-a-day world advocating false doctrine and living the life of a reprobate while claiming to be a child of God. Christ admonishes us in today's church to be careful; be very careful. When people come into the church, they should be "tested" before offering them places of leadership, especially positions where they can have a significant influence on other Christians. Make it difficult for the "practical" Christian to inspire others, especially young believers. Encourage "lifestyle" Christians to teach and lead and continue to live their God-honoring lives in the world outside the church.

In cases where a person's behavior has reflected ill on the church, we must not condone, but must employ a style of biblical discipline that uplifts and encourages that person to live closer to Christ. To do so is to exalt the name of Christ above all other considerations and to declare unequivocally His greatness and glory. TODAY IS THE DAY OF SALVATION!

SARDIS 3:1-6

Sardis was a remarkable Greek city and one of the most important Persian cities in Asia Minor. It could well have been called "glorious Sardis." Its claim to fame was that it was the hometown of Xerxes, King of Persia. During its history, it was captured by both Cyrus and Antiochus; it was essentially destroyed in AD 17 by an earthquake. Today, only a small village, Gediz, can be found on the site of the ancient city of Sardis.

Little is known about this church. There is no record of its pastors or anyone who may have founded the church. As with the other churches in the "Revelation Circle," it could have been founded by Paul. What we do know is that the church's passion for Jesus had waned; it maintained a façade and became nothing more than a magnet and a trap for spiritually hungry people.

TITLE.—Jesus orders John: "Write to the angel of the church in Sardis: The One who has the seven Spirits of God and the seven stars." Characteristically repetitive of the attributes of Jesus Christ from chapter one offered in every letter, these can be found in 1:4 and 1:16. Jesus identifies Himself in two respects: (1) "One who has the seven Spirits of God." These seven spirits represent the completed ministry to the church of the one Holy Spirit.[30] (2) "And the seven stars." These are none other than the "angels" of 1:20, the pastors of the churches. These are not words of criticism by Jesus. He is simply saying that His method, His strategy is to work through the authority of dedicated pastors that have been called to preach the spirit of light to a lost world. "This is who I am," He says to the church at Sardis.

PRAISE.—The Lord offers a word of approbation to the church at Sardis. There is not a whole lot about which to commend the church at Sardis, but a few in the church had not participated in pagan worship or in the worldliness of the city of that day. "Clothes" (KJV, "garments") is a picture of character, and there were many who had "defiled," had "soiled" their character by unrighteous living. But Jesus commends those "who have not defiled their clothes." They will remain alive to continue their refusal to partake in the pagan worship which was so much a part of the life of that city. They will stand with

Jesus Christ in their white, undefiled clothing, testimony to their faithfulness and righteous living.

BLAME.—Jesus shares a grievance about this church that was peculiar to it. "But you are dead," He said. Sardis had the reputation for being a church of considerable energy, hustle and bustle, fervor and activism. But underneath that active exterior lay a spirituality, a real vitality, that was lifeless. It was dead. Christ describes it as a church that has a "reputation for being alive, but you are dead."

Have you ever known churches in this condition? So much activity; Sunday School bursting at the seams; the church growing and all of its organizations thriving; the budget being met, even exceeded; the recreation program better than anywhere else in the city; the senior adults traveling everywhere; expansion to multiple campuses; but the church inwardly is spiritually dead.

The church at Sardis possessed no real devotion to the cause of Christ. Such is the danger to the post-Christian church. We contrive all the activities, and we lose our spirituality. The church at Sardis was a modern-day "walking dead" church. Little would have been required for this church to close its doors and exist no more. Prompt action was required, therefore, for the church at Sardis to be revived. The forms were all there; the function was lacking. The outward appearance was there, but these people needed to be filled once more with the true power of and sincere devotion to Jesus Christ. The church had a name for doing good works. It was well-known in the community. Often heard would be such words as, "That First Church at Sardis is wonderful. Look at all the things it does." But Christ has a way of judging churches not by their activity but by their purpose and meaningful intent. Christ observes that which underlies all the activity. In terms of spirituality, in terms of genuine faithfulness to Christ and their primary mission, Sardis failed the test.

COUNSEL.--Then Christ instructs the church. Three measures are demanded: (1) Be watchful. Jesus says, "Be alert," because, like a thief who doesn't announce his presence, so I will come unannounced. (2) Hang on. Jesus knows what is to happen, and He advises that they "strengthen what remains," hold fast to the hand of the One who can help them overcome. (3) Remember and repent. Christ wants every Christian to maintain a lifestyle that reflects the life He lived. If Christians do not reflect Christ, repentance is the only alternative.

The death rattle of the Sardis church had not yet sounded. There remained a few who remained spiritually alive, but it would require immediate, emergency action to return the church to its once powerful, spiritual influence.

WARNING.—Jesus warns the church that "if you are not alert, I will come like a thief." Unless the church at Sardis remembers the real content of religion as it was first received, unless and until the church returns to those first principles that it acknowledged when it first came to know Jesus, and practices them, if it fails to do this, then Christ will come upon it in judgment and destruction.

PROMISED REWARD.—For those who had not bowed to the ways of the world, Jesus affirms three promises: First, "they will walk with Me in white," white being a symbol of salvation and purity. That purification comes as a result of washing their garments in the blood of the Lamb. What a reward awaits those who are faithful in the face of trouble and persecution, those who are deeply spiritual in their hearts, those who are complete in Jesus Christ. They will trade in all their filthy rags of this world for the white clothes of a new nature.

Second, Jesus will never blot their names from the book of life. In antiquity, cities often registered their citizenry. Ways to have one's name erased from such a registry was by death, by moving to another city, committing a capital crime or the act of treason against the government. Jesus says, "I'm not like an earthly king. For those who are faithful to me, who honestly and sincerely carry the spiritual load of this church, those are the names that will be written in the Lamb's Book of Life." Those are the names that shall never be erased because of the power and commitment of their spiritual lives.

Third, He promises to "acknowledge his name before My Father." Jesus will acknowledge the names of the faithful to the Father of Light. Recall the words of Jesus in Matthew 10:32 (Luke 12:8): "Everyone who will acknowledge Me before men, I will also acknowledge him before My Father in Heaven." He declares to those who are spiritually dead to come back to life. Renew your faith and strengthen your resolve to live for Me. But He also says, if you are unsaved, today you have an opportunity to repent and come to Me. In either case, He promises that those who are spotless, those who have repented, those who are perfectly righteous, those who are carrying the load of the church, whose spirituality is commendable, they will be the ones who will know perfect security and honor.[31] And such is the promise to the post-Christian church.

APPLICATION TO OUR POST-CHRISTIAN WORLD

Is the modern church bowing to the pressures of today's rapidly changing culture? Many millennials criticize the church because it is too settled and unadventurous. Yet Christ calls for the church to be apart from the world. The church is called to be distinctive in, not characterized by the world. It is to be "in the world but not of the world."

So many churches boast about programs and opportunities offered to members without associating the fundamental purpose or mission of these activities, namely, to proclaim Christ and Him crucified. Singing beautiful music in a choir without a corresponding ministry purpose is empty. I once observed a minister of music actually ask for several already robed singers in his choir room to go sit in the congregation on a particular Sunday because the chairs had already been arranged in the loft, and he did not want the choir to appear unbalanced. That is activity without purpose, mission and ministry.

Traveling on a mission trip without understanding the "Who" for whom you are traveling and serving is ineffective. Form without substance results in a "walking dead" church. TODAY IS THE DAY OF SALVATION!

PHILADELPHIA 3:7-13

The church at Philadelphia was a marvelous church. Located in the city of brotherly love, it was well-known from 159 BCE to the time when John wrote this letter. It had originally derived its name from the relationship of Attalus II, King of Pergamum, with his brother Eumenes II, a co-regent of Pergamum and King of Lydia. He so loved his brother that he became known as a "brother-lover,"[32] hence, Philadelphia, city of brotherly love. It was a center of Greek culture, reputed as the epicenter to spread the Greek language, a city known for promulgating Greek customs. It was the Greekest of all Greek cities. In later years, Philadelphia became known as "little Athens" because of its Greek reputation. Like other cities around it, Philadelphia suffered greatly in the earthquake of AD 17, so much so that, three years later, the historian Strabo wrote that numerous of the inhabitants of the city were now living in the countryside surrounding the city for fear of aftershocks.

The church at Philadelphia, like most of the churches of the Revelation Circle, possesses a somewhat scant history. We do not know who founded the church, who might have been its first pastor or who comprised any of its leadership. We do know, however, that like the city in which it was located, the church was a soul winning, missionary and evangelistic church, dedicated to sharing the witness of Jesus Christ to the Greek world.

TITLE.—Of all the letters to the seven churches, this is the only one of which good alone is spoken. It is also the only letter to depart from employing the characteristics written in chapter one to designate the Lord Jesus. Perhaps Jesus did not see this church as He did the others, dead, lacking in faith, teaching unsound doctrine. To those churches He became a judge. His goal was not to judge Philadelphia, He was content with the church and its missionary zeal.

Rather, Jesus harks to Isaiah 22:22 and identifies Himself with Eliakim, the son of Hilkiah. By giving Eliakim the "key of the house of David," he becomes the steward of Hezekiah with all the power and authority of a king's steward. In Isaiah, Eliakim is a "type" of the Messiah. "The Messiah, who is the son of David, holds the keys of the messianic kingdom. It is his authority to open these doors."[33] These doors of opportunity become open for the church at Philadelphia, and it pursues that missionary purpose with passionate enthusiasm.

PRAISE.—John writes, "I know your works. Because you have limited strength, have kept My word, and have not denied My name, look, I have placed before you an open door that no one is able to close." Jesus is placing before this church the opportunity to occupy a strategic role in the evangelization of the world. Acknowledging that they are a weak congregation, physically and financially, yet they have been faithful and are strong spiritually because they have not succumbed to the brow beating of the "synagogue of Satan" by denying His name. These fake Jews will eventually find themselves bowing before the feet of this church.

PROMISED REWARD.—Jesus promises His sustaining grace during the forthcoming time of Tribulation. Because of their loyalty under weakness and under severe difficulty, the Lord promises to justify them completely. He will make the persecuting Jews, the Jews who say they are Jews but are not, the persecuting Jews who are doing Satan's work—He will make them understand and recognize that His true love is reviled most by these persecuting Jews. The ones upon whom others frown are the ones whom God really loves, and because they have been faithful, He promises His sustaining mercy and divine grace to encourage them when suffering seeks to consume them and the world. And consume them it did. A terrible time of persecution encompassed them, but it was a time of suffering that would not conquer these zealous Christians.

The promise is also for the time of Tribulation to come in the last days. The rcal church will not go through these trials; the false church, the apostate church will know and experience the Tribulation in all its pain and misfortune. But in the Tribulation, Jesus says, "I will also keep you from the hour of testing." His promise is to take His children before that dreadful era of misery; they will be happily in the presence of Christ as declared in 3:10b.

WARNING.— Christ makes a promise. "I am coming quickly." In the middle of this promise, Jesus injects a warning, "Hold on to what you have." He admonishes them to remain steadfast and honorable in the face of persecution. Here is a people who, in the face of persecution, are bursting with spiritual enjoyment, who are seeking every opportunity for service in the name of Jesus.

Following this warning, Jesus completes His promised reward. To the faithful servant of the Lord Jesus Christ, He will make him a "pillar in the sanctuary of My God." Jesus will offer strength and stability like the pillars of the temple offer sturdiness during the earthquakes that ravaged the region. No longer must they leave their homes for fear of crumbling in on them. They had Jesus' assurance.

Finally, He promises to memorialize their name. "I will write on him the name of my God." It was common for pagan rcligions to inscribe the name of their god on the structure in which they worshipped. But Jesus says, I will write on you the name of My God, emphasizing the "authority of Jesus Christ to bestow upon his faithful followers the designation "children of my Father."[34] He will even go so far as to inscribe the name of the city of His God—the new Jerusalem—marking him as a citizen of the heavenly kingdom. Both the name of Christ and the name of His abode will be conferred upon all who are called faithful and will offer an assurance of a heavenly home.

The Philadelphians are the antithesis of the church at Sardis. The church at Sardis sought the opportunity to serve, but they served out of a selfish motive. The church at Philadelphia sought the opportunity to serve also, but they served in the name of Christ for the simple, shear, spiritual enjoyment that they received from serving Jesus. Christ knew that the church was weak, but He also knew that the church had been faithful, so no condemnation was forthcoming for the church at Philadelphia, only commendation.

APPLICATION TO OUR POST-CHRISTIAN WORLD

As I look at our world, and especially our country today, I think what a marvelous opportunity our country has possessed for almost 250 years, and yet it appears to have been squandered. We have been put in the position to declare to the world the thriving culture of a nation whose motto is "In God we trust." This nation has been tendered the opportunity to show the world how living a life of morality and faith can bring peace and tranquility. Yet, in many ways it has been wasted. Even in times of difficulty—financial depression and world war—our nation has unified and recovered but, at the same time, failed to show the world the real reason behind such unity and recovery, God Himself.

In much the same manner, how often has the church failed in its mission to evangelize the world by compromising its convictions to seek the approval of society and its culture. The opportunity to bring Jesus to the world, the chance to make the earth a more peaceful planet and the ability to employ our knowledge and scientific progress to provide holy nourishment to an otherwise morally and spiritually bankrupt world appears to have vanished. With evil lurking all around the globe, "America has ceased to be great because America has ceased to be good."[35]

A time of testing is coming. Is the church today prepared for the onslaught of evil? Are you as an individual ready to take on the face of evil and persecution? Even some of the latest polls proclaim that many Americans no longer believe the United States to be a Christian nation. Whether statistically or spiritually, it is time for the church to rise in power and show the world the mercy and grace of God. Only then will God justify us even as He promised to the Philadelphians. TODAY IS THE DAY OF SALVATION!

LAODICEA 3:14-22

Laodicea was founded in 250 BCE by Antiochus II who named it after his wife, Laodice. Chiefly characterized by exceeding riches, Laodicea was one of the best-known centers of commerce in this geographical area of the world. It was the crossroads for three major Roman highways which approached the city from three different directions. As a commercial freeway, its distinction was well established, opening it to the cultural and religious influences of all who traveled through the region.

Laodicea's commerce included the production of special garments and carpets, and it soon became the Paris of its day. Its prosperity in commerce led to the development of the city as a financial and banking center.[36] Philanthropy thrived in the city. Even after the earthquake of AD 60, Laodicea requested no assistance from the ruling Romans but rather reconstructed the city with money from its wealthy citizens. Such wealth inspired an appreciation of the arts and promoted the advancement of science and literature, as proven by the existence of a medical school. As a result of such an attitude of self-sufficiency, "the spirit of the town had made itself felt in the church."[37] The city developed a form of godlessness along with its riches.

Little is known about the church at Laodicea. We are not told who founded it, yet from textual evidence in the New Testament, we can infer that Epaphras, one of the apostle Paul's disciples, likely planted it or at least introduced the Gospel there. We know that Epaphras founded the church at Colossae (Colossians 1:6–7), Laodicea's close neighbor to the east. Therefore, it seems plausible, if not probable, that he would also be responsible for planting the church at Laodicea.

TITLE.—Jesus begins by pronouncing the source of the message to follow. He is the "Amen." The Greek word ἀμήν (*amēn*) means "so be it" or "so let it be." Jesus declares that the Word of God is true and all that will follow is true, and He confirms by "Amen." Since Jesus Christ is the "so be it" of God, the last days will be just as

He says. He says further, "I am the walking, living, incarnate visible proof that the Word of God is true—so be it." He is the great I AM; the truth is in Jesus Christ.

Harking back once more to chapter one (1:5), He proclaims Himself to be "the faithful and true witness." Witness to what? Witness to who and what the Father is; witness to the Word (John 1:1); witness to truth (John 14:6); witness to what He will do in the last days. His is a witness on which one can stake his life and future. It is a faithful witness, trusted when other witnesses fail; it is dependable, can be counted on. It is a true witness, when other witnesses disappoint; it is truth incarnate.

Finally, He says that He is the "Originator of God's creation." He is the ἀρχή (*archē*), the original cause of the creation of God. "All things were created through Him, and apart from Him not one thing was created" (John 1:3). He was not created first because He was not created. He has always been and is the original means through which God accomplished His work of creation. Paul echoes these thoughts in Colossians 1:15-18: "He is the image of the invisible God, the firstborn over all creation. For everything was created by Him . . . and by Him all things hold together." Jesus can truthfully claim to be the designer and creator of all that is. No truer words were ever spoken.

PRAISE.—Unique to this letter is the fact that there is not a single word of commendation for this compromising, ingrown, unbelieving, self-serving church. It was a church in name only, a church that was grinding away at doing its own thing, rich in resources but immensely poor in spiritual energy. Furthermore, the Laodiceans were completely oblivious to the fact that Christ had no part in the pitiful performances they put on every week. There was no praise to be shared!

Christ says to the church at Laodicea: "I know your works, that you are neither cold nor hot. I wish that you were cold or hot. So, because you are lukewarm, and neither hot nor cold, I am going to vomit you out of My mouth. Because you say, 'I'm rich; I have become wealthy and need nothing,' and you don't know that you are wretched, pitiful, poor, blind, and naked, I advise you to buy from Me. . ." Jesus knows this church inside and outside.

BLAME.—Observe the statement of blame. Christ's complaint referred to the spiritual lethargy of the church. You see, as a church it was not entirely cold, i.e., it was not completely and utterly indifferent. In fact, Jesus wishes that it had been cold, for as a cold church it could have repented of sin and returned to a strong faith in Christ. But neither was it hot; it was not characterized by a fervent heat and passionate zeal for living and being and doing for Christ. Jesus would have preferred that they be hot, on fire for Him. Yet, because the Laodiceans were neither cold nor hot, they became distasteful to Christ. They were sick unto death. Christ counsels them in verse 18 with several interesting admonitions, all based upon the three chief business activities that characterized Laodicea.

First, Jesus says that "I advise you to buy from Me gold refined in the fire so that you may be rich." Laodicea was a wealthy financial center. Because of the scope of its banking empire, Laodicea enjoyed the spoils of a thriving investment environment. Even the church possessed material wealth, yet with all that material wealth, they were absolutely and spiritually poverty stricken. They may have inhabited a place high on the material possession food chain, but with respect to their spiritual condition, they placed much lower. Thus, the Lord counsels them in verse 18 to buy "gold" from Me." The word "gold" here refers to the deity of Jesus and His imputed righteousness. He pleads with them to buy from someone who will not just take their money. He urges them to buy from Him who knows what they desperately need to purchase, He who has already paid the supreme price on the cross.

Then He says, "white clothes so that you may be dressed and your shameful nakedness not be exposed." A second thriving business in the city was the textile industry or more specifically the black wool market. Like the "Fifth Avenue" of today, the clothing produced from these fine wools was in great demand throughout the known world. Laodicea could boast, and rightfully so, that it was the fine clothing capital of the region. And many Christians had benefitted from the success of this industry.

But the Lord acknowledges that they are being blinded to their own plight. Christ asserts that, in spite of being overburdened with wool and clothing and cloth, yet they are spiritually "naked." They need to come to Christ and obtain from Him the covering that will genuinely hide their exposed condition before God. What these people called exquisite clothing left them bare before God. As with "gold" above, "white garments" here also refers to Jesus' imputed righteousness. The Laodicean church had religion but lacked relationship. They had attempted to substitute their own righteousness for the righteousness that can only come from God. They were naked but unable to see their nakedness. They needed to purchase from God the righteous robes of rectitude.

Finally, Jesus says they need "ointment to spread on your eyes so that you may see." Near Laodicea was located a famous medical center and medical school most specifically recognized for its ophthalmic treatments, especially the ointments developed by the two physicians practicing there. If one required eye treatment, even eye surgery, the medical school at Laodicea was the preferred choice. Developed at this medical center was an eye salve sought throughout the Roman world. People would come from near and far to obtain the salve to bring comfort and healing to their eye troubles.

Jesus refers to this characteristic of the region to highlight their paucity of spiritual enlightenment and devout shallowness. "You are so blind," Jesus says, "you need to come to me, and I will give you an eye salve that will really allow you to see." Christ possessed all that the church sorely lacked, spiritual wealth, spiritual clothing, spiritual eye salve.

WARNING.--Next comes the warning in verse 19. "As many as I love, I rebuke and discipline. So be committed and repent." The Lord warns them to repent, recognize their dullness and to allow the spirit of God to motivate them to a life of passion for the kingdom rather than to lead a mere lukewarm existence.

Then one of the most poignant pictures in all Christendom is painted by Jesus Christ in verse 20, "Listen! I stand at the door and knock. If anyone hears My voice and opens the door, I will come in to him and have dinner with him, and he with Me." The church had it all—wealth, power, fame—everything except Christ. He was on the outside seeking entrance, asking only that He be allowed to enter, to commune and to share *koinonia*, fellowship.

To the one who opens, Christ promises an unimaginable reward. Even as Jesus ascended to and sat down at the right hand of the Father in heaven, so also he who opens the door to Christ will have the privilege of accepting a place of honor beside the Lord. It is a promised glory alongside a glorified Christ. What a future!

APPLICATION TO OUR POST-CHRISTIAN WORLD

Laodicea represents the church of post-Christian America that is willing to compromise fundamental beliefs of salvation to accommodate an ever more worldly culture. Jesus is not a God of compromise on the issues that count most. Yet there are churches today that bow to the pressures of society and water down their theology to the point that it becomes ineffective.

A church that preaches any gospel less than truth is, like Laodicea, an apostate church. Belief in the virgin birth of Jesus, His atoning death on the cross, His resurrection to new life, His ascension to the Father in heaven and His promise of a New Heaven and a New Earth for believers—all of these dogmas must be believed and lived out before an unbelieving world. A church that advocates anything less is a traitor to the Gospel. TODAY IS THE DAY OF SALVATION!

POSTSCRIPT

Viewed in its entirety, the Book of Revelation is not a book of history, it is a book of prophecy. In verse 19 of the first chapter, Jesus offers an outline with respect to what is to follow. The vision is divided into three parts: The Past, "what you have seen," The Present, "what is" and The Future, "what will take place after this."

The past has to do with the Revelator, Jesus Christ, chapter 1. It is all about His plan of Redemption and His atoning death on the cross. From Genesis to Jude, the details of the past are described, and God's plan for fallen man is revealed and executed.

The present has to do with the seven churches that existed in Asia Minor and to which the letters were addressed, chapters 2-3. What we know from the letters provides a wealth of information on the status and condition of those churches.

The future refers to the seven periods of the church age, chapters two-three; the judgment of Israel and the coming king, chapters 4-19; followed by the judgment of Satan, the Millennium, the New Heaven and the new earth, chapters 20-22. These seven churches represent seven ages through which the church has journeyed. These ages or church types represent all churches in all generations for all times, and as such, they also represent all church members. This idea was advanced by Reverend C. I. Scofield, a 19th and 20th century theologian and minister, and Clarence Larkin, a Baptist pastor and Bible teacher. It is also the position of one of Southern Baptists' most beloved and dynamic preachers of the 20th century, Dr. John Bisagno. Dr. Bisagno was pastor of the First Baptist Church of Houston, Texas, for more than thirty years. To get a better idea of this history, consider this summary.

The church ages are defined as:

Ephesian Age—AD 50 -AD 150. This age, which begins at Pentecost (the beginning of the church age) and ends with the coming of Christ (the end of the church age) is described as a time of slow, diminishing zeal for Christ. The love of the church slowly cooled.

Smyrna Age—AD 150-AD 312. This age is defined as the age of persecution of content. If you were a Christian, you could expect persecution and even death.

Pergamus Age—AD 312-AD 600. This church age emerged from the edict of Emperor Constantine that everyone in his kingdom was required to become a Christian. Church and government were in collusion, and in every way, the church was married to the world.

Thyatira Age—AD 600-AD 1500. This age is characterized by false doctrine. No real truths were being taught. Life and culture, religion and philosophy, science and education became so ineffective that this period in world history has come to be known as the Dark Ages. The church of the time was no different.

Sardis Age—1500-1750. This period principally saw a dead church. It had become rotten to the core from false doctrine. But toward the end of this age, the church had new life breathed into it through the preaching of such men as John Knox, John Calvin, Huldrych Swingli, Martin Luther and George Whitefield.

Philadelphia Age—1750-1925. This age was marked by evangelism and missions. It is the age of the outreaching church. During this period, revival erupted with preachers and evangelists dedicated to declaring truth and righteousness. It was also during this age that the modern missionary movement began. Churches rekindled their desire to proclaim the truth of God. Men like William Carey, Adoniram Judson, Hudson Taylor and Lottie Moon started what has become a missionary movement unparalleled in world history.

Laodicean Age—1925-Return of Jesus Christ. This is the age of an apostate world, the age during which we are moving toward the appearance of the Antichrist. It will be the age of unity—one world government, one world currency, one world court, one system of communicating, and ultimately one world church.

As we study this marvelous book, keep these thoughts in mind. You may or may not agree with this idea but keep an open mind with respect to its relevance for us as we move forward during what, perhaps, are the end times.

APPLICATION TO OUR POST-CHRISTIAN WORLD

Let me sum up these letters to the seven churches. Taken as a composite, the messages to these seven churches of Asia Minor constitute a fair warning from Christ himself, as expressed in the exhortations to each of these churches. He warns the churches of our post-Christian world, indeed He warns the churches of the 21st century and beyond to hear the message offered by the spirit to the churches. These letters may have been penned more than 2,000 years ago, but they speak as passionately to the post-Christian church as they did 2,000 years ago. Jesus continues to exhort the church to *listen to what the Spirit says to the churches*.

The church at Ephesus represents the danger of losing one's first love, that fresh passion for and devotion to Christ that characterized the early church. Jesus began with eleven dedicated men who willingly laid their lives on the line to share the "good news" of Jesus. Because of their commitment and perseverance, the Gospel spread like a wildfire until it encompassed the globe. How many of us today would be willing literally to give up our lives for what we believe? The church at Ephesus had abandoned that zeal felt at first, bowing to the pressures of the culture around them. How many post-Christian churches are closing their doors because their members have been influenced by the culture of the world invading the spiritual atmosphere of the church?

The church at Smyrna represents the danger of the fear of suffering. They were exhorted by Christ not to fear the idea of suffering.

Since its founding on Judeo-Christian principles, our country and our churches have enjoyed unprecedented freedom to worship and believe as led by the Holy Spirit. But, oh my, how our nation has changed! In post-Christian America where the latest polls indicate our loss of character as a "Christian" nation, Christ followers are being ridiculed and persecuted as never before. Inevitably, to continue down this road of perdition, the relatively mild persecution of today will lead to severe persecution by government and/or other groups. Throughout other parts of the world, Christians are dying for their faith. It is imperative that the church hear the words of the letter to the church at Smyrna and heed this admonition not to fear the coming of suffering.

The church at Pergamum illustrates the constant danger of doctrinal compromise. Doctrinal compromise does not refer to the importance of ideas that form non-foundational or non-absolute tenets of the Christian faith but are considered important enough to divide a congregation or church body. Differences with respect to music and worship styles, the Tribulation, speaking in tongues, or any other doctrine that centers on opinion and interpretation rather than the truth would not be considered doctrinal compromise. Doctrinal compromise refers to those beliefs that can best be described as unstable and unhealthy. They apply to the basic beliefs of the faith, the creeds that are common to the Christian faith and that are often recited in the Apostles' Creed.

The church at Pergamum had become "Hell's Headquarters."[38] The church was so infiltrated by heresy that it had lost its vitality. Mixed up by the teachings of heathen neighbors, many in the church accepted spiritual compromise as the norm. Like the church at Pergamum, cultism and the post-Christian New Age movement that is so immeasurably influencing the 21st century church, are a first step to complete defection from the faith. The Lord's clear call to the modern church is to heed the warning to the church at Pergamum.

Similar to the church at Pergamum, the church at Thyatira is a monument to the danger of moral compromise. The church at Thyatira accepted a willingness to harbor a sinful woman who advocated for principles of heresy. Claiming to be a mystic to whom God offered a special revelation, Jezebel wielded a misleading influence upon the church. Do you know of any churches today that have tolerated, and in many cases, have encouraged compromise of biblical moral truths and standards? Are there churches that you know that support cohabitation without marriage, defend abortion or view morals as an outdated list of "don'ts"?

All too often, the children of our post-Christian world are permitted to engage in activities and live lifestyles that are completely foreign to that supported by Scripture. Moral compromise! The tendency of many modern parents is simply to take the easy way out and say, "Well, it won't hurt just this one time." Moral compromise! I know when compared to today's thinking, the church is rapidly abandoning the "old time religion," a faith focused on the mind of Christ, not compromise. We must return to the times when our faith was not up for sale to the highest bidder. Jesus cannot and will not tolerate the compromise of morality and clean living simply to appease a reprobate world.

The church at Sardis is not unlike so many post-Christian churches. Observe any church website and notice the glut of activities being offered. A choir tour here, a mission trip there, a senior adult dinner and entertainment, or a Wednesday night "prayer" service. All of these activities are worthwhile and encouraged unless they lack inner spirituality.

To the church at Sardis, Jesus issued a warning against spiritual deadness. Orthodoxy without life, alive yet dead. Mere outward appearance, no inward reality; that is the church at Sardis. Concerned more with appearance, the post-Christian church has often been more interested in being "seen" for doing good than for actually pleasing God. While the post-Christian church is more concerned about influence and form, Jesus seeks real substance.

Philadelphia. Oh, how we are encouraged by the church at Philadelphia to endure with patience, to maintain the little strength that we may have that we can wait patiently for the Lord's return. In our post-Christian world, the church at Philadelphia should serve as an example to every church to love the Lord and work tirelessly for His Kingdom.

The final message to the church at Laodicea is the crowning indictment. It is a warning against the danger of lukewarmness and self-sufficiency. Like a tepid bottle of soda, a lukewarm church is unpalatable, indifferent, lethargic.

Perhaps the desire for fervency is present, but the coldness caused by outside influences affects that fervor to the point of being distasteful. God declares that He will *vomit you out of My mouth*. Whether we think we can do it on our own, whether the power of the "new age" negatively impacts our faith or whether we become unconscious of a desperate spiritual need, we are in trouble.

The invitation given then to the seven churches of Asia Minor is to hear what the spirit says. What the spirit says is extended to all men, to all churches everywhere, then and now—yesterday, today and tomorrow. Only a loving God would have men hear and believe and turn from their idols of sin and self and look in faith to the Son of God who loved them and who gave himself for them. TODAY IS THE DAY OF SALVATION!

CHAPTER 5
THE SOVEREIGNTY OF GOD
4:1-5:14

The drama of this great book begins to unfold in the revelation of the eschatological calendar. Here John sets the stage for us to see the vision so well-prepared by the living, preeminent, righteous and victorious Lord. It is time for the Lord Christ to assure His persecuted followers that all is not lost. The struggle may be harsh, and the battle may be difficult, but in the final analysis, absolute triumph over evil and the world is assured.

THE THRONE, THE ELDERS AND THE LIVING CREATURES, 4:1-11

Between chapter three and chapter four, the Christians of earth have been Raptured to heaven. The vision of John, at this point, is to reveal what heaven will be like for those who have been Raptured and how the last days will play out.

So, what is the Rapture? It is that time in God's plan when, immediately before the Tribulation, all who have accepted Jesus as Christ and acknowledged Him as Lord will be "snatched away" from this worldly plane to live with Christ in the heavenlies. While the word "Rapture" does not occur in the Bible, its meaning is clear from the use of the Greek ἁρπάζω (*harpadzō*) meaning to "seize," "snatch up" or "catch away." Rapture is the clear meaning in the writings of Paul in 1 Thessalonians 4:16-17. Here he employs *harpadzō* to describe how we, as believers, will be "caught up" with Jesus at the time of the Rapture. Two other key passages present the idea of *harpadzō*. In one passage Jesus offers a glimpse of the heavenly glory in John 14:1-3, and Paul, once more, in 1 Corinthians 15:51-52 offers a descriptive preview of what the Rapture will be like.

In the tradition of "semper paratus," Jesus' words from the Olivet Discourse in Matthew 24 make the Rapture a real event. In Jesus' Discourse, He illustrates in detail the manner in which the Rapture will occur. No conditional clauses, no uncertain avowals, no vague proclamations. Jesus is clear that, one day—date and time known only to the Father—the snatching away of the faithful will suddenly and unmistakably occur.

You may ask how we can be confident that the Rapture occurs at this point in the story? Let me offer four reasons for including it here.[39]

1) Revelation, chapters 4 and 5, show us a vision of heaven, while chapter 6 introduces the period of the Tribulation. Jesus has promised in 3:10 to keep those in the church at Philadelphia from the coming "hour of testing." It would be most appropriate then to exit believers before presenting a vision of what they will be doing in heaven.

2) There is no mention of the church in the remainder of the Revelation, indicating that the church is not on the earth during the Tribulation. While there are 16 occurrences of the "church" in chapters 1-3, all references to the church are absent in chapters 6-18.

3) The use of Old Testament language and symbols in chapters 4-18 points to Israel, not the church. After all, the age of the Gentiles (Christian age) is no more, and the Tribulation fulfils the prophecy of Jeremiah 30:7, during which the "time of Jacob's trouble" will occur and God will deal with His chosen people through a time that is unparalleled in history.

4) There is considerable similarity between the events of Revelation 4:1-2 and other scriptural teachings on the Rapture like 1 Thessalonians 4:13-18.

Beginning here in chapter four John sees the future of humankind as the door of heaven is opened to him. Through this door he observes the very throne of God upon which "the One" is seated. And so begins a vision, indescribable in earthly terms, but divinely inspired in heavenly terms initiating an experience that the Seer would narrate in acute detail over the next chapters.

John sees with heavenly clarity of the glorious throne of God where we as believers will join the angels and the elders in praise and adoration to the One on the throne. "After this" (v. 1) refers to the Rapture when the door of the heavenly kingdom is opened, and, through the words of John, we are given a glimpse of glory as it will be for the believer. And then the voice of One like a trumpet—none other than the voice of Almighty God Himself—sounds and invites John to "Come up here, and I will show you what must take place after this." The church will be no more, the church age will have expired, and the trumpet shall serve as the clarion call for all Christians to depart their earthly abode.

Immediately John finds himself in the throne room of God. He witnesses the presence of a glorious figure on the throne who is the Lord God Almighty, the Triune God. Who else could it be? Consider the description.

In the Old Testament, the High Priest wore a breastplate on which were placed twelve stones, representing the twelve tribes of Israel. The first stone was carnelian (sardius), representing the tribe of Reuben. The last stone in the breastplate was jasper, which symbolized the tribe of Benjamin. But these stones not only represented their respective tribes, but they also represented the first and last stones of the breastplate, the Alpha and Omega, the Beginning and the End, the great Creator God. Jasper, with its pure white color and clarity speaks to the holiness of God, while the sardius, a brilliant red stone, is a picture of the Messiah, our Lord Jesus Christ and His vicarious atonement, redemption—the price paid—by the righteous One who occupies the throne.

Here we have God the Father, the First and the Last, Jesus Christ, the living, breathing human sacrificial source of our redemption, and then in verse five, John writes about seven fiery torches which are the seven spirits whom we met earlier. This figurative language harks back to Isaiah 11 where the prophet writes about the Holy Spirit in all His attributes. Taken collectively, a picture of God in all three of His Trinitarian manifestations emerges.

Around the throne is a rainbow, God's reminder of the covenant He had made with His creation. It is a circular rainbow, complete, perfect, unlike the partial rainbow that we observe on earth, and it offers a visual reminder of the living hope that is found in relation to God through His Son, Jesus Christ. Just as the rainbow was a sign to Noah that God would never again bring judgment in this form on the earth, so the rainbow of Revelation affirms that God has already judged the earth spiritually, and He will never judge that way again. God is as good as His Word, and this rainbow offers a vibrant hope in the midst of judgment.

In verse 4 John notes that the throne of "the One" was surrounded by twenty-four other thrones upon which were seated "elders." What do these thrones and elders represent and does the number have any significance?

Priests were established in Israel to provide an intermediary between God and the people. The Tribe of Levi was designated as

Jehovah's Levitical agents. From 1 Chronicles 24:3-5, we learn that King David divided the Levitical priesthood into 24 orders. Each order not only represented itself individually but also represented the entire priestly tribe. With the death of Jesus, no longer was a priestly intermediary needed to act on behalf of the people before God. As true believers in Jesus Christ, we are individual priests before God and can approach His throne of grace independently.

The thrones and the corresponding elders of chapter four, therefore, represent the twelve tribes of Israel and the twelve disciples, which together, symbolize the Judeo-Christian tradition and the blood-bought church of the Living Christ, the body of Christ, all the redeemed of all the ages. These elders are robed in "white clothes," suggesting the purity and righteousness of the Redeemed of the Lord. They are adorned with "gold crowns," not crowns of royalty or governmental authority but στέφανος (*stephanos*), crowns of victory, honor, glory.

"Flashes of lightning and rumblings of thunder came from the throne." These occurrences can be found throughout Revelation: 8:5; 10:2-3; 11:19; and 16:18. In them the voice of God peals throughout the earth striking fear in all those who dispute the truth of redemption. Take heart, believer, God declares that He will not leave you alone but will bring the power and authority of His throne to encourage you, offer stability and guarantee security.

Toward what do the lightning and thunder point? Judgment; the final judgment; the Great White Throne Judgment that will occur after the thousand-year reign of Christ on the earth. At that judgment, we too will be seated, not to give an account of our sins (for we will have already been judged on that account) but to explain what we did with our salvation. Rather than a judgment on our sins, ours will be an "audit"[40] of our Christian life.

In the seven lamps God has assured all believers that the Holy Spirit, the perfect Holy Spirit, demonstrates God's dominion and His faithful companionship. The "sea of glass," acting like a moat surrounding a castle, illustrates God's unapproachable nature, His preeminence. Yet, because we can now approach God directly, the sea, which once separated us from God is no more (21:1).

John introduces us to "four living creatures covered with eyes in front and in back (who) were in the middle and around the throne." While numerous scholars view these creatures as real "beasts" and so translate the text, the Greek word employed here is ζῷον (*zōon*) which means "living being." In Ezekiel 1:5f the prophet describes a vision that includes חַיּוֹת (*chawyot*), creatures similar to that shown in Revelation 4:6-8, non-descript living creatures. He adds yet another picture of such creatures in Ezekiel 10:14-15. The prophet explains that these creatures are angels (cherubim). The most reasonable interpretation (using the Bible to explain itself) is that the creatures in Revelation 4 are angels.

Their features might sound frightening, but they actually represent the attributes of God. The lion represents God's courage; the young bull represents His power; the man embodies God's intellect and wisdom; the eagle symbolizes God's quickness in protecting and redressing His people. As representative of the essential characteristics of God, these creatures demonstrate His eternal vigilance on behalf of His people.[41]

These angels are there to do God's will, to protect God's people, to worship God. Unlike the elders who worship God out of relationship, these angels worship God because they are created to do so. They worship God ceaselessly with "Holy, holy, holy, Lord God Almighty, who was, who is, and who is coming."

Worship continues as the elders join in. These who represent the Bride of Christ, with devotion and praise, worship the Creator, adoring Him as the eternal God. And like the victorious athlete who offers his crown to his sovereign, so the elders cast down their crowns before the Sovereign of the universe. They cast their crowns at his feet, in recognition that they owe their triumph to Him. To His divine dealings, to His prudent and compassionate authority they owe their victory, and the most appropriate manner to acknowledge their gratitude is to worship Him by placing their crowns at His feet.

This is worship in spirit and in truth. Worship is not being caught up in the form of a church service. Worship is not singing along as the worship leaders lead. Worship is not having our minds cluttered with the insignificant. Worship is a total investment of one's entire person, the immersion of mind, body and spirit in praise. Worship is seeing a holy God, confessing that He is THE God. We should humble ourselves before Him, acknowledging Him as the One who created us. It would be sin not to bow in reverence to Him.

Verse 11 closes this scene in heaven with a song seemingly echoing down through the ages from Isaiah 6. The Great Creator is on the throne and is both worthy of and commendable to be praised and glorified by all of creation. He is the focus of all activity and will protect, defend and encourage those who suffer for His sake.

APPLICATION TO OUR POST-CHRISTIAN WORLD

Talk with any atheist, and he will tell you that "there is no God." Only the foolish, simple-minded and ignorant believe that there is a being greater than man or any form of life after death. And while this attitude may not be that of the church in general, a form of it exists in the 21st century apostate church that bends to the culture of the day and submits to the pressure of society by diluting the Gospel and its message of redemption. John reveals the truth of today's reality and tomorrow's prophetic end. To dismiss this truth, as increasing numbers do, is indeed, to deny that God has ever existed or will ever exist. What a contemptuous and self-aggrandizing attitude!

Today's world also seems to have lost the ability to recognize the miraculous. The gift of creation should produce wonder and amazement as well as praise and glory to its Creator, yet much of the awe of today's world is lost on the curiosity of technological advancement. How often does a sunset at the Grand Canyon inspire a sense of wonder? How the Creator must mourn the lack of acknowledgment. Revelation 4:4-11 reminds us that the Creator is still on the throne and, like the twenty-four elders, we must offer Him praise, glory and honor.

The true message here is from Jesus Himself. He tells the believer: (1) Do not be afraid. There is to be no fear of the present or the future. Paul reminds us of that fact in 2 Timothy 1:7.[42] For the believer, victory over the now is assured, however uncertain it may appear.

(2) Do not look forward with sentimentality. Heaven will be absolutely everything God has declared that it will be. Your happiness will never, ever be so fulfilled as when you meet Jesus face-to-face in the Eternal City. But do not live your life outside the bounds of reality. Live life with the knowledge that

your future is made certain through the promises of the "One" who is on the throne.

(3) Do not concede defeat. We have God's immutable Word that, as Christians, we will never see the Tribulation. So, as reassuring as God's Word is, victory in this life over death and over hell in the next life is guaranteed. Whatever life throws at you in these post-Christian times, never give up. TODAY IS THE DAY OF SALVATION!

WORTHY IS THE LAMB, 5:1-14

From a literary perspective, chapters four and five should be considered as a single unit. In chapter four God is presented in all His creative power, and His worshippers so declare in the great oratorio of 4:11-12. Then in chapter five, God is presented in all His redeeming power. In fact, chapter five becomes a prologue for all that will follow in chapters six through 22 where God will redeem His people, His planet and His universe. Recall the words of Paul in Romans 8:23, "We also groan within ourselves, eagerly awaiting for adoption, the redemption of our bodies."

Today, our souls have been redeemed by the blood of Jesus Christ on the cross, but ultimately our bodily redemption will be in heaven. I remember so well, from an early pastorate, the prayer of a member of my church when he closed his prayer with, "And now, O Lord, save us at last in heaven." He may have been a ruddy, sunbaked tenant farmer with little education, but he was a theological giant. He understood that our final redemption will be through the work of our Lord Jesus Christ when He Raptures us to glory, and we reign with Him for a thousand years.[43]

The curtain now rises, and the scene opens once more on the throne room of God. "Then I saw in the right hand of the One seated on the throne a scroll with writing on the inside and on the back, sealed with seven seals."

God is at center stage. Once more He is surrounded by the four creatures and the 24 elders who continue to worship Him. In His right hand, considered to be His hand of strength and power, He holds a book. More likely a scroll fabricated from papyrus, it has writing on both sides demonstrating the fullness or completeness of its contents. The scroll is closed and sealed with seven seals. The word "sealed" appears linguistically here as a perfect participle indicating total and complete security. Only One with the power and authority to do so would be able to break the seals and open the scroll.

What is this book that appears to be so important and meaningful? It is nothing less than the "last will and testament of God to this world."[44] In the ancient world, wills, like many official documents, were signed and sealed with a signet signifying the writer's authenticity and authority, thus assuring its legitimacy. Contained in this particular scroll observed by the Seer of Patmos is an account of the last chapter of man's existence on earth, the climax of the human experience and the judgment of God upon what was once His perfect creation. It is the bequest of God to a world that has blotted Him out. The executor of this last will and testament is none other than He who sits at the right hand of God, Jesus Christ, the Messiah.

From the sin of man in the Garden of Eden until this present day, the world has belonged to Satan. And look what he has done with it. Overrun by sin, sickness, disease, death, the threat of atomic annihilation, inflation, antagonism—the devil has simply messed it up. And this will not change until someone comes that is worthy to possess and inherit it by cleansing this world of Satan's mess and declaring judgment on it. As the title deed to the world which He created, this scroll authorizes Jesus to return to earth with all His saints and claim once more what rightfully belongs to Him.

Now the search is on for someone who can open the scroll and break the seals. Even the mighty angel, Michael, acknowledging the impossibility of the situation, cries out, "Who is worthy to open the scroll and break its seals?" No one comes forth.

Now notice the breadth of the search. "No one in heaven" could be found. This means that even the redeemed of God who have joined Him in heaven did not possess the power to open the scroll. Then "no one on earth," i.e., no living being possessed the might to open the scroll. And finally, "no one under the earth" could rise up and open the scroll. Even Lucifer himself, the prince of darkness was unworthy to open the scroll. The search was futile.

Not only was no one identified who could open the scroll, but also no one could "look in it." The word used here is βλέπω (*blepō*), meaning to "see," "perceive" or "discern." It is more than simply casting one's eyes on an object or observing. It means to comprehend, to understand deeply and genuinely. Who could comprehend the contents of the scroll? Who could interpret the contents of the scroll? No one could be found.

As he observed the scene unfolding, John became discouraged. Being the dramatist we know him to have been,[45] he wept over the gravity of the situation. But his weeping was not a mournful cry. The words he uses are ἔκλαιον πολὺ (*eklaion polu*) which means to weep as a "sign of pain and grief for the thing signified."[46] In this case the thing signified was the absence of someone to open the scroll and break the seals. And it was not a quiet cry. The word πολὺ (*polu*) refers to weeping greatly, almost ceaselessly. John was so affected by the situation that he simply could not cease his crying.

John saw a threat to his redeemed inheritance; he wept over the possible fading of the glory of God; he wept that Satan might not be expelled; he wept that the world might not ultimately be redeemed; he wept that the righteousness of Christ might not be authenticated; he wept out of fear that the world would end up as it was at that moment.

Then the answer comes. "And one of the elders said to me, "Stop weeping; behold, the Lion that is from the tribe of Judah, the Root of David, has overcome so as to open the book and its seven seals."

Praise God, the answer came from one of us. Recall from our previous chapter 4 that the elders represent the church of Jesus Christ, and we as Christians are a part of that church. So, it was one of our very own that told John to stop weeping and see that there truly was someone capable of opening the scroll and breaking the seals.

That One is the Lion of Judah. The writer of Genesis 49:9-10 observes, "Judah is a young lion . . . the scepter will not depart from Judah or the staff from between his feet, until He whose right it is comes and the obedience of the peoples belongs to Him." Judah was the son of Jacob, and, from this Scripture, the lion became an ancient symbol of his tribe. Judah became the tribe of the kings, and out of Judah the Messiah—the King of Kings—was prophesied to emerge. This verse speaks, then, to the victorious Lord and His right to remove His people and gather them to Himself in eternity. Jesus, as the "Lion of Judah," holds the authority to open the scroll.

That One is also the "Root of David." Isaiah prophesied that from the stump of Jesse would appear one whose heritage would be celebrated throughout all Judah. David, the son of Jesse, fulfilled that prophecy of Isaiah, became Judah's greatest king and provided the lineage through which the Jesus Messiah of history was born. This Root of David has now come to open the scroll and break the seals.

In an instant the vision is transformed from one of disappointment, discouragement and despair to one of optimism and enthusiasm. Christ suddenly is brought into the forefront. Christ is pictured in his atoning sacrifice. He is here to break the seven seals and to open the book.

But then, what a change in focus! John now sees Jesus as a slaughtered lamb standing among the creatures and elders. This Lamb, the One so declared by John in his Gospel (1:29), is now the taker of the scroll and the breaker of the seals. He is the perfect Lamb with seven horns. Remember now, horns in the Book of Revelation always represent power, and these seven horns represent extreme power, promised power, complete power. Christ is perfectly equipped to put down any kind of opposition to his Kingdom, and His power is absolute and complete.

His eyes represent the seven spirits of God which are the seven manifestations of the Holy Spirit, the invisible, spiritual presence of Jesus Christ. He is a dead Lamb—bloody, beaten, maligned, bruised, sacrificed—but innocent. The very word employed for "lamb" implies its innocence and gentility.

Follow the action in verse seven. The Lamb takes the scroll in a spirit of real determination. John writes that He "came," a verb in the aorist tense. The aorist means that it is a completed action that took place in the flash of an eye. It was not a protracted action. Then the lamb "took the scroll," a verb in the perfect tense. He grabbed it out of the hand of Him who sat on the throne. The idea of the perfect tense is an action that is completed but the effects of which continue. The lamb took the scroll from the hands of Him who sat on the throne, but the effects of that "taking" will continue to the end of time. More will be evident as the scroll judgments are revealed.

Then happiness and enthusiasm turn to praise in verse 8 where the Lamb is worshipped by the four living creatures (angels) and by the twenty-four elders, with harps of praise and offerings of prayers of the saints as they fall before him and sing the song of redemption. Notice in verse 9 that this is a "new song."

Two words in the Greek can be translated "new." νέος *(neos)* refers to a new point in time; καινός *(kainos)* refers to a new quality, new in kind. The word used here is *kainos*, a new kind of song. It is a song never heard before, a unique refrain proclaiming man's redemption by the blood of the lamb.

The number of those singing praise is also not inconsequential. The Greek words written to describe the host of those praising the Lamb mean innumerable. They literally mean thousands of thousands. John saw every known creature joining in chorus to offer praise and tribute to the victorious Christ. As I read these words of praise, I can hear the harmonious voices of a mass choir as they sing *Messiah*, the extraordinary oratorio by George Frederick Handel. Together, these angels, these creatures around the throne and these elders join in chorus: "The Lamb who was slaughtered is worthy to receive. . ." To receive what?

John describes seven attributes that He is worthy to receive. Let's take a look at these attributes, objects of His worthiness: First, "power." This is the Greek word δύναμις (*dunamis*) which refers to physical force. It is the same power that He employed in creating the world; the same power that allowed Him to heal the sick and raise the dead; the same power He possessed to redeem an unregenerate people.

Second, "riches." John writes the generally accepted word for wealth, πλοῦτος (*ploutos*). It points toward royalty and immense wealth, both material and spiritual. And while He is worthy to receive material wealth, He possesses no need for any material acumen for He is the source of it all.

Third, "wisdom." The Greek here is σοφία (*sophia*), meaning "insight," "skill," "intelligence" and "wisdom." It is a kind of spiritual knowledge, a sort of heavenly knowledge. Christ possesses the wisdom beyond that of any known creature. In fact, He IS wisdom, and because He is wisdom and possesses the spirit of wisdom and knowledge, He is the author of all wisdom.

Fourth, "strength." The word used here to describe His strength is ἰσχύς (*ischus*), which refers to "power," "might," "force" and "ability." Inherent in His nature is His strength and ability to control, to issue orders to the world. He it is who saves and redeems His people with a mighty hand and outstretched arm; whose power defeats and subdues all His enemies; and whose might gives strength to them to discharge their duty, resist temptations, oppose corruptions, and do their generation work.

Fifth, "honor." The original word is τιμή (*timē*) which actually possesses several meanings. Literally meaning "price," other meanings include "honor," "respect," "perceived value" or "worth." When we stand in the presence of the Lord Jesus Christ, we should be awed by the image of His glory and His honor.

Sixth, "glory." John writes the word δόξα (*doksa*) here, referring to His renown, an especially divine quality. It can also denote the unspoken manifestation of God, His splendor or that which possesses intrinsic worth. It is His charisma that emanates from His very being.

Seventh, "blessing." The word translated as "blessing" in the Holman version is actually the Greek word εὐλογία (*eulogia*) which means "adulation," "praise," "blessing," "gift." He alone is worthy of all praise. Our adulation of Him compels us to fall to our knees before Him and offer Him blessing and praise. For one day, the kingdoms of this world will become "the kingdom of our Lord and of His Messiah."

Then sounds the mighty chorus from every corner of heaven and earth: "Blessing and honor and glory and dominion to the One seated on the throne, and to the Lamb, forever and ever!" So mighty and powerful is this chorus that all the people cried out, "Amen!"

For the Christians of this historic period, these words must have offered considerable encouragement. Hope was renewed as they were assured that the God of the universe would not only redeem their souls but also their bodies. He would one day come back and reclaim His world for Himself, and they would share in that reclamation.

APPLICATION TO OUR POST-CHRISTIAN WORLD

Much of our post-Christian world and especially post-Christian America has bought into the narrative that we occupy a planet that was formed, along with all life on it, by the random, coincidental arrangement known as the Big Bang Theory. You may ask, but what really is the Big Bang Theory? Well, simply put, it is an attempt to explain the universe as we know it, starting with a small singularity then expanding continuously over the next 13.8 billion years to the cosmos that we know today. That action supposedly emerged from "nothingness." It is thus an effort to explain what happened during and after that moment. Yet, in spite of all of the attempts of science to explain how we came to be, science still cannot describe what existed before the "Big Bang." And although today's most intelligent scientist continues to be unable to offer such an explanation, any one Christian can.

Beginning with Genesis 1:1, the source of the origin of the universe is clearly declared. What was before the "Big Bang" and afterwards, was God. He created the universe, a perfect world and offered it to man to enjoy forever.[47] As Creator, it belongs to Him, and He owns the title deed to all that we see and in which we delight today. Pity for the man or woman who does not acknowledge the power of God and His ownership of all that we are and have.

Think of your own life. When you go to an attorney to prepare your will, do you tell him, "Just leave everything I have to whomever you wish"? No, of course not. You are having a will prepared because you care about your family, your children and grandchildren. You carefully plan out what you will leave to each and authorize your attorney to draw papers that legally empower the course to distribute your assets following your death.

What John is describing here is no different. From before time, God the Father planned to leave the universe—created by Himself, His Son and the Holy Spirit—to His Son, Jesus Christ. He carefully prepared a scroll, a title deed, that would allow Jesus to stake His claim on the world. In these prophecies of John, he is describing how Jesus will come one day to acknowledge that claim and take back what is rightfully His. But He will not take back a sin-soiled and rebellious world.

Today's earth is decidedly under the control of Satan, and Jesus Christ will not wish to inherit such a corrupted world. But although today may be characterized by evil, there will come a day when the Eternal King—Jesus—is coming again, and He will take charge of all that belongs to Him and redeem it to Himself. The scroll of chapter five, then, is that title deed authorizing Jesus to return with His saints and His holy angels to redeem what is His by right and title. But His coming will occur only after the world is cleansed of all sin and rebellion.

Post-Christian America, now is the time to arise, recognize and confess the truth of God's ownership of all creation. Avoid the pain and suffering of the Tribulation to come by accepting His free offer of salvation. Assuredly, Christ will return to claim what is rightfully His.[48] TODAY IS THE DAY OF SALVATION!

CHAPTER 6
THE SCROLL AND THE SEVEN SEALS
6:1-8:6

There is no fear among Christians; they are not around anymore. Christ has come in all His glory and at that point in time all those, dead or alive who were Christians, have been called up to join Christ in the air. In the twinkling of an eye you and I will have united with Christ in heaven where we will worship Him day and night. Those of our beloved who have gone on before us have already taken on a changed kind of body, one different from but not unlike the body in which they will live eternally. Since death, they have been with Jesus in a spiritual body but will now be with the Lord in their glorified and eternal body. They receive that eternal body only after the Rapture.

With chapter six, the Rapture has already occurred, and the only people remaining on the earth are those unrepentant, unsaved. disobedient sinners who have refused to acknowledge Jesus Christ as the Messiah and Saviour of the world. Christians now occupy the portals of heaven and enjoy its peace and security as well as the joy of being in the Father's presence as the Tribulation on earth begins to unfold with its terrible sequence of events that will ultimately lead to the Battle of Armageddon, the Millennium, the Great White Throne Judgment and Eternity. Worshipping God on His throne is the schedule of the day for the Bride of Christ as the Tribulation engulfs the earth, and sinful mankind suffers the excruciating pain of a living death.

It is not as though Jesus has not warned the world of the difficulties to follow. In speaking with His disciples in Matthew 24:4-9, Jesus warned, "Watch out that no one deceives you. For many will come in My name, saying, 'I am the Messiah,' and they will deceive many. You are going to hear of wars and rumors of wars. See that you are not alarmed, because these things must take place, but the end is not yet. For nation will rise up against nation, and kingdom against kingdom. There will be famines and earthquakes in various places. All these events are the beginning of birth pains."

The time has arrived for God to pour out His avenging judgment on the earth. God reveals His plan to us through John's vision beginning with the opening of the seven seals. These seals represent God's initial judgment of unbelievers on the earth during this seven-year Tribulation period. The purpose of this terrifying time is to dispense out justice to unbelievers for their sin and their continuing rejection of Jesus as the Christ and to draw a remnant of the faithful to Him.

As the first seal is broken, the sound of thunder can be heard. Thunder has often been used to describe the voice of God as in Psalm 29:1-11 and Job 37:2-6.[49] It has also been used to portray God's judgment on His people.[50] But now God is about to sound His voice and issue judgment on those who have refused to call Him Lord. He will not be deterred, and He will speak clearly through the images of the horsemen that will follow.

The first four seals portray the images of four horsemen. Why four horsemen? The number four is important in Hebrew numerology, for it denotes the creation formed by God, in other words, all the things you see around.[51] It represents totality, universalism, the whole truth. The appearance of the four horsemen signifies a universal message, available to all people. These four horsemen are not unlike the four horsemen of Zechariah 6. In fact, this is a duplicate vision of the identical horses that we read about there. And when asked to identify the horsemen, the angel replied to Zechariah, "These are the four spirits of heaven going out after presenting themselves to the Lord of the whole earth."

Each of the first four seals, represented as a horseman is not to be identified with any specific person. More commonly recognized as the Four Horsemen of the Apocalypse, these horses and their riders represent first the peace that shall initially engulf the earth followed by the calamities that will rain down on the unrepentant at the beginning of the Tribulation. They are progressive in their brutality and represent the four phases of judgment that God will employ to purge society of its spiritual rebels. In every sense, these horsemen and the Tribulation itself are a preview of what hell will be like.

SEAL NUMBER ONE.—THE SEAL OF THE WHITE HORSE, 6:1-2

Christians and the church have been removed from the earth, and the Tribulation can now commence. With the removal of the Christians, a vacuum is created into which the Antichrist adroitly inserts himself. At this point the first seal is opened with "the voice like thunder" commanding the appearance of the first horseman. At the opening of each of the first four seals, the Lamb says, "come," as though commanding the horsemen to appear on the stage. What is to follow, then, is the unfolding of the divine plan of God for the end of time.

"I looked, and there was a white horse. The horseman on it had a bow; a crown was given to him, and he went out as a victor to conquer." The first seal is the seal of the white horse. Many believe it to be Jesus Himself. But no, it cannot be Jesus, for He sits among us in Heaven at the right hand of the Throne of God. He is with His saints. Further, Christ is not due to come again until the end of the Tribulation according to 19:11. The description here suggests, rather, that this rider is an imposter Christ, a false Christ. Notice the differences. The true Christ, described in 19:11-15, wears many crowns as well as a blood-stained robe. He carries a sword in His mouth and possesses a name known only to Himself. The rider of this first seal is a pretender who wears a single crown and carries a bow as his weapon.

Who, then, is it? This white horse represents an unparalleled era of world peace. The world will have been in tumult and war for such a period of time before the Tribulation that people wish only for peace, peace at any cost. People are anxiously waiting for someone to bring peace, and this peace will be ushered in with the appearance of several false messiahs, concluding with the arrival of the Antichrist, the great deceiver. To the world he will be the answer to everything, but in reality, he will be the solution to nothing. Nevertheless, the world will hail him, and he will rise to power. This horseman then represents this Antichrist who, through deception and skillful scheming will successfully introduce a false, but short-lived peace to the world.

He carries a bow but no arrows. Although he is depicted as a mighty, Parthian warrior, he did not carry the primary weapon of the Parthians, arrows to accompany the bow. Nevertheless, he is victorious in his quest as seen in the "crown" of verse two. As in 4:10, this is a στέφανος (*stephanos*), a crown of victory, honor, glory. But his victory is not a result of war; his is a victory of diplomacy. Like a bloodless coup, he will achieve peace in the world by covenant, treaty and agreement, a peace that will last for three and a half years.

He will bring the whole world together in peace with a program of unification. One world government, one world army, one world bank and financial system, one world measurements and standards, one world economy, one world court, one world system of communication—all will be the result of the work of the Antichrist. Does he live among us today? I am not prepared to say. The signs of his work appear all around us, and the signs of his existence—or at least his soon coming—cannot be discounted.

APPLICATION TO OUR POST-CHRISTIAN WORLD

Peace can be defined from several perspectives. However, generally peace represents the harmonious absence of hostility and violence. This typically means the nonexistence of war. But peace is more than that. We often speak of "peace of mind," meaning a stable, undisturbed feeling of well-being, tranquility and quietude. The rider of the white horse, the Antichrist, will be skilled in offering and providing such peace and tranquility. By agreement, nations will not lift swords against each other, and individually, life will be peaceful and serene.

In 1920, following the "Great War," world governments attempted to bring world peace by the establishment of the League of Nations. It lasted only until World War II and its unimaginable atrocities in both the European and Pacific Theaters of Operation. Once more, following the war, world governments attempted to bring peace by the establishment of the United Nations. And here we are today, a world still under the threat of annihilation because there is no real peace in the world.

When the Antichrist appears, his compelling and enigmatic leadership will result in a peace that will reign on the earth for three and a half years. But it will be a false peace (a bow with no arrows). This leads me to believe that the Antichrist does not live among us at the present. We must yet await the rise of a world leader that will emerge from the ashes of a war yet to be fought. War is God's instrument of peace, and this world leader, with his charismatic manner and his unique ability to persuade and manipulate, will achieve what no one else has been capable of achieving—negotiating a peace acceptable to all governments. Albeit a short-lived peace (three and a half years), it will provide him sufficient time to advance his plan toward world domination. We must be vigilant in our outlook and smart in our choices of government leaders in order to avoid his conquest. TODAY IS THE DAY OF SALVATION!

SEAL NUMBER TWO.—THE SEAL OF THE RED HORSE, 6:3-4

Once the Antichrist has filled the void left by the removal of the Christians and Christ's church, universal peace engulfs the earth. But not for long. It is now time for the opening of the second seal.

"Then another horse went out, a fiery red one, and its horseman was empowered to take peace from the earth, so that people would slaughter one another. And a large sword was given to him." The second phase of God's judgment is seen in seal two, the red horse, symbolic of war.

During the first three and a half years of the Tribulation, the period of time immediately following the Rapture, the world will experience a kind of peace that belies the underlying tumult that is brewing, a false peace created by the Antichrist. It is a time of no laws, no war, hedonistic living, a "do as you please" attitude. His most ingenious and crowning achievement, perhaps, will be when he establishes a peace accord between Israel and her Arab neighbors, empowering even more the person of the Antichrist.

At the end of the three and a half years of peace, the second seal will be opened, and the rider of the red horse will appear and snatch peace from the earth. Based upon the words of Ezekiel 38-39 and Daniel 11:40-44, there will be such severe war and suffering as no man has ever known. A "holocaust of war" would not begin to describe the horrors to be experienced. Men will rise up against one another and slaughter each other. The Greek word used here is σφάζω (*sphadzō*) meaning to "murder by violence," "slaughter," "butcher." The complete phrase contains the Greek word ἵνα (*hina*) meaning "in order that," thus providing a reason for peace being removed from the world, namely, in order for the slaughter to occur.

He is given a "sword." This sword was not like the long broad sword described in the letter to the church at Pergamum. That sword would have been a long sword employed for beheading an enemy.

This was a short-bladed sword, the kind carried into battle and used for hand-to-hand combat or for close, personal assassinations. It would be the kind of sword that would efficiently accomplish the slaughter that is here prophesied.

Could this be a prophecy of World War III? Perhaps! The Antichrist will oppose all with deadly force and crushing defeat. The results will be unthinkable. Only since the beginning of the atomic age has such massive, incredible and swift destruction on a massive scale been possible.

The Antichrist will now declare himself to be the messiah and will ring true the words of Paul in 2 Thessalonians 2:3-4: "Don't let anyone deceive you in any way. For that day will not come unless the apostasy comes first and the man of lawlessness is revealed, the son of destruction. He opposes and exalts himself above every so-called god or object of worship, so that he sits in God's sanctuary, publicizing that he himself is God." Such will be the fulfilment of the prophecy of Daniel 9:27f where Daniel describes the "abomination of desolation."[52]

Ultimately, with her Arab allies, Russia will invade the Middle East and attack God's people, Israel. The war will escalate until it involves all the major powers on earth, and it becomes the greatest battle in the history of mankind, the Battle of Armageddon. At the end of this seven-year period (three and a half years of peace and three and a half years of war), the battle to end all battles will occur on the Plains of Megiddo.

APPLICATION TO OUR POST-CHRISTIAN WORLD

Have we seen or experienced the red horse of Revelation? The answer depends upon your interpretation of the "abomination of desolation." If you think of the Antichrist as a specific person, then it would appear that we have not experienced his presence or at least evidence of his presence. No one sits on the throne in Jerusalem, and no one has established a divine reign in a rebuilt Temple. However, since the crusades Muslims have occupied and administered the Temple Mount under the approval and security of Israel. For a time, Israel once more controlled it, but after the Six-Day War, they returned its administration to the Muslims, and it remains under their management today. Does this condition qualify as the “abomination of desolation”? I do not consider it as such. The Antichrist is not described as a group of people or a movement or religion. It is a person. We are to anticipate the arrival of an actual person whose attractiveness and charismatic quality will so captivate earth’s population that he will convince the world of his divinity and be hailed as the messiah. TODAY IS THE DAY OF SALVATION!

SEAL NUMBER THREE.—THE SEAL OF THE BLACK HORSE, 6:5-6

War has reigned supreme. And while war is brutal in itself, murderous on its combatants, it also produces collateral damage to those who do not carry the sword. After all, worldwide war can and does destroy or strictly reduces the food supply. And as was observed during World War II, rationing and starvation result.

“I looked, and there was a black horse. The horseman on it had a set of scales in his hand. Then I heard something like a voice among the four living creatures say, ‘A quart of wheat for a denarius, and three quarts of barley for a denarius—but do not harm the olive oil and the wine’.” The third seal is opened, then, to reveal the black horse. This horse pictures the results of the war(s) of horseman number two—famine, economic depression, catastrophe. When the consequences of war come to the people, they are no longer able to function because they do not have enough to eat. And where there is enough to eat, the price is so inflated that they cannot afford it.

This horse represents the beginning of a scarcity of all of the commodities needed to sustain life—food, fuel and other life supporting products. Food will be so inadequate that the scales will be devoted to so carefully assessing each item that it is quantified to the most minute measure. And even when available, the price will be exorbitant—a denarius, the normal pay for one day’s work. It will be the worst possible inflation in the extreme ever to embrace the whole world.

But one group will be saved. “Do not harm the olive oil and the wine,” said Jesus to the horseman. During the time of the Tribulation—during peace and during war—there will be among the population those who will experience God’s protection.

Among biblical scholars two positions of interpretation seem to arise. The first interpretation is that the “olive oil and wine” represent wealth, and therefore, the rich will do quite well during this period of the Tribulation. The other line of thought is that "oil and wine" refers to Spirit-filled believers who, during the Tribulation, acknowledge Jesus as their Lord and are filled with the Holy Spirit. It is thus possible that these words refer to those who have totally sold out to Christ and are to be spared from the harm of the Tribulation. God's Divine hand will protect them, and they will be saved "in" the famine but not "from" the results of famine. Perhaps He will establish centers of protection where they can find sustenance and spiritual nourishment.

APPLICATION TO OUR POST-CHRISTIAN WORLD

In some places in the world today there is a scarcity of food. People are thirsty from a shortage of water resources and starving from an insufficiency of food stuffs. It doesn't take much for people to panic when deficiencies appear on the horizon. For an example we need only remember the COVID-19 scare of 2020 when, just based upon reports by the media of the possibility of shortages of certain commodities, there was a run on the grocery stores, empty shelves and hoarding of cleaning supplies and food staples. Think what it will be like when the whole world literally—even the United States—has nowhere to turn to obtain supplies to sustain life. Yet such circumstances will only be the beginning of the pain and suffering that the unbelieving world will experience.

Thank God, the message of the Gospel will not have been extinguished. During this time in the Tribulation, the Gospel will continue to go forth, and wise men and women will repent and believe. And to reward them for their faithfulness, they will be protected. TODAY IS THE DAY OF SALVATION!

SEAL NUMBER FOUR.—THE SEAL OF THE ASHEN HORSE, 6:7-8

The final, natural result of what has gone before—war and famine—is death. This fourth rider represents the culmination of the work of the three riders who have preceded the fourth horseman.

"I looked, and there was a pale green horse. The horseman on it was Death, and Hades was following after him." This horse is aptly described here by the Greek word χλωρός (*chlōros*) from which we derive the English chlorophyll. It actually means "pale green," the color of sickness and death, and so this fourth horseman represents pestilence and death, the natural outcome of war and famine.

Death is followed by Hades. Does this mean that there are actually two horsemen identified as a single fourth horseman? Not likely. Death and Hades are often personified together as in Isaiah 28:18 where they signed a covenant. Hades naturally follows Death as the destination of the unsaved.

This seal reveals that the Tribulation period will include mass death. In fact one fourth of the world's population will be destroyed within a matter of days—by war, by famine, by sickness and by wild animals gone mad.[53] Only the unbelievers will perish in this phase of the holocaust; only the unrepentant will hear the voice of God say, "Too late, sinner. Too late."[54]

APPLICATION TO OUR POST-CHRISTIAN WORLD

Let's summarize what has happened. First, the Tribulation has been initiated by the removal of Christians and the church from the world. Second, the Tribulation has created a vacuum characterized by turmoil, disorder and anarchy. Third, into this vacuum the Antichrist inserts himself as the answer to the world's problems. Fourth, the Antichrist offers and successfully negotiates a peace among the nations of the world—albeit a false peace. Fifth, this peace, because it is false, brings war back to the world. Sixth, the war results in extreme shortages of all the world's resources, including food and water, with famine as the aftereffect. Seventh, the consequence of famine is death. And by the end of the opening of the fourth seal, one-fourth of the world's population will have died. What a world in which to live! TODAY IS THE DAY OF SALVATION!

SEAL NUMBER FIVE.—THE SEAL OF THE MARTYRS, 6:9-11

Beginning with the fifth seal, the symbolism changes. "Up to this point, we have observed the means of judgment; we now see before us the reason for judgment."[55] Revelation 6:9 reads: "When He opened the fifth seal, I saw under the altar the people slaughtered because of God's Word and the testimony they had."

In these words we view concurrently a picture of what is happening in heaven and on earth. The picture painted by this seal finds its origin in Leviticus 8:14-15. Aaron, his sons and Moses are following the commands of Yahweh by offering the sacrifice of an innocent, spotless animal. But notice what Moses did with the blood: the blood from the sacrifice was poured "at the base of the altar." The image is not unlike that written by John in this fifth seal, where those martyred for their faith are seen "under the altar." They represent the innocent lives of those who have responded to the continuing proclamation of the Gospel, have come to Christ during the Tribulation and who, because of their faith in God and loyalty to Christ have paid the ultimate price.[56]

These innocents cry out to God, "Lord, the One who is holy and true, how long until you judge and avenge our blood from those who live on the earth?" They have faced persecution and death at the hands of the forces of the Antichrist during the Tribulation. They now cry out for God to avenge their deaths. But they are told to "just sit over here in the corner for a little while longer." More will suffer death and will sacrifice their lives for the sake of Christ, and when the number of martyrs reaches a specific number, then God will intervene. That reassurance is echoed by Paul in 2 Thessalonians 1:6-8.

These who have been sacrificed in the name of the Kingdom of Heaven will not face death again, but rather they will have washed their robes in the blood of the spotless Lamb of God and openly wear those white robes which represent their victory, holiness and purity won by their faithfulness unto death. They have persevered and can claim victory through the power and authority of Jesus Christ.

APPLICATION TO OUR POST-CHRISTIAN WORLD

As during the end times, so today, there seems to be no spiritual security in the world. One need only look at the Middle East and Africa to see that Christians are dying, being martyred, for their faith. Their blood cries out from beneath the altar of sacrifice for Christ to avenge their blood. Throughout other parts of the world, Christians are ridiculed, mocked, isolated, disparaged and set apart.

We may not be living in the Tribulation at this specific moment in history, but the obedient and faithful are still dying for their testimony to Jesus Christ. Oh, how we all long for the coming of Christ and the Millennium, when we can see a preview of what heaven will be like as a deposit of the Holy Spirit, a down payment of the Spirit in our hearts even today. And if the Millennium is a preview of heaven, then the Tribulation will be a preview of hell with all its pain and suffering, sorrow and sadness, torment and torture. The souls of the martyrs who will come to Christ during the Tribulation cry out evermore for God to avenge their deaths, and soon. TODAY IS THE DAY OF SALVATION!

SEAL NUMBER SIX.—THE SEAL OF THE EARTHQUAKE, 6:12-17

Exodus chapter five through chapter twelve chronicles the struggle of Moses to lead the children of Israel out of the bondage of Egypt. The judgment of God descended upon Pharaoh and Egypt as plague after plague devastated the people and the landscape. With each plague, Pharaoh hardened his heart toward Yahweh and refused to let the people go. The final straw was personal, and Pharaoh finally released God's people from their 400-year bondage.

What John is describing in this sixth seal is much the same drama as that of the Exodus. The first five seals have been opened and serve as a precursor to the full ferocity of the Day of the Lord. To this point the judgment of God has been poured out on unbelievers as a result of human activity, yet with little success. In fact, the heart of mankind has been hardened to the message of Christ.[57] Now God intervenes with Divine wrath and initiates His final judgment on unrepentant mankind.

John writes in verses 12-13: "Then I saw Him open the sixth seal. A violent earthquake occurred; the sun turned black like sackcloth made of goat hair; the entire moon became like blood; the stars of heaven fell to the earth as a fig tree drops its unripe figs when shaken by a high wind; the sky separated like a scroll being rolled up; and every mountain and island moved from its place." Wow! What a description of the final judgment that God will pour out on His earth. It is nothing less than the initial phases of the collapse of the physical universe.

God's final judgment then will commence with a massive assemblage of natural calamities, beginning with a "violent earthquake." Numerous passages throughout the Bible have illustrated the calamities of the Day of the Lord. Note especially Matthew 24:7, Luke 21:26, Isaiah 2:19, Isaiah 13:9-10, Ezekiel 32:7-8 and Joel 2:30-31. The quake of this final judgment, however, will be of such ferocity that "every mountain and island will be moved from its place." Its magnitude will upset the very balance of nature.

Has the earth not experienced this kind of activity before? Yes. Scientists tell us that the land masses of the earth were, at one time, connected. But because of seismic activity, the tectonic plates upon which the landmasses rest have shifted over time, and the continents have been formed as we see them today. This earthquake, however, will make all other earthquakes minor in comparison and be so strong that mountains will flatten, and islands will literally disappear into the sea.

Combine this enormous earthquake with other natural catastrophes and the outcome will be a complete alteration of the universe. The violent shaking of the earth will, perhaps, trigger volcanic eruptions of unprecedented magnitude, causing the sun to be hidden because of the ash being spewed into the atmosphere. This same ash and debris will change the color of the moon from a reflective white to a blood-red hue. Asteroids and meteors will rain down upon the earth, and the sky will roll up like a window shade pulled down and suddenly released.

This final shifting and rumbling of the earth will be of such massive proportion as to cause unrepentant men to fear shamelessly and run for their lives. If Herbert Morrison were reporting about it on radio, he might say, "Oh, it's the most terrible disaster in the world."[58] But such an account would come nowhere close to picturing accurately the final judgment of God on the world. Running for their lives and hiding in caves and among the rocks, impenitent man suddenly recognizes that the phenomena originate from the hand of God and so cry out for death. After all, death would be preferable to what man shall face.

Beginning with the wealthy and influential, the message will be loud and clear—wealth and position have no place in God's economy of redemption. He is not impressed with importance. And so it will be with the poor and underprivileged as well. Physical security will not matter, only spiritual security. Silver, gold, influence or position will not save the unsaved from the wrath of God.

Suddenly many people will realize their mistake in not accepting faith in Jesus. But now it is too late. They have rejected Him for the final time. They would rather die than face the "One seated on the throne" and learn the hellishness of their fate. Eternity awaits!

APPLICATION TO OUR POST-CHRISTIAN WORLD

Where can the voice of God be better heard than in an earthquake? Have you ever witnessed firsthand the effects of a major earthquake? I recall some of the "large ones" that have occurred even during my lifetime. For example, in 1964, a 9.2 magnitude quake hit Alaska killing 131 people. That quake was so strong that the Space Needle in Seattle, Washington, wobbled on its base, and the landscape of Alaska was forever changed.

Or a more recent event in Japan where an earthquake and tsunami caused enormous damage and death in 2011. Known as the Great Sendai Earthquake, this 9.0 magnitude seismic event killed more than 19,000 people and caused uncounted billions of dollars in damage.

But beloved, these occurrences are a mere minor ground temblor compared to the earthquakes that shall encompass the whole globe during the last half of the Tribulation. The earth will be so affected by the shaking of its foundations that the stars and the heavens will be altered as well. The continents will drift, and the ecological balance of the earth will be transformed forever. So agonizing will be these events that everyone, great and small, royal and common, rich and poor, powerful and insignificant will wish for death.

All of these "birth pains" will be signs of the coming of the Lord in all His glory. For the unrepentant, the only words to be heard will be, "Depart from me into everlasting darkness, down into the bottomless pit. And the wicked, like lumps of lead will start to fall, headlong for seven days and nights they'll fall, plumb into the big, black, red-hot mouth of hell, belching out fire and brimstone."[59] Fortunately, Christians will experience none of these occurrences. For we will be enjoying the peace of Christ in the heavens where Christ is seated on the throne. TODAY IS THE DAY OF SALVATION!

GRACE PERICOPE—7:1-17

Just as John the Gospeler often wrote a pericope (pronounced per-í-co-pee) in the Fourth Gospel, so John the Apocalyptist writes an interlude just before the opening of the seventh seal. Here he places a parenthesis of thought in the chronology of Revelation in order to highlight the availability of God's grace and mercy during this time of judgment. It is a pause for the sake of grace.

The chapter opens with a picture of four angels restraining the four winds of the earth until commanded by God to release them. The angel announces, "Don't harm the earth or the sea or the trees until . . ." The purpose of God's restraint is to allow sufficient time for the sealing "of the slaves of our God in their foreheads." These "slaves" are none other than Jewish evangelists whom God has appointed as very special servants. The seal received by these special servants—from the Greek σφραγίς (*sphragis*) as in signet ring or proof—is a visible mark to designate God's ownership and protection. This sealing is a symbol of the protection of these believers from the Satanic or destructive forces that are to come upon the world during the Tribulation time. But when does this sealing occur in the end time chronology? Most likely immediately before the Tribulation era begins. God delays His judgment to take occasion to seal His servants as a means of protecting them during the calamitous times that shall befall the earth and its inhabitants.

"And I heard the number of those who were sealed: 144,000 sealed from every tribe of the Israelites." Does this mean that only 144,000 will be saved and secured from disaster? Perhaps, but when the Gematria (Hebrew numerology) is considered, the number more likely represents completeness, thus indicating that a vast multitude of Jews could be included. Suddenly and miraculously these Jews will become committed followers of Jesus much as did Saul of Tarsus on the Damascus road. Like those today who are called to share the Gospel in ministry, so these 144,000 are called of God and "sealed" (protected from the onslaught of the Antichrist and his forces) by the Father to comprise a missionary force of redeemed Israelites who will preach the Gospel during the Tribulation and draw multitudes of other Jews and Gentiles to salvation.[60] They can expect to be under the scrutiny and constant attack of the demonic forces of Satan and the Antichrist during the Tribulation, but the protection provided by God will safeguard them from death. Their ministry will meet with success as revealed in verses 9-10.

The scene now shifts from the earthly realm to heaven. "After this I looked, and there was a vast multitude from every nation, tribe, people, and language, which no man could number, standing before the throne and before the Lamb. They were robed in white with palm branches in their hands." Who are these people? Many have debated the identity of this "vast multitude," but no consensus has ever been reached among scholars. By connecting the first seven verses of this chapter with these verses, my conclusion is that this crowd comprises the successful results of the labor of the 144,000 (verse 14). These are the people reached by the missionary efforts of the redeemed Jews and represent their converts. They have professed their faith in Jesus Christ and many of them have paid the ultimate price of death. Angered by their abandonment of evil, Antichrist has released his forces upon them, and they have been martyred for their faith in Christ. Now, after being Raptured to heaven, they have gathered at the throne of God for a great revival.

Why does God point specifically to this group? Simply to underscore the importance of professing faith in Christ NOW. This image reveals that the Tribulation will be a time of severe suffering. Unlike those who acknowledged faith in Jesus before the Tribulation, these people have experienced the brutality of the Tribulation and died because of their belief in Christ. They came to believe in Christ during the Tribulation time, but they came to know Him nonetheless. And because they experienced His grace and mercy, because the times were evil and because the destructive forces of the Antichrist were concentrated during the time of the Tribulation, these people became martyrs to the name of their personal Saviour. Now they gather to rejoice and offer praise to the One on the throne.

They are attired in white robes signifying holiness and purity—robes that have been made white in the blood of the Lamb. They join with the throng that was Raptured before the Tribulation in praise, honor and thanksgiving to Him who sits on the throne. They raise palm branches, a sign of victory and celebration.

No more will they experience the pain and suffering of the first four seals, for "they will no longer hunger; they will no longer thirst; the sun will no longer strike them, nor will any heat." They will never again know the agony of the four horsemen, but rather they shall weep no more and enjoy "springs of living waters." What a glorious day!

In summary, chapter seven actually communicates three lessons. The first is the story of the ancient people of God, the Jews. Though they failed repeatedly to fulfill God's purpose in choosing them, here God provides one final opportunity for obedience to Him. This time the remnant of 144,000 Israelites, handpicked by God, enjoys success in dispersing throughout the world and evangelizing that world.

The second lesson concerns the new converts of these evangelists. Unquestionably, during the first years of the Tribulation, the preaching of the Gospel will produce a vast harvest of faithful Christians. Despite unprecedented tribulation, despite unparalleled persecution, despite eventual martyrdom, these believers from both the tribes of Israel and every ethnic group of the world, evangelized by the 144,000, remain loyal to Jesus Christ.

The third lesson is the record of God's grace and mercy in judgment. Even while God is justly punishing the earth, allowing destruction and the satanic forces to rain down in an extraordinary way upon the world, because of mankind's unrelenting rejection of Christ, God continues to offer both the Jews and the Gentiles yet another opportunity to repent and come to know Him as their personal Saviour. The Tribulation time is not a time for giving up, not a time for giving up on the Gospel, not a time to abandon evangelizing the world. Rather it is a time to acknowledge that, however God ends time, He will still be King of Kings and Lord of Lords. He is a God of love as well as a God of wrath, and He is a God of the second chance.

APPLICATION TO OUR POST-CHRISTIAN WORLD

We serve such a wonderful God! After He has released the first six judgments upon the earth, He pauses to offer grace to those still in sin. Similar to the door on Noah's ark at the time of the flood, God's mercy is still available, albeit, for a short time. His purpose is to bring unrepentant sinners to repentance. And so the winds of God's judgment are held back by the angels as He offers mercy and grace to a remorseless world.

God is still in the business of pausing judgment for the sake of grace. Even in your sin, as long as you remain on the earth, God is withholding His judgment for the sake of His mercy. But just as a parent will not give a child unlimited opportunities to change behavior, so God's patience has a limit as well. In the meantime, His grace is available and sufficient.

I'm reminded of that wonderful song made so popular by Larnell Harris, "Were It Not for Grace."

Were it not for grace
I can tell you where I'd be,
Wandering down some pointless road to nowhere
With my salvation up to me.
I know how that would go.
The battles I would face,
Forever running but losing the race,
Were it not for grace.
TODAY IS THE DAY OF SALVATION!

SEAL NUMBER SEVEN—THE SEAL OF SILENCE, 8:1-5

Before addressing the seventh seal a bit of explanation might be appropriate. As we approach the seventh seal, it is important to note that the bulk of the Book of Revelation deals with the seventh seal. The reason is that the trumpet judgments are a part of the seventh seal and the bowl judgments are a part of the seventh trumpet. The writing is so masterful as to seamlessly segue from one series of judgments to the other, thus connecting all of them as though they consisted of one judgment. Consequently, when all of the judgments are considered, most will comprise this seventh seal.

Now, the final hammer is about to fall. "When He opened the seventh seal, there was silence in heaven for about half an hour."

The usual cacophony of heaven—joy, worship, praise, glory, honor, thanksgiving—has given way to silence. A deafening silence. It is a silence of anxiety. Like a calm before the storm. It was a silence "of trembling suspense, a silence of reverence, expectancy, and prayer."[61] It certainly was a dramatic silence. It was as if John, the dramatist, says, "Let's pause and take a breath."

These moments of silence are a prelude to what is about to happen. God has initiated His judgment on the earth and has opened six of the seals to His title deed to the world. Now He is about to unleash the greatest judgment yet in the form of the seven trumpets which are a part of the opening of the seventh seal. The silence is a preamble to the devastating judgment, the demoralizing destruction and the tremendous turmoil that will result from the blowing of the seven trumpets. The greatest judgments are yet to follow, and the seventh seal is both an introduction to and an execution of these great judgments.

There now appear seven angels. "Then I saw the seven angels who stand in the presence of God; seven trumpets were given to them." Actually, they were likely there all along, simply awaiting an assignment; in their hands are trumpets. In ancient times trumpets were often used to declare war, call the people to assemble for worship or proclamations, introduce a king or high governmental official and announce the fall of a city in battle. John presents seven angels and their trumpets to introduce the judgments of God on His fallen world.

I'm reminded of the Battle of Jericho[62] when seven priests with seven trumpets marched around the city of Jericho seven times for seven days, and on the seventh day, the great walls of Jericho fell. Here seven angels with seven trumpets at the close of the first half of the seven years of Tribulation blow their trumpets and the world falls. "The trumpets announce everything at once, the Rapture, the assembling of the people together, the announcing of the coming of the King, the declaration of war on this world and the fall of civilization."[63] We have reached the conclusion of the first half of the Tribulation period. What will follow will be of such magnitude and severity as to make the first half seem like a party. Just as the earth has endured the wrath of the Antichrist and his forces during the first half of the Tribulation, now it will suffer the wrath of an Almighty God.

Another angel appears. "Another angel with a gold incense burner, came and stood at the altar." In His pre-incarnate state, Jesus is often depicted as "the angel of the Lord" who presented the prayers of the people to the Father. Now Jesus is depicted as "another angel" who was prepared to present the "prayers of all the saints" before God.

The portrait painted by John is of an Old Testament High Priestly function, when he offered the prayers of his people before God. The High Priest of Revelation 8 is Jesus Christ Himself, who mixes the sacrifice of the martyrs who have died in the Tribulation with the prayers for mercy and release of the remaining suffering saints of God. In John's portrait, Christ stands before the altar, golden censer in hand, prepared to offer the prayers to the Father. In this role, He is our advocate, our Saviour, our intercessor, adding our prayers to His shed blood.

The angel now returns to the altar, “filled (the censer) with fire from the altar and hurled it to the earth.” Christ, the Saviour, is now Christ, the Judge. His patience has been exhausted, and He responds with “rumblings of thunder, flashes of lightning, and an earthquake.” The fire indicates that the prayers of God’s persecuted saints have been accepted by Him. But God is angry; His tolerance of sin and an unrepentant spirit is depleted. The natural disasters that follow the hurling of the incense burner are a reaction of God’s anger to a sinful and reprobate generation. The time has finally come to release that anger and punish those on the earth who have rejected Jesus Christ.

Now that the seventh seal is opened, God’s final and severest judgments will encompass His world and its unregenerate people. The wrath of God has thus begun as He explodes His righteous anger upon the earth in The Great Tribulation.

APPLICATION TO OUR POST-CHRISTIAN WORLD

Have you ever heard the phrase, “calm before the storm.” Having lived in Florida for so many years, I have experienced numerous hurricanes. None is fun, but they all seem to behave the same. Hours before landfall, the birds go silent, apparently seeking a safe haven to ride out the coming maelstrom; wild animals herd together in sheltered places. But the most eerie occurrence is an uneasy calm that seems to engulf an area before a storm actually begins to make landfall.

This kind of encounter is similar to what is described in the seventh seal, the calm or silence before the full wrath of God is poured out on the earth. This silence is more than an eerie silence; it is an atypical silence. Heaven is not generally silent, so silence is uncharacteristic of a place where God is continually praised and the glory of God lifted by the voices of its inhabitants. So why silence in heaven?

God was about to witness the end of the human race where rejection of God has resulted in moral bankruptcy. As an American citizen, I truly believe that America is the last great bastion of freedom, of godliness, of education, of power and influence, of decency, of all that demonstrates what civilization should be like. But we are living in a day when it seems that, in spite of ourselves, in the words of Paul in Romans 7:15, "I do not practice what I want to do, but I do what I hate." We need the silence to contemplate more deeply our need for grace and then possess the fortitude to seek that grace in Jesus Christ.

To ignore God's grace and to continue in unbelief will invite God's wrath upon you. For God will judge the earth. Yet just before hurling His judgment on the earth, we see an angel (Jesus Christ) intervening on our behalf. But salvation is a two-way street; like any gift, it must be received and accepted. If not accepted, then the only alternative is judgment. So, what you do with Jesus determines what He does with you. Contemplate the refrain of a hymn written in 1905 by Albert B. Simpson:

What will you do with Jesus?
Neutral you cannot be;
Someday your heart will be asking,
"What will He do with me?"[64]

Remember, you will ultimately deal with Jesus as your God or as your judge. The choice is ours. TODAY IS THE DAY OF SALVATION!

CHAPTER 7
THE SOUND OF THE TRUMPETS
8:7-11:19

The seventh seal is opened, and seven angels stand in the portals of heaven with trumpets in hand prepared to blow them at the command of the One on the throne. Prayers are offered by the persecuted saints remaining on earth, the censer of coals is cast down and the judgments of God are about to be poured out upon the earth. Since the trumpet judgments are now to be of a greater gravity than the previous six seals, grand ceremony attends the moment. What is about to happen is only a prelude to the final catastrophe that will follow with the bowl judgments.

The seven trumpets are divided into two distinct groups just as the seals were divided into two groups of four and three. Note that the number seven here once more pictures completeness, perfection, maturity. What God does here will be in perfect harmony with His plan for the last days.

The first four of the trumpets sound warnings only, and they are singularly restricted to their effect upon the earth. Reminiscent of the Egyptian plagues, their impact is only upon nature and the environment, representing the realms generally known to exist by humankind in that day: land, sea, freshwaters and celestial bodies. They also "depict the continuous operation in history of the effects of sin and evil."[65]

The last three of these judgments concern more specifically the inhabitants of the earth. They are a warning to impenitent sinners in the Tribulation to repent or suffer even greater judgments.

THE FIRST TRUMPET, 8:7

At the sound of the first trumpet "hail and fire, mixed with blood, were hurled to the earth." The words of this verse remind me of two particular Scriptures, Joel 2:30 where the prophet writes: "I will display wonders in the heavens and on the earth; blood, fire, and columns of smoke"; in the other Moses describes the seventh plague of the Exodus in Exodus 9:24: "The hail, with lightning (fire) flashing through it, was so severe that nothing like it had occurred in the land of Egypt." The idea of fire and hail was not new, for it had been observed previously in history.

Two possible interpretations have been advanced to explain what is happening here. The first interpretation suggests that mankind, who presently has the capacity to unleash atomic and nuclear weapons of war, has now been allowed to deploy these weapons unrestrained upon humans and the result is nothing less than a nuclear winter in proportions never experienced by man. The second interpretation submits that John is illustrating catastrophic forms of nature involving volcanic eruptions that result in calamitous pyroclastic flow engulfing a "third" of the trees and all of the grass. The result is loss of food sources and a deficiency of oxygen production, both necessary for productive human existence. Supporting this idea of such natural disasters, one must only view a map of the world where active volcanic activity currently occurs. Today, there exists ample numbers of active volcanoes throughout the world to fulfil this prophecy many times over. Nevertheless, do we know the exact calamity being expressed in this first trumpet? Could this depiction simply be a "type" for an unutterable event? Whether it is one of these interpretations or yet another undescribed happening, God's judgment is harsh. So blows the first trumpet.

THE SECOND TRUMPET, 8:8-9

"The second angel blew his trumpet, and something like a great mountain ablaze with fire was hurled into the sea. So, a third of the sea became blood, a third of the living creatures in the sea died, and a third of the ships were destroyed." As with the first trumpet, two lines of thought emerge. One interpretation holds a literal view of these words.[66] Like the fiery events of Sodom and Gomorrah, the conflagration may be the result of a large meteorite crashing into the sea causing a tidal wave of such enormity that a third of the ships are destroyed, and the heat from the meteorite revives inert algae causing red tide. A second view considers this to be a nuclear holocaust which, due to a nuclear winter, causes ice to form in the atmosphere and fall in large chunks to the earth.[67] Can we describe the specific event? No, but we do acknowledge that, whatever the specific occurrence, the results will be disastrous to the world and humankind. So sounds the second trumpet.

THE THIRD TRUMPET, 8:10-11

"The third angel blew his trumpet, and a great star, blazing like a torch, fell from heaven. It fell on a third of the rivers and springs of water. The name of the star is Wormwood, and a third of the waters became wormwood. So many of the people died from the waters, because they had been made bitter." Once more, these same two schools of interpretation offer explanations of this third trumpets. One states that this is yet another meteorite that falls at the headwaters of key rivers, turning them "bitter" or undrinkable. The other suggests that there will come a time on this earth when one country will wage thermonuclear war on another country in a nuclear warhead exchange, with radiation fallout so enormous that it will have devastating effects on the rivers and lakes of the earth.

The word choice by John is interesting. The word rendered "Wormwood" is the Greek ἄψινθος (*apsinthos*). It refers to a plant that is intensely bitter. Remarkably, it is the same word that translates the Russian/Ukranian word "Chernobyl." When that explosion occurred in 1986, the environment surrounding the Chernobyl nuclear power plant as well as the water, both ground and surface, immediately became poisonous and unfit for human consumption. And it remains so today. Perhaps John is describing such an event but on a worldwide scale. Whatever the actual event will be, life-sustaining, potable water will be at a premium, if available at all. The event or series of events will be of such calamitous proportions that life will become unbearable. So closes the third trumpet.

THE FOURTH TRUMPET, 8:12-13

"The fourth angel blew his trumpet, and a third of the sun was struck, a third of the moon, and a third of the stars, so that a third of them were darkened. A third of the day was without light, and the night as well." To get his message across, John employed images that his readers would have understood. Only a few years earlier, 79 AD, Mount Vesuvius had erupted after a major earthquake, pouring lava and ash onto cities and even out to sea. Many people were consumed by the pyroclastic flow or choked by the sulphur-laden air that surrounded the mountain, and the day became black as night from the rain of ash.

On another occasion, prior to the Christian era, the volcanic island of Santorini had violently erupted in one of history's largest volcanic eruptions. Eyewitnesses of the time testified as to how the fiery blasts of the mountain destroyed all surrounding vegetation and how the sulphureous gases killed enormous numbers and varieties of sea life. They even affirm that the sea turned red like blood. John's readers would have "gotten it"; they would have understood this message quite clearly.

At the sounding of this fourth trumpet, John writes that the world will be less visible, for a third of its light—sun, moon, stars—will be extinguished. Can you imagine the meteorological effects of the loss of one-third of the light and warmth of the sun? Crops, which require intense sun to thrive, will wither and die from lack of adequate light to produce fruit. Biological cycles will be disrupted, and animals, both wild and domesticated, will become confused. The drastic reduction in temperature will produce a radical effect on all living beings.

Perhaps the reduction of light is a result of the tremendous pollution from a post nuclear winter. Carl Sagan, along with several of his colleagues, published an article in *Science Magazine* in 1983 in which they describe some of the effects of a thermonuclear exchange. How for days, even months, the world would be bathed in a cloud of dust that just simply would not dissipate.[68] Which leads to the real possibility that this fourth trumpet is a great dust cloud that forms around the earth as a result or consequence of a nuclear exchange so intense the sun cannot penetrate the darkness.

"I looked again and heard an eagle flying overhead, crying in a loud voice, "Woe! Woe! Woe to those who live on the earth, because of the remaining trumpet blasts that the three angels are about to sound!" First let's clear up the translation a bit. The translation "eagle" in verse 13 is an accurate translation of the Greek text. A majority of the most reliable Greek manuscripts read ἀετός (*aetos*) meaning "eagle" or "bird of prey." The eagle was often used to symbolize vengeance and would be apropos to the thoughts being rendered.[69] Plenarist interpreters view this eagle as simply a flying messenger informing men that the gravest destruction, the most ruinous experiences and some of the severest persecution is yet to come. Others actually consider that the eagle is Christ Himself, but such a position seems untenable since Christ remains seated at the right hand of the Father.

Fair warning, however! For whether an angel or an eagle, these last three trumpets will make the first four seem like a cakewalk. The severity of these trumpets is emphasized by the three "woes" that are announced, one for each of the final trumpet blasts. They are designed to put pressure on those who have steadfastly refused God's mercy throughout the period of the seal judgments and continue to harden their hearts and blaspheme God. This wrath of God likely will occur near the end of the Tribulation, during the last three and a half years. So ends the fourth trumpet.

APPLICATION TO OUR POST-CHRISTIAN WORLD

The warnings are clear to a world that is increasingly sinful. Can you remember the time when curse words and other foul language were not allowed in radio, television and the movies? Recall the "flap" over the use of a "curse word" in the final line of *Gone with the Wind*. Or do you remember when references to any kind of sexual activity was anathema to any entertainment storyline? I could go on, but these are sufficient to get the idea across. My, how circumstances and culture have changed! Watch television shows, especially those attractive to youngsters with impressionable minds, shows that should be portraying healthy and moral role models, and you will often observe a string of "four letter words" (sometimes "bleeped," but not always) along with innuendo and suggestive content that, only a few years ago, would never have been tolerated by the public and would have found its way to the cutting room floor. With nothing uplifting or positive in the way the principals conduct their lives or their language, such appears to be the norm today.

Will filthy language send one to hell? No. But the use of such language certainly is an indicator of where one's heart lies, his/her commitment—to the world or to Jesus. Imagine Jesus using such language or offering such suggestive activities! And while I would never judge anyone on this basis, this kind of behavior does not seem fitting for the life of a committed Christian who wishes to "be like Jesus." Yet our post-Christian world doesn't even frown upon such behavior, and if someone calls attention to it, that person is ridiculed and called old-fashioned. For the networks and movie studios, this behavior is often encouraged for the sake of ratings and profit.

But ah, unrepentant sinner, he who makes a habit of sinning, who denies Christ by living an immoral existence and/or who ridicules those who live Christ-like, woe to you. A just and righteous God will one day pour out His wrath on you just as He promised, and you will reap the reward of the trumpet judgments, finding God's blameless anger to be all that He claimed it to be.

The world may attempt to stifle the truth; mass media may hinder, distort or falsify the truth, but the truth, God's truth, will always be victorious. We live in a world where trust is no longer assumed to be the norm. And when trust is gone, so is truth. Jesus said in John 14:6, "I am the way, the truth, and the life." Until our world recognizes this one principle, it is doomed to experience the catastrophic results of the judgments of God. TODAY IS THE DAY OF SALVATION!

THE FIFTH TRUMPET, 9:1-12

Beginning with this fifth trumpet, a foretaste of hell is unleashed upon the world in The Great Tribulation. Comprising the final three and a half years of the Tribulation, the woes that shall befall unrepentant earth will be of such severity as to defy description. God will inflict upon sinful mankind everything He has in judgment.

Let me pause here to remind the reader that, throughout Revelation and especially the trumpet and bowl judgments, John is attempting to describe what he observes using images with which he and the people of his time would have been familiar. What he saw and what he says about what he saw are vastly different. He had never seen anything like what he was witnessing. He resorts, then, to anthropomorphic, entomorphic and theriomorphic terms. He writes in expressions that ancient peoples of his day would understand.

"The fifth angel blew his trumpet, and I saw a star that had fallen from heaven to earth. The key to the shaft of the abyss was given to him." The "star" of John is not a celestial body as many would think. The use of the personal pronoun "him" demonstrates that this entity is a living being. It is a star like unto the stars of 6:13 whose order is evil and whose destiny is hell. The star is Lucifer (Satan), a fallen angel presented in Isaiah 14:12f as the "destroyer of nations" and he who will "make myself like the 'Most High'."[70] But Jesus Christ holds the key to the "bottomless pit." "Pit" here translates the Greek word ἄβυσσος (*abussos*), "abyss." It describes the lodging place of evil, angel spirits. But the abyss is not accessible, not opened. A key is required.

Jesus received the key when He descended into Hades after His death but before His resurrection. This journey of Jesus is acknowledged by Peter's quotation of Psalm 16:9-10 in Acts 2:25-31. It is also referenced in Ephesians 4:8-10 and Romans 10:7. This One who holds the keys to heaven, hell and death has handed over the key of hell (the "abyss") to Satan. Satan did not forcefully wrest it from the hand of Jesus, but it was willingly given to him. Just as Satan needed God's approval to trouble Job, so he needed God's permission to inflict these terrible judgments on the earth and His people.

Once the portal to the abyss was opened, John saw smoke like that emitted by a blast furnace. The smoke was so thick that the sun was obscured and the air darkened. Notice that John does not write that it was real smoke that belched from the abyss, but he employs the Greek adverb ὡς (*hōs*) meaning "like" or "as." The smoke was actually "*like* smoke from a great furnace." And out of the smoke came the locusts—swarms of locusts.

"Then locusts came out of the smoke on to the earth, and power was given to them like the power that scorpions have on the earth. They were told not to harm the grass of the earth, or any green plant, or any tree, but only people who do not have God's seal on their foreheads." What appeared to John as locusts was most certainly an army of demons commanded by Satan to emerge from the abyss like a plague of locusts.

In the realm of demons, two types can be identified. The first type is those demons commonly found on earth. Luke 8 relates the story of demons encountered by Jesus in the man from the Gerasene region. Jesus cast out the demons and sent them into a group of pigs. Another example is in Luke 4 where, in the synagogue, Jesus confronted a man possessed of multiple demons, hence the word "us" in Luke 4:34. Such demons are quite real and evident even today.

A second type of demon belongs to a much lower order of Satanic angels, a worst, more powerful, horrific order of evil spirits. According to Jude 6-7, these demons have been "kept with eternal chains in darkness for the judgment of the great day." These demons (verses 7-9) are given physical forms so that they may execute their destruction and torment. They have been sitting on the bench reserved in the "abyss" waiting to be released on the earth. Now John sees them covering the earth like a plague of locusts. But they are not locusts; they are demons that do not eat vegetation but only torment people who have not been sealed by Jesus. For a period of five months (the normal life cycle for locusts), they are given the power of scorpions whose sting produces agonizing pain, intense convulsions, blurred vision, difficulty breathing and an irregular heartbeat. Perhaps, in this context, John is writing as much about the spiritual pain inflicted upon them as he is the physical pain resulting from the bites of the scorpions.

"In those days people will seek death and will not find it; they will long to die, but death will flee from them." For the unsaved person, the longer he lives with and thrives on sin, the more intolerable life becomes. His torment will realize no relief. Even efforts at suicide will be in vain. His pain and suffering, both physical and spiritual, will be of such intensity that he will wish to die, but death will elude him.

"The appearance of the locusts was like horses equipped for battle. Something like gold crowns was on their heads; their faces were like men's faces; they had hair like women's hair; their teeth were like lion's teeth; they had chests like iron breastplates; the sound of their wings was like the sound of chariots with many horses rushing into battle." John is describing a massive attacking military force. The horses, in their warlike character, symbolize the power of an army or ground force; the gold crowns denote them as unstoppable, victorious in their conquest; "men's faces" probably refers to them as rational, intelligent creatures; "hair like women" could, perhaps, refer to vapor trails that might be emitted by jet airplanes; their ferocity, power and lethality can be explained in the lions' teeth; breastplates suggest their imperviousness; and their wings were like chariots, suggesting the sound of tanks and vehicles of war rushing into battle. These demons are impossible to destroy; resistance is futile; there will be nowhere safe to hide.

John is observing an organized battle, and in any organized effort someone must be in charge. The commander of this force is the Prince of Darkness, Satan, Lucifer. He is identified here as Abaddon, the Hebrew word for "destroyer." He is also known by the Greek name Apollyon, which also means "destroyer." Once he was a beautiful angel before his fall, but now his sole intent is to oppose Jesus and those who follow Him.

Against what force are they battling? The Scripture defines that force as all humanity. But notice that they are denied the option to harm nature and those "who do not have God's seal on their foreheads." Are these the 144,000 Jewish evangelists. Yes and no. The "sealed" are not only the Jewish evangelists who have previously been "sealed" but also those who have become followers of Christ during the Tribulation and sealed by Him. The demons hurt and torment only those unrepentant souls who deny Jesus. Notice that they torment only. Death does not come, only continual torture, distress and suffering.

Satan recognizes the power and authority of Jesus and wishes to be like Him. In his efforts to be like Jesus, he develops into a master counterfeiter. Dr. John Bisagno paints a poignant picture comparing Jesus to Satan. "Jesus says, 'I'm the Father of incarnate truth.' Satan says, 'I'm the father of incarnate lies.' Jesus says, 'I am the water of life.' Satan says, 'I offer a thirst that can never be quenched.' Jesus says, 'I put My seal of protection on My people.' Satan says, I put my 666 on the foreheads of my followers.' Jesus says, 'I give life." Satan says, 'I destroy life.'"[71] Satan's masterful manipulation of evil highlights his ability as a deceiver, as a faker, as a fraudster. No deed, thought or word is beyond his malevolent intent to obtain the results he desires. He will do whatever is required to achieve his malicious objectives.

Satan possesses, at least temporarily, the key to the Abyss, and he has created and advanced the strategy for evil, and now Jesus has unleashed him on the world to execute judgment on unrepentant mankind. He is the "star" from 9:1 who has been ejected from heaven and cast into hell. God alone can stop Satan, but for now, he brings his judgment down on all who have taken pride in their sin. Thus sounds the fifth trumpet and ends the first of the three "woes."

APPLICATION TO OUR POST-CHRISTIAN WORLD

Could John be observing a prelude to the Battle of Armageddon? Could he be viewing a preview of an invasion of Israel? With modern weaponry developed to the point of human annihilation, John could very well be explaining a world gone mad from sin and disobedience. With the opening of each subsequent trumpet, he witnesses a progressive advance from the devastating environmental affects that resulted from the first four trumpet judgments. TODAY IS THE DAY OF SALVATION!

THE SIXTH TRUMPET, 9:13-21

At the sound of the sixth trumpet, God focuses His judgment on humanity. "From the four horns of the gold altar that is before God, I heard a voice say to the sixth angel who had the trumpet, 'Release the four angels bound at the great river Euphrates'." Recall that the number six represents man, signifies something less than perfection, denotes weakness, implies sin. So here, at the sound of the sixth trumpet, man alone becomes the object of God's judgment.

The golden altar to which John refers is the altar of incense ordered by God in Exodus 30:2. It was a place of grace, where God responded to the prayers of His people. It is a figure of Christ in His intercessory role, and because the altar stood in front of the veil behind which the mercy seat was located, it is also a symbol of His grace to redeem and restore.

Out of the horns came a voice of authority ordering the angel to blow the trumpet. The voice had always been there giving orders throughout the book. This voice that cries out to the angel is none other than Jesus Christ, the very source of the judgment to follow. The voice is pictured as the exalted High Priest of the Old Testament. Jesus had already declared Himself equal with God,[72] now He is heard as the Great High Priest.

Who are the four angels at the Euphrates River? They are a part of Satan's army that has been bound by God until He orders them freed at the appropriate time. They command an army of 200 million who ultimately kill a third of the souls on the earth. They are bound at the command of God, and they will be freed at the command of God. At this point, they are holding back the judgment of God until He is prepared to unleash His harshness on a people devoted to their sin. They are bound at the Euphrates River that comprised one of the four rivers in the Garden of Eden. It is also the eastern border of the land God promised His people.[73] It is a geographical feature that God considers to be the dividing line between east and west. East of the river is considered to be the Far East and Asia, and west of the river is generally cited as the Near East and Asia Minor. It is a region that, today, is menaced by war and terror, and it is here that a battle, the proportions of which cannot be fully described, will occur.

This army is unlike any other army, and its number represents ultimate completeness. It is an army arrayed against those who have rejected Christ and aligned themselves with the Antichrist. Pictured as the Parthian cavalry, it is not a human army, but rather it is a supernatural force; it is an army of demon-like, evil spirits that have emerged from the abyss and advanced on humankind under the leadership of the formerly bound angels. Its appearance is fearsome, and the result of its efforts is the immediate death of a third of the world's population. More specific details will be described in Revelation, chapter 16.

In verses 17-19 John envisions three ways in which humans are killed by this army of demons. "The heads of the horses were like lions' heads, and from their mouths came fire, smoke, and sulfur." From out of the pits of hell the horses gallop into battle spewing forth fire from their mouths as they incinerate people in their paths. They expel fire, smoke and sulfur (like balls of brimstone) searing those whom the fire touches and suffocating those who oppose them or stand in their way. They are killing machines whose ability to torture and destroy life is powerful and obsessive. They are good at what they do, and those who have scorned the pleas of Christ to turn from their evil ways now suffer unspeakable agony and death. Remember, too, that these are not actual horses but are so represented.

These horsemen also kill with the tails of their horses. "Their tails, which resemble snakes, have heads, and they inflict injury with them." So ahead and behind, these horses could let loose their deadly powers. While the tails, too, are not actual serpents, they have the ability to act as poisonous snakes, striking at will those who are unrepentant. John's language here is quite conclusive. These are deadly serpents, and their bite is fatal. Unlike the experience of Israel in the wilderness,[74] there is no salvation from the effects of these bites.

After suffering from the effects of the seal judgments, after experiencing the judgments of God on those who refused the testimonies of the 144,000 Jewish missionaries, after witnessing God's wrath on nature in the first four "woes" and after the calamitous effects of the fifth trumpet, one would think that sinners would carefully consider their fates and turn to Christ. But these people will not repent. "The rest of the people, who were not killed by these plagues, did not repent of the works of their hands to stop worshiping demons and idols of gold, silver, and bronze, stone, and wood, which are not able to see, hear, or walk" (9:20). So caught up in the culture of the times, so committed to their own worship of inanimate gods, so dedicated to the elevation of themselves over anything else in their lives, they refuse once more to repent and turn to their only source of salvation, Jesus Christ.

Their hedonistic behaviors also present a stumbling block. "They did not repent of their murders, their sorceries, their sexual immorality, or their thefts" (9:21). They cannot suppress the desire for vengeance and go on murderous rampages, seeking revenge or simply getting what they want. They are dedicated to their "sorceries." The word used here is the Greek word φαρμακεία (*pharmakeia*) which means "magic" or "enchantment." It is the word from which our English "pharmacy" is derived. These people will not give up their drugs, their means of escaping the pressures of life and a potion widely used in their cultic worship.

Sexual immorality is commonplace in this post-Rapture world. The Greek word used by John here is the word πορνεία (*porneia*), from which we derive our English "pornography." These people are addicted to their immoral ways, and giving up those behaviors is not an option for them. There will be a total breakdown in the institution of marriage. Rape and sex outside of marriage will be commonplace, and same sex relations will be considered to be normal. Such will be the pleasure-seeking world of the sixth trumpet.

Because of the effects of the previous "woe," food, shelter, water, and other necessities of life will be inadequate, so they will yield to the temptation to steal. And with all sense of morality faded into extinction, all manner of thievery will be rampant. And so concludes the second "woe."

APPLICATION TO OUR POST-CHRISTIAN WORLD

Today, both Russia and China have armies that number more than 2 million. On May 14, 2021, Former United Nation's Ambassador Nikki Haley said about China: "China is now building up their military. They have the largest naval fleet in the world, they have more air defense systems, they are modernizing their military. At the next Olympics [to be held in

China], they will be showing that they are the new superpower in the world."[75]

With this new standing in the world, China and Russia, along with their allies, would have a relatively effortless mission to raise a mighty force of 200 million. It becomes possible, therefore, for these two armies to consolidate, drive through the middle of Iran and attack Israel. Later in Revelation 16:12, John writes that the "kings from the east" will traverse a drained Euphrates River to enter the land of the Israelites as promised in Genesis 15. Even today, China would welcome the ability to build a road from Beijing to Israel through the main crossroads that have existed in the Middle East for millennia. Could we be seeing the early stages of development of these plans?

One conclusion can be determined—the people of the post-Christian world have not and apparently will not repent even when death seems to appear on their doorsteps. The judgment of God, even today, does not bring people to repentance. That can only be the result of the love of God.

And so God's judgment continues. How does America measure up to the standards set by God? In July 2012, Billy Graham authored an article in which he wrote, "Some years ago, my wife, Ruth, was reading the draft of a book I was writing. When she finished a section describing the terrible downward spiral of our nation's moral standards and the idolatry of worshiping false gods such as technology and sex, she startled me by exclaiming, 'If God doesn't punish America, He'll have to apologize to Sodom and Gomorrah'."[76] This trumpet should be a wakeup call to all of us. TODAY IS THE DAY OF SALVATION!

TRIBULATION PERICOPE, 10:1-11:2

So much has been prophesied to this point that John needs a bit of rest. So just as he wrote an intermezzo between the sixth and seventh seals, he now takes a pause and includes a pericope between the sixth and seventh trumpets. Since this pause occurs where it does, we can only assume that the visions of this interlude are related in some way to the time period covered by the first six trumpets or during the first twenty-one months of the second half of the seven-year Tribulation.

"Then I saw another mighty angel coming down from heaven, surrounded by a cloud, with a rainbow over his head. His face was like the sun, his legs were like fiery pillars, and he had a little scroll opened in his hand" (10:1-2). These verses present several interpretive dilemmas. For example, who is the "mighty angel? How do the cloud and rainbow add evidence for a suitable interpretation? Do his face and legs offer hints as to who he might be? And what is the little scroll that he holds in his hands?

Let's see if the language of the verse offers any clarification. This being is described as "another mighty angel." The word for "another" is the Greek word ἄλλος (*allos*); it is a primitive word meaning another of a similar kind or type. While some scholars assert this being to be Christ Himself, the language of the verse and the words of verse six where he swore an oath to Jesus, would preclude the Lord as embodied in this angel. Rather this presence is an angel from among the highest ranks of heavenly beings and certainly unlike the angels who are blowing the trumpets. His identity is of far less importance than his rank. He is a "mighty" angel, from the highest order of angels, who possesses power and strength, implying that the task to which he is assigned is one of divine importance.

John, in his most dramatic fashion portrays the angel as being "surrounded by a cloud," representing majesty and glory. As a special messenger of God, he is appropriately clothed in magnificence and splendor. "He was invested with the credentials of divine authority, which his vestures symbolized. This display was not for the execution of judgment, but rather to be clothed and attired with the glory befitting his portfolio and comparable to his commission."[77]

The rainbow is a reminder of the fulfillment of a promise made to Noah in days of old. God is true to His word, and He has declared that judgment would befall those who refuse to turn to Him. The rainbow, then, is a sign that this angel is an agent of mercy offering assurance that God will keep His promise to protect His own.

With a face like the sun and legs like pillars, this angel is a formidable being. The "sun" face implies that he reflects the brilliance of the Son of Man even as one who possesses the glory of God. His flaming feet, like pillars, may suggest the state of the church and the fiery martyrdom of so many Christians. They may also epitomize the coming judgment of God on the unredeemed. But more important is the location of these feet—"his right foot on the sea, and his left on the land"—a picture of the universality of God's judgment. It is an image of God's complete judgment over the entire world.

The angel holds in his hands a little scroll. What is this scroll? It is the Word of God, the Bible. It is both the sweet message of salvation to those who willingly accept Jesus as Lord and the bitter message of judgment and tribulation for those who refuse to accept the redemption offered through His death. John is ordered to eat the scroll, to literally make it a part of himself. The sweetness of the savor, in verse 9, speaks to the joy of receiving this revelation from God. The bitterness, however, is the nauseous feeling that result from the delivery of God's message of judgment and condemnation.

The angel now declares in verse 6, "there will no longer be an interval of time." There is to be no delay in the judgment of God on the world. At the sounding of the seventh trumpet, the world will progress toward the realization of all of biblical prophecy, climaxing in the glorious coming of Jesus Christ to reclaim His earth. There will be no additional delay in the establishment of the millennial reign of Christ. The opportunity for repentance will have passed, and unredeemed man's fate will have been sealed.

Chapter 11 continues the Tribulation pericope of John begun in chapter 10. Here John is asked to participate in the vision and is given the tools to perform his task. Then he is ordered to "measure God's sanctuary." Over history several temples had been built. Solomon's temple that was destroyed in 587 BCE was followed by the rebuilding of the temple about 70 years later by Zerubbabel. This second temple was built on a smaller scale than Solomon's temple, so Herod had it refurbished. It was eventually destroyed by the Romans in 70 AD. Neither of these temples is being referenced here. The temple about which John writes is a third temple that will be built by unbelieving, unsaved Jews during the Tribulation. The measurements commanded of John, then, offer evidence that this third temple will also be razed, and a final temple will be built upon the site of Solomon's temple. From this temple the glorified Christ will reign during the millennium.[78]

Notice, however, that John is not to measure the "courtyard outside the sanctuary" because it "will be given to the nations, and they will trample the holy city for 42 months." The phraseology of this passage parallels that of Daniel 9: 27f [79] where the period of the Tribulation is described as the 70th week. The week of Daniel denotes seven years in God's frame of reference for the end times. Thus, John is asserting that the courtyard and the city will be overrun for three and a half years, during the last half of the Tribulation.

The outer courtyard of the Gentiles probably suggests that John is pointing to both unbelievers and Christians in name only. The language of this verse offers hints as to the timeframe being implied here. John is told not to measure the outer court because it "has been given" (NASV). The Greek verb δίδωμι (*didōmi*) is in the aorist tense, meaning a completed action. During the first half of the seven years of Tribulation, the Antichrist honors his covenant with Israel and allows them to continue worshipping and offering sacrifice on the altar. Then John is told "they will tread," from the Greek πατέω (*pateō*), the future tense of "trample." Such "trampling" would seem to include the abomination of desolation—the cessation of worship and sacrifice—which leads to the destruction of both the city and the temple.

It seems unlikely that these actions would have taken place simultaneously, thus placing these verses chronologically in the latter half of the Tribulation. By not measuring this outer courtyard, therefore, God is declaring His condemnation of those who have tormented His chosen people as well as believers in Christ. But the worst is yet to come!

APPLICATION TO OUR POST-CHRISTIAN WORLD

Over the centuries, several attempts to rebuild the Temple have been undertaken.[80] Beginning in the fourth century, Roman Emperor Julian promised to rebuild the Temple in Jerusalem. Then again, in the 7th century, the Sassanid Empire ordered Jewish sacrifices reestablished and a Temple rebuilt. Later, in the 13th century, renewed fervor arose to rebuild the Temple and restore the city of Jerusalem. Even today, a group of Orthodox Jews has organized The Temple Institute and initiated an intensive effort to rebuild the Temple. For many, the rebuilding of the Temple is important not only to retaining the system and traditions of the past but also to fulfil prophecies for the future. TODAY IS THE DAY OF SALVATION!

THE PERICOPE CONTINUES, THE TWO WITNESSES, 11:1-14

The Tribulation is full on; Christians have been raptured to glory; 144,000 Jewish evangelists have been dispatched to share the Gospel; Tribulation saints have been martyred for their faith; and judgment continues. But God's grace and mercy prevail in the commissioning of two witnesses to preach with energy and passion the love of Christ and judgment. Like the prophets of the Old Testament, these witnesses are clothed in sackcloth, demanding penitence; without penitence comes doom.

These two witnesses are an oriental symbol of strength, i.e., like strands of thread, one could be broken, two could not; two are stronger than one. The two witnesses symbolize a witness of great power, and no matter how evil the world becomes, Christians will be protected, and the Gospel will be preached. The witnesses also represent that militant spirit of all true Christians, that unabashed desire to preach the Gospel.

While the identity of these witnesses is really immaterial to the account, scholars have speculated as to who they might be. From Elijah and Moses to contemporary preachers with the spirits of Elijah and Moses, no identity is provided by John. Elijah is often identified as one of the witnesses because of the writings of Elijah in Malachi 4:5-6. Moses is mentioned in connection with the first plague upon Egypt. Nevertheless, we do know that these were preachers of extraordinary passion and power. They are described as "olive trees and lampstands," indicative of light and that which holds the light. Because they hold the light of God's truth in themselves, they demonstrate remarkable zeal to provide that light to a dark world.

They live deeply spiritual lives in a very unspiritual environment. Nevertheless, they preach, proclaiming God's grace and mercy to unrepentant Jews and Gentiles. They are threatened by evil around them, but they are protected by the hand of God. Individuals cannot come against them, armies cannot attack them, kings and princes cannot touch them. God has empowered them supernaturally so that they can shut off the rain, turn water into blood and call down plagues upon the earth. But oh, how this intensifies the hatred of the people against them. They even have the power to kill those who would do them harm.

For 42 months these witnesses will preach the grace of God, then their mission will be fulfilled. Once fulfilled, the protection of the Lord will depart. From the abyss, the Beast, or Antichrist, of 13:1-7 will emerge from the pits, engage in a war against the witnesses and kill them. Their deaths will occur in Jerusalem, which is now known as the Sodom and Egypt of its day, Sodom representing the worst kind of sin and Egypt representing bondage to sin. Jerusalem is seen as sin city.

Here their dead bodies will be put on display, with their images being transmitted around the world through the most modern technological means. Is that already possible? Absolutely! For three and a half days, their lifeless bodies will be defiled and disparaged for all the world to observe. Celebrations will take place; people will send and receive gifts not unlike Christmas or at a birthday party. It will be a time of great glee and gaiety.

Then the most supernatural of miracles will cross those same airwaves. After three and a half days, God will vindicate these witnesses, these great preachers of the Gospel, these two missionaries to millions, by resurrecting them. Great fear ensues! And even while unredeemed man stands around watching, these two witnesses are summoned by the voice of the Lord to "come up here." What an invitation! Even the observing mob hears the voice of God as He beckons them. It has always been the invitation of Jesus Christ to all of mankind, "come." The whole world watches by satellite television and internet as they are immediately Raptured to heaven in a cloud. There they join all the saints who have gone before, the angels and the Lord Jesus Christ. And this world of mankind who refuses to believe in a resurrection or a Rapture now watches with fearful attention as these witnesses are physically resurrected and Raptured to glory.

Then in 11:13 God puts an exclamation point on this time in history with a disastrous earthquake. Geologists tell us that today there exists a significant geological fault beneath the Mount of Olives. So in God's timing, it is scientifically possible for such an earthquake to occur. The result will be devastating. Seven thousand of those who have continued to reject God are caught up in the devastation and death of the earthquake. Could this be an actual death toll? Perhaps. But the seven thousand could also represent death on a massive scale, for it symbolizes totality or absoluteness. Many, but not all, of those who remain repent and turn to Jesus, glorifying Him and praising Him. Thus passes the second woe!

APPLICATION TO OUR POST-CHRISTIAN WORLD

Daniel 12:4 declares, "Many will roam about, and knowledge will increase." Man has always possessed such innate curiosity that he could use his mind to develop new ways of accomplishing tasks. Whether it was the invention of the wheel, learning how to make fire, or inventing the automobile and airplane, man has never stopped advancing technology for his own betterment. At one time it was thought that knowledge doubled about every ten years; today scientists tell us that progress advances at such a pace as to double our base knowledge every two years. The advances in technological knowledge make the fulfillment of future Bible prophecy all the easier to accomplish. With the invention of radio, television, satellites, the global internet, and advances in other fields like medicine and physics, mankind has increased his knowledge here in the end times just as the Bible forewarned would happen.

It is little wonder that the prophecies of the Two Witnesses are now within man's technological capabilities. With satellites and GPS (Global Positioning System), these prophecies are well within the scope of man's achievement. No longer can we simply deny such prophecy as the daydreams of a demented mind. The truth is there for the taking. Which begs the question: If these prophecies, written centuries ago, can be shown to contain truth or even the possibility for fulfillment, then why not accept that the promised judgment of God is equally possible? TODAY IS THE DAY OF SALVATION!

THE SEVENTH TRUMPET, 11:15-19

Recall that, earlier, I emphasized the fact that Revelation is not written in chronological order. The seventh trumpet is a good example of that element. For while we read of the blowing of the seventh trumpet here in chapter eleven, it does not actually reach its conclusion, foretold in 11:19, until we come to the end of chapter sixteen. Here we also read of the establishment of the millennial reign of Christ, a bit out of order since the final bowl judgments, which are a part of the blowing of the seventh trumpet, have not yet been poured out. In these verses we have the entire seventh trumpet. Here John describes the glory and the blessings that shall abound once time has ended, and the final judgment of God has been declared and executed.

Keeping this fact in mind, the seventh trumpet sounds and offers a preview of all that is coming. Loud voices in heaven proclaim, "The kingdom of the world has become the kingdom of our Lord and of His Messiah, and He will reign forever and ever!" The words of this proclamation offer an interesting interpretive puzzle. At what point in time, in the mind of the author, does the rule of God in Christ over the world become a reality? Based upon the language of this proclamation, I believe it has already, in part, become a reality. The second "kingdom" in this above translation does not occur in the original language. Further the Greek word translated "has become" is γίνομαι (*ginomai*) and is written as an aorist indicative verb. While the aorist often is translated as a purely completed action, when combined with an indicative mood, it can be translated in a variety of ways. Here it expresses the individual phases of a continuous process (narrative aorist). Thus the "vision is a representation of the establishment of God's kingdom in Christ with the birth of the Messiah and the completion of his work upon the earth. From this passage, then, we are led to the conclusion that the *basileia* [kingdom] of God in Christ began with the incarnation."[81]

This "kingdom" proclaimed by the loud voices leads ultimately to the establishment of the millennial reign of Christ when the kingdom of this world will be totally defeated by the coming kingdom of Christ.[82] The thousand years is mentioned by Paul in 1 Thessalonians[83] and is the time when Jesus takes back His earth and reigns with His saints for a thousand years. We are the saints, and we will have the privilege to rule with Jesus during this time. But this period for Him will be only a foretaste of eternity, for His reign has always been and always will be.[84]

"The 24 elders, who were seated before God on their thrones, fell facedown and worshiped God." Remember that these elders represent all believers, you and me. We are sitting around the throne praising God for His final victory, grateful that He has taken back His power over the world and thankful that we have been spared the judgments of God. We speak of God's future vengeance with assurance of its inevitability. The persecutors have become the persecuted, and as a penalty for not accepting Jesus Christ in faith they will be destroyed along with the earth.

In the estimation of many scholars, verse 19 introduces a new narrative that actually begins in chapter 12. This verse aptly comprises the conclusion of the seventh trumpet vision, however, it serves also to initiate a separate vision in the chapter to follow.

The scene changes, and we are offered a glimpse of God's temple in heaven.[85] When the door is opened John observes the heavenly Holy of Holies where God dwells in all His magnificent glory (*shekinah*). He is allowed to view its most hidden mysteries. There he sees the Ark of the Covenant.[86] This most holy piece of furniture was a symbol of the presence of God, a representation of forgiveness and a sign of God's covenant with His people. Where the Ark went, God was leading. The Ark made God's people feel safe, secure and strong because it meant that the presence of God was near.

But today the earthly Ark cannot be found. This sign of God's mercy and atonement has been lost to time and history. But like the tearing down of the curtain that separated the Holy of Holies upon Jesus' sacrificial death, so the heavenly Holy of Holies embodies the saving power of the New Covenant and redemption in the midst of wrath.

The final words of this verse express a disturbing reality. Actually a part of the seventh bowl judgment, the "flashes of lightning, rumblings of thunder, an earthquake, and severe hail" occur at the conclusion of the seventh trumpet. "Nothing remains hidden or concealed. The ark of the covenant so long hidden from view, is now seen. That ark of the covenant is the symbol of the superlatively real, intimate, and perfect fellowship between God and His people—a fellowship based on the atonement."[87]

More calamity, in fact worse calamity, is yet to come. John is commanded to prophesy again about judgments that are still not complete. He continues with this prophecy in chapter 12.

APPLICATION TO OUR POST-CHRISTIAN WORLD

I recall having the following conversation with an atheist friend of mine. While very intelligent and most discerning, he could never understand my position as a Christian. He would say, "How can you believe in a God you can't see, you can't feel and, quite frankly, I don't see any evidence of him?" I never tried to argue with him; he was too intelligent for me and my ordinary capacity to try to convince. But I do remember asking him this question: “If you were a betting man, would you rather take a chance on the possibility that I could be right? Consider this. If I am wrong, and you are right, I have lost out on nothing. If I am right, and you are wrong, you have lost the most precious commodity available to you, an eternal future in happiness and peace. On which of these would you bet? Will you take a 50/50 chance?” I recall how stunned he was at the question and how he spent a lot of time discussing it with me. I do not know if he ever came to know Christ, but the question is as relevant today as it was when I first posed it to him.

The time for Christ’s judgment *will* come. Would you rather be on the debit side of that judgment, or would you rather be on the credit side of the ledger? TODAY IS THE DAY OF SALVATION!

CHAPTER 8
THE SEVEN APOCALYPTIC FIGURES
12:1-13:18

The first eleven chapters of The Revelation deal with the judgment that comes on earth as God purges it at the end of time in order that Christ might ultimately fulfill the will of God while ruling it. It has all been from heaven's point of view as judgment rains down. Beginning with chapter twelve the scene changes, and judgment shifts from heaven's viewpoint to activities and events transpiring on earth as society responds to the judgment of God. In the first twelve verses of this chapter we have the most complete perspective from the farthest back from before creation to the farthest into the future until finally the kingdoms of this world become the kingdoms of our Lord. They truly offer a microcosm of history. Behind it all is an eternal conflict between right and wrong. The action from here to the close of the Apocalypse moves at a significantly quicker pace. It begins by introducing us to the first three of the seven figures whose identity will hold the key to understanding the message of The Book of Revelation.

THE WOMAN, 12:1-2

Once again the dramatic character of the Prophet of Patmos emerges with yet another scene change. Peering into heaven John sees a "sign" ("wonder," KJV). The word he employs here is σημεῖον (*sēmeion*), a favorite word of John's and the same word he uses in his Gospel to identify the seven miracles that point to Jesus as the Christ. By applying this Greek word, he attaches considerable significance to what he is about to write. Interestingly, he makes use of this word seven times in this Apocalypse.[88]

We are now carried back to the beginning of the story of salvation. A new series of visions, or a montage, portrays significant figures and occurrences from the series of events written in Revelation 5-11. The mystical language of these figures paints a picture that is neither intended to be interpreted literally, nor is it meant to relate directly to literal, historical occurrences.

John first observes a pregnant woman who is "clothed with the sun, with the moon under her feet and a crown of 12 stars on her head." Who is this woman and what does this unique description mean? Scholars for centuries have speculated on her identity. She has been variously identified as the Virgin Mary, the Church, and even Mary Baker Eddy, founder of the Church of Christ, Scientist. All of these hypothetical views fall short of the most obvious truth.

The woman observed by John is not a real woman but a spiritualization, a symbol of Israel much like the writings of the Old Testament where Israel has been portrayed in the feminine gender.[89] The imagery with which she is depicted also points to Israel as her identity. Being "clothed with the sun" addresses the honor and exalted status of Israel as God's chosen people and speaks of a nation whose God has promised to save them and provide them an everlasting kingdom. The "moon under her feet" symbolizes God's pledge of dominion and His covenant relationship with Israel.[90] The twelve stars represent the twelve sons of Jacob who became the twelve tribes of Israel.[91] The Scripture here is referring spiritually to the birth of Christ and Christianity.

The time for her delivery is at hand. She is in travail and cries out in "agony." These screams of agony reflect the pain suffered by Israel throughout history. From the Pharaohs of Egypt to the Holocaust of the 20th century to the threats and attempts to destroy Israel today, this band of people has suffered the pains of existence and survival. And because Israel gave us Jesus, the Jews will never see a time void of suffering.

Recall that, at the beginning of the Tribulation, the Antichrist established worldwide peace by agreement and treaty. At the midpoint of the Tribulation, the Antichrist will break his covenant, especially with Israel, will halt all worship in the Temple, will set up the abomination of desolation as prophesied in Daniel 9:27 and will ravage Jerusalem. The Jews will flee for their lives to the wilderness in adjacent Gentile nations which God will spare from the assaults of the Antichrist. God will protect these Jews for three and a half years during the Great Tribulation period.[92]

APPLICATION TO OUR POST-CHRISTIAN WORLD

To this day, Israel remains God's chosen people. Though most of the world comes against Israel, though her one-time allies abandon her, though her neighbors distance themselves from her, yet she will garner the favor of God. God will offer His people every opportunity to turn to Him in repentance, faith and acceptance.

It is my firm belief that the clock of the end of time as we know it began its final countdown in 1948 with the re-establishment of Israel as a sovereign nation. Her national identity has always been important to God, and her spiritual faithfulness has been His divine burden. Throughout the centuries, God has made a way for Israel to return to Him in obedience. Today, God offers a way through Jesus Christ. TODAY IS THE DAY OF SALVATION!

THE DRAGON, 12:3-4

John sees a second sign in heaven, a "great fiery red dragon having seven heads and 10 horns, and on his heads were seven diadems." Identified in verse 9, this dragon is depicted as a figure of great wisdom as attested by the seven heads. He is a wise, cunning and powerful individual. Satan is, after all, a personal force.

On its head are seven diadems, which, unlike the crowns of chapter four, are crowns of a king, of royalty. They represent the profound authority that resides in sovereigns. These seven crowns indicate a figure of immense, universal might and authority. The color of the figure is red, representing the color of blood, for Satan has been the instigator of all the terrible wars that have ever been fought, all the countless slaughters of history, all the great inhumanities of man to man.

On the dragon's head are ten horns, reminiscent of the fourth beast in Daniel 7:7. It is Satan, fallen from heaven[93] who, when he rebelled against God, was cast out of heaven. The "third of the stars in heaven" swept away by his "tail" are created angels, his angelic warriors, who followed his commands in open, demonic rebellion against God.[94]

Another clue to the dragon's identity can be found in verses 4b-5. The picture painted by John here depicts a demonic figure lying in wait to strike and destroy. Satan knows that Messiah will come through the line of David, so he has constantly attempted to destroy the lineage of David. History, and even the Bible itself, confirms that every effort was employed by Satan to kill the child Jesus.[95] But Jesus was protected by the Father because the revelation of His Messiahship was yet to be, His "time" had not yet come.

APPLICATION TO OUR POST-CHRISTIAN WORLD

Satan is alive and well in our post-Christian world. As the people of the earth become less and less spiritual in their attitude toward Christ, Satan revels in his victory. Nothing will halt his efforts to turn the world against God and toward worship of himself. He has already declared himself to be God, and he will continue to escalate, by every means possible, his deception of the world until he has accomplished his intended goal—to be the sole object of worship.

So many nations, once bastions of Christianity and faith, have fallen away from their spiritual roots. Since 1930, for example, church membership in England has declined from 10.6 million to 5.4 million in 2013. It is expected to decline to 2.53 million by 2025. This same survey revealed that only 28 percent of United Kingdom inhabitants believe in any kind of God.[96]

In Scotland, one of the hotbeds of evangelism for the past 150 years has experienced a significant decline in church attendance. In 2016, only 7.2 percent of its population attended church regularly, down from 17 percent in 1984. During that same period, the number of congregations decreased by 9.7 percent.[97]

From these statistics alone, the labor of Satan to deceive and lead astray has been most successful. But where does America stand? Well, let's take a look. In a 1944 Gallup Poll, 96 percent of Americans responded that they believed in God.[98] Today, Gallup reports that responses depend solely on the wording of the question. In 2018, a poll conducted by Pew Research indicated that 89 percent continued to believe in a god or a higher power, a decline of 7.3 percent. Of that 89 percent, only 56 percent believed in God as described in the Bible.[99] Regardless, however, all of Gallup's and Pew's questions about belief in God show declines from previous decades.

From these statistics, which are only examples from a limited number of nations, Satan's agenda is being achieved on a massive scale. His power and authority to defraud the nations and suppress good is overwhelming. He will continue his quest until he finally encounters the risen Christ and is ultimately defeated. TODAY IS THE DAY OF SALVATION!

THE MAN-CHILD, 12:5-6

The woman gives birth to a male child who is prophesied to rule with an iron scepter. Recall the words of Psalm 2:6-9: "'I have consecrated My King on Zion, My holy mountain.' I will declare the Lord's decree: He said to Me, 'You are My son; today I have become Your Father. Ask of Me, and I will make the nations Your inheritance and the ends of the earth Your possession. You will break them with a rod of iron; You will shatter them like pottery'."

This "rod of iron" is a symbol of Jesus' reign as king over the nations, for He reigns as King of Kings.[100] John also envisions Jesus as the Good Shepherd,[101] and recalls His ascension into heaven.[102]

APPLICATION TO OUR POST-CHRISTIAN WORLD

One need only to read or to listen to the news each day to know how far our world has fallen with respect to the gift of life. In our post-Christian world, 42.3 million babies were aborted worldwide in 2019.[103] That accounts for more deaths than from cancer, HIV/AIDS, traffic accidents, suicides and numerous other causes combined. During that same period, just under one million abortions were recorded in the United States.[104] Each of these babies represents a living human being whose life was violently destroyed in their mother's womb. What if abortion had been so rampant at the time of Jesus' birth? Would He have been born?

God's planning was perfect. No such casual attitude toward life existed at that time, and our blessed Saviour was not only born but also protected from the attempts by the Roman government to have Him murdered. What a perfect plan!

That same Jesus, born to a poor, humble couple who perhaps, could not afford to have children, will now rule the world from a reclaimed and renewed kingdom. He is the Man-Child whose rule will be eternal. TODAY IS THE DAY OF SALVATION!

MICHAEL, THE ARCHANGEL, 12:7-12

Suddenly John sees a war that has broken out in heaven. This war is to be a prelude to Satan's expulsion from the heavenlies and his limitation to earth during the last half of the Great Tribulation. The leader of the angelic forces of God is Michael, the archangel, who directs his army against that of the dragon—Lucifer, Satan—the commander of the fallen angels. The result of this tumultuous battle will be the casting out of Satan and his forces from heaven and confining all of them to their evil activities in the earthly realm.

Notice how John has applied four designations to this evil one. He calls him a "dragon," referring to his monstrous character as the enemy of God. He refers to him as an "ancient serpent," connecting him with the clever deception of Eve in the Garden of Eden (Genesis 3). He declares him to be the "Devil," meaning "slanderer." And he calls him by his name, "Satan," which means "adversary."[105] However, regardless of his designation, regardless of his power, regardless of his deceptive nature, he could not overcome the forces of Michael, the great angelic commander of God's forces for good.

Satan has continuously brought before God indictments of God's faithful children. His loss as a consequence of this encounter with Michael means that he and his angels are denied access to heaven—barred from heaven—limited to an earthly existence and never again allowed to come before God with accusations against God's children. Since this war occurs in the middle of the Tribulation, Satan is turned loose on this earth during the last half of the Tribulation to carry out all of his evil trickery.

APPLICATION TO OUR POST-CHRISTIAN WORLD

In our post-Christian world, a battle for the souls of men is being waged. Satan is working overtime to destroy Christianity and to manipulate all of us to do his will. He employs every means to get mankind to pursue every want and desire, live as though there is no tomorrow and simply never think about eternal life or its consequences. He promotes cultural acceptance, the apostate church so heavily influenced by the fads of the day and public opinion as the norm. He employs busyness to divert our attention from the Word of God and prayer, and he encourages a lifestyle of profligate living.

But Satan will be the loser. If we do not allow Satan to influence our lives, then he can have no sway over us. Live your life immersed in the blood of the Lamb. TODAY IS THE DAY OF SALVATION!

PERICOPE: DOXOLOGY OF TRIUMPH, 12:10-12

The words of these verses form a doxology celebrating the final victory over evil. The opening words of this doxology allude to the coming of the millennial kingdom of Christ. Words like "salvation" (σωτηρία, *sōtēria*, "deliverance," "salvation"); "power" (δύναμις, *dunamis*, "force," "might," "power"); "kingdom" (βασιλεία, *basileia*, "sovereignty," "rule," "kingdom"); "authority" (ἐξουσία, *exousia*, "influence," "authority,") speak to the ultimate reign of Christ and an eternity of praise and exultation for all believers. Satan is cast down, and the salvation of the people of God is finished.

What a celebration that will be! For at the conclusion of the war won by the blood of the Lamb of God, when Satan has been expelled from heaven and "kicked to the earthly curb," then "every knee shall bow . . . and every tongue confess that Jesus Christ is Lord to the glory of God the Father" (Philippians 2:10). Hallelujah!

THE JEWISH REMNANT, 12:13-17

Now we see yet another attempt of Satan to annihilate Israel. After all, history is replete with attempts by the Devil to destroy Israel. Beginning with their bondage in Egypt for 400 years, the plot of Haman to destroy the Jews by false witness, the decree of Herod that all Jewish males should be killed, the attempt of the Romans led by Titus in AD 70 to extinguish all things Jewish by destroying the city of Jerusalem, the siege of Masada, the organized work of the Nazis of World War II to achieve "The Final Solution," even today the attempts by so many Arab nations and Muslim extremists to bring an end to Jewish existence, and finally the Battle of Armageddon, when all the evil forces of the world will come against Israel—all of these have been, are, and will be concerted efforts to completely exterminate the Jews and conquer and terminate the Jewish nation. Remember, however, that Israel is God's chosen people, His timetable, His calendar. All will happen only in God's time.

In spite of the Devil's attempts to destroy her, the woman (read Israel) will experience supernatural protection as she flees on "two wings of an eagle." Now, notably, in the Scriptures, eagles have represented God.[106] So as God rescued His people in Exodus 19:4, so He will protect His people as they flee to the wilderness for three and a half years. How? We cannot know for sure what John saw, but could it be a massive modern airlift? In any case it will be a specific location that God has designated for her protection.

However, Satan is still not ready to surrender. He has yet another tactic up his sleeve. The Scripture reads: "From his mouth the serpent spewed water like a river flowing after the woman, to sweep her away in the torrent. But the earth helped the woman." This flood observed by the Apocalyptist represents overpowering wickedness and torment, for Satan does not submit easily. But what is this river seen by John? Through the centuries numerous explanations have been offered. Some scholars believe it to illustrate an earthquake in which the earth opens and catches the Jews, allowing them to find safety. Others believe that, since water is a symbol of the Word of God, it could be a flood of propaganda or false doctrine preached by Satan to lead the Jews astray. Could it be a type of overpowering military force that will come against the Jews? Perhaps. Nevertheless, whatever this river may be, it will be unsuccessful, and the Devil, once again, will fall short.

During the last half of the Tribulation, Satan will turn his wicked and deadly tactics against the "rest of her offspring." With disregard for Jews who have taken the mark of the Devil, with disregard to the 144,000 who are sealed by God and protected by Him, with disregard for the Jews who have fled into the wilderness, Satan will focus his diabolical efforts on a small remnant of the people of Israel who have not fallen victim to the false doctrines being preached by Satan, those who "keep God's commands and have the testimony about Jesus" as a result of the witness of the 144,000.[107] Read Zechariah 13:8-9 to learn that only a third of Israel will actually survive the Tribulation and enter into the Millennium.

Does this mean that Satan will not torment believing Gentiles? No. All believers, Jews and Gentiles, will suffer extreme danger and devastating persecution during the last half of the Tribulation.

APPLICATION TO OUR POST-CHRISTIAN WORLD

If the woman represents Israel, and the male-child represents Christ, then this phrase must suggest the next generation of her "seed" (KJV) or all Christians. The very idea of the "rest of her offspring" refers to any person who has believed on the Lord Jesus Christ during the Tribulation and has become an obedient servant of the Saviour.

Even today, though we do not find ourselves in the Tribulation, Satan, nevertheless, seeks to destroy Christianity. If he can divert the attention of Christians away from Jesus, his efforts will be complete. To avoid the torment and maltreatment of Satan, TODAY IS THE DAY OF SALVATION!

THE BEAST OUT OF THE SEA, 13:1-10

Chapter 13 acquaints the reader with the final two characters or personages that define the message of The Revelation. Both of the beasts that emerge here are actually agents or instruments employed by the dragon, Satan, to accomplish his evil ends. The first, the beast from the sea, is described in the first ten verses of this chapter. This grotesque creature arises from the sea and is reminiscent of the fourth beast of Daniel 7. It has been described as "Satan's hand . . . and represents the persecuting power of Satan operating in and through the nations of this world and their governments."[108] It is, in fact, not an animal or a creature but a person affirmed by the use of the personal pronoun "he."

What is the significance of the source of this beast, the sea? From Revelation 17:15 we learn that the "sea" represents the Gentile nations of the world out of which this person, the Antichrist, will arise. Therefore, understanding that this beast symbolizes a real person, and "the sea" indicates the milieu out of which this person will emerge, he will be a Gentile sovereign who will come out the disorder of the nations[109] and will receive his power and authority directly from Satan. He is characterized by ten horns representing his great power, or perhaps ten nations that will form a confederacy over which the beast will rule during the Tribulation. He will possess seven heads symbolizing his wisdom, and ten crowns signifying his great authority.

This beast resembles the leopard, the bear, and the lion of Daniel 7 where the empires of Babylon, Medo-Persia, and Greece are introduced. This beast combines the distinguishing features of all three from Daniel. He will be "like a leopard," reminding us of the swiftness of the Grecian Empire under Alexander in defeating foe after foe and bringing them under subjection. His "feet were like a bear's," indicating considerable strength. Like the brutal power of the Medo-Persian Empire, domination will be accomplished without a fight. He will also possess a mouth "like a lion's mouth," with an all-consuming power and fierceness, combined with strength and cunning, to overpower all governments and religions. This last great kingdom will embody all the philosophy, the power and swiftness of control of all the other empires combined. This Antichrist will be powerful and invincible, and just as Jesus was the indwelling incarnation of God the Father, so the Antichrist will be the indwelling incarnation of Satan.

Now Satan has one final card to play. This beast will suffer a mortal wound of some kind—what it is we are not told—but he will die. Appears now Satan who performs a miracle, brings the beast back to life, and to the amazement of the people of the world, heals the mortal wound. The allegiance of the people is now sealed, and Satan can end the period of peace and prosperity that he promised and delivered at the beginning of the seven-year Tribulation. He is now free to act with reckless abandon to bring all his demonic power to bear on the world.

Satan will be invincible; after all, "who is able to wage war against him?" Beginning as verbal warfare (verses 5-6), he will ultimately resort to physical warfare. And he will be prodigiously victorious over all against whom he wages war. All who have not been bought by the blood of the Lamb of God will fall down and worship him. Christians will be martyred[110] and non-Christians who do not worship him or who do not accept the mark of the Beast will meet a fatal end.

As the latter 42 months of Revelation 13:5 dawn, the triumph of evil will appear to be nigh. Believers are admonished to accept intense persecution from the Antichrist with ὑπομονή (*hupomonē*), the "endurance of the saints." They will suffer and die as did the Tribulation saints who were martyred before them. Those whose names are written in the Lamb's Book of Life, those who have experienced a genuine saving faith, will gladly endure the persecution with "perseverance and faith."

APPLICATION TO OUR POST-CHRISTIAN WORLD

While Satan is the power behind all evil, in the last days, he will empower the Beast—the Antichrist—to do his evil bidding. Can we identify this person who will declare himself to be God, demand that he be worshipped and sit upon the altar of the Temple in an act of supreme sacrilege? Not right now. But when he is revealed, every human being on earth will know his name and will be given the choice to worship and serve him or not. We do know that he will likely be a Gentile that will originate from a revived Roman Empire nation and his name will symbolically be 666. Seek to be vigilant, keep your eyes toward Europe.

Is he alive today? Perhaps. As we continue to see our world sink increasingly into the muck and mire of sin and degradation, could it be due to the impact of a "Beast" who is already casting a compelling influence on the world? Such is certainly possible. Without doubt he has the power to perform miracles and execute an agenda of evil that can influence mankind. One day the unbeliever shall know precisely who he is and shall make the choice to follow him or not to follow him. What will you do? TODAY IS THE DAY OF SALVATION!

THE BEAST OUT OF THE EARTH, 13:11-18

We know from our study thus far that Satan is a master counterfeiter. He imitates Jesus, the characteristics of Jesus, the actions of Jesus and the persona of Jesus. In chapter 13 we find perhaps the supreme counterfeit of the Father and our Lord in Satan's unholy trinity. Just as the Holy Trinity is expressed as God the Father, Jesus the incarnate Son and the Holy Spirit as Prophet and Presence, so Satan expresses himself in three forms, complete counterparts of the persons of God. In verses 1-10 Satan, embodied in the "dragon," declares himself to be a god. He has given power and authority to the first beast, the Antichrist, who demands that he himself be worshipped and who brings death to those who refuse to bow to him. Now, in verses 11-18, we find the final person of this unholy trinity, the False Prophet.

John begins this section by writing, "Then I saw another beast." John connects this beast with the dragon and the first beast by employing the Greek word ἄλλος (*allos*) denoting an entity of the same kind or type. This creature, the second beast, the anti-spirit, possesses all the DNA of both Satan and the Antichrist. He is a symbol of false or apostate religion and false thinking. His assignment will be to convince people to worship the Antichrist.

John includes five characteristics of this False Prophet. (1) He will come out of the "earth." While many scholars believe this refers to a Jew from Israel, it is highly unlikely that the Antichrist, who is also intensely anti-Jew, would allow a Jew to hold such a prominent position. More likely he will be a well-known religious figure who represents an expanding spiritual and ecclesiastical movement.

(2) He will be seen to have "two horns like a lamb." Not only does this characteristic parallel Jesus who is the "Lamb of God," but it is also reminiscent of the sacrificial lamb which was so much a part of the Jewish sacrificial system. He will attempt to impersonate the true Lamb, Jesus. This person will, indeed, be a wolf in sheep's clothing.

(3) Though he will possess the meek and mild appearance of a lamb, his speech will belie his true nature. What he says will reveal his real thinking, his genuine self, the very essence of his actual character. He will speak "like a dragon," but the power of his speech will be derived from Satan.

(4) He will "exercise all the authority of the first beast." There will be such a close relationship between these two evil personages that the Antichrist will imbue this False Prophet with the same power possessed by the Antichrist.

(5) He "compels the earth and those who live on it to worship the first beast." Such will be the basic purpose and function of the False Prophet.[111] He will force people to worship the Antichrist under penalty of death.[112] He will seek to merge every religion on earth into one. Could this characteristic be the modern effort at ecumenism—to bring all religions into one?

If, through the efforts of the False Prophet, Satan can convince us to amalgamate all religions, he will know that success is nigh. Let me illustrate.

Salt is a common seasoning that all cooks use to release flavor. But what happens to salt when it is added to food? Eat salt directly from the saltshaker, and it is inedible. It will cause thirst and a variety of adverse physical responses. However, add that same salt to food, and the salt can no longer be tasted. If Satan can do the same with Christians, what a marvelous victory he could claim. If he can unite all religions into one through ecumenism, he will have won a remarkable victory. We would no longer be identified as God's children.

The False Prophet will accomplish his goals through deceit. He will perform great "signs" that counterfeit those of Christ. Once more John uses the word "signs," the same powerful Greek word, σημεῖον (*sēmeion*). By employing signs, the False Prophet will convince the world that the Antichrist is as powerful, if not more powerful, than God.

Reminding us of the fickleness of humanity, the False Prophet will persuade the world to make an image of the Antichrist. Do you remember the "golden calf" of the Sinai experience? Or the image of Nebuchadnezzar? The False Prophet will go one step farther by magically empowering the image of the Antichrist to speak as a man. By trickery he will demand that this image be worshipped.

In verses 16-18 one of the most frequently discussed subjects is introduced—the mark of the beast. In order to understand this concept, we must look at history. Branding or marking for ownership began with the Egyptians as early as the third millennium BCE. In Exodus 21:6 we read that, when a Hebrew took a slave for life, that slave was marked by driving an awl through his or her ear. Even in John's day slaves were branded by their owners, so it was a natural segue for John to see that the mark of the beast would indicate that you are sold in slavery to Satan.

Precisely what this mark is we do not know. However, we can infer at least two conclusions. The first is that it will have an economic impact as well as significance in a worship system. If one is willing to worship the beast, then that person will be allowed to function economically without interference. Accepting the mark will be tantamount to rejecting Jesus.

The second conclusion is that anyone accepting the mark of the beast will do so of his/her own free will. By assenting to take the mark one denies the Messiahship and sacrificial atonement of the Lamb of God and willingly chooses permanently to disqualify himself from eternity in heaven.

While we do not know the precise form the mark will take, we are simply told that it is the number 666. This mark will be a distinguishing mark, perhaps a tattoo, visible only under ultraviolet light and will be placed either on the right hand or on the forehead.

Many scholars over the centuries have meditated on, calculated and pondered the identity of 666. From identifying him as Nero Caesar[113] to associating the number with Hitler, all efforts to identify him have been speculative. The most reasonable explanation comes from Hal Lindsey when he writes, "Since the number 6 in the Bible stands for humanity, I believe the meaning of 666 is man trying to imitate the trinity of God (three sixes in one person). Anyone who acknowledges this blasphemous trinity by worshipping the 666 Beast will be separated *forever* from the true triune God."[114]

APPLICATION TO OUR POST-CHRISTIAN WORLD

Both Beasts will possess nothing but malicious intent in all that they do. They are empowered to carry out the orders and schemes of Satan. They will be triumphant when they can convince humankind that Jesus is not real, His life either never happened or was fictionalized, that the church is old fashioned and is no longer needed, that obedience to Christ no longer takes precedence over New Age culture or that real religion is found in the Antichrist. Many of these objectives can be successfully achieved by bringing all religions together into one based upon the premise that nothing is wrong as long as it is performed in the name of Satan or the Beast.

In order to achieve a "one world religion," the Beast from the Sea," the Antichrist, must first create a consolidation of religions from throughout the world. That effort is already underway. In its purpose statement, the World Council of churches declares: "The World Council of Churches is a fellowship of churches which confess the Lord Jesus Christ as God and Saviour according to the scriptures, and therefore seek to fulfill together their common calling to the glory of the one God, Father, Son and Holy Spirit. It is a community of churches on the way to visible unity in one faith and one eucharistic fellowship, expressed in worship and in common life in Christ. It seeks to advance towards this unity, as Jesus prayed for his followers, 'so that the world may believe'."[115] Today, the World Council of Churches sees its role as sharing "the legacy of the one ecumenical movement and the responsibility to keep it alive" and acting "as a trustee for the inner coherence of the movement."

But you may ask, how would Christians give up beliefs simply to join forces? The answer to that question can frequently be observed in today's society. Read the newspaper or watch television, and you might see articles or reports like this: A Christian pastor invites a Muslim imam to speak in his pulpit, or a church may get together with a Hindu temple to hold a joint prayer service. That is ecumenism at it root source. And yet such examples are common.

Or from solely a Christian perspective, are those with whom we join truly Christians in the biblical sense of the word? There are many denominations and organizations that declare the name of Jesus Christ and may even avow that He is Lord and Saviour, yet they clearly reject what the Bible says about Him. Examples of these would be the Latter Day Saints (Mormons) and the Jehovah's Witnesses. In both cases, they claim to be followers of Jesus Christ, and they claim to be "Christian," yet they reject and disavow what the Bible clearly proclaims about the nature of Christ and His work. A not-so-obvious example is apostate Christianity. Apostate Christianity is liberal theology, plain and simple. Liberal Christianity is found in almost every denomination, and, although it may claim to be Christian, it generally denies certain essential truths, leading to apostacy. For example, liberal Christians will often deny or diminish the inspiration and authority of the Bible, the exclusive nature of salvation in Christ, and the total dependence upon God's grace, apart from human works, for salvation. By joining with any or all of these religions for the sake of ecumenism, one positions himself to be deceived by the Antichrist and be drawn into his web of evil and sin.

With respect to the economic plan of the Antichrist, how close are we today to the conditions prophesied by John? With our ever-increasing cashless society, our identities now singularly associated with our Social Security numbers, technology involving microchips and barcodes, it is easy to understand how this kind of state could be created. Only when the clock of God is approaching midnight will we finally understand clearly this great prophecy. TODAY IS THE DAY OF SALVATION!

CHAPTER 9
MID TRIB
14:1-20

Throughout the Book of Revelation John has taken a breather to make certain that his readers are current with what he has written. Here in chapter 14 we encounter the third of his pauses where John encourages the people of God to "persevere" in the face of intense persecution and great tribulation. The Revelator wants his readers to know that good will win and evil will suffer.

VICTORY PERICOPE, 14:1-20

Have you ever gone to a movie you had been waiting impatiently to be released only to find when you get to the theater that you must "endure" preview after preview before the movie actually starts? In chapter 14 we read a microcosm of such an experience. John offers a preview of times to come. His desire is to convince his readers that he knows the end of the story and that victory ultimately belongs to Christ and His followers.

Occurring at the midpoint of the Seven-Year Tribulation, John sees the "Lamb," none other than Christ Himself. John has already glimpsed the victory of the Lamb and the glory of a world under the reign of Christ. He now places this detail immediately following chapter 13 as a means of contrasting the rule of the false lamb who declares a false god with the rule of the true Lamb who declares a true God.

The Lamb stood on Mount Zion. Understand that we do not have biblical evidence of a Mt. Zion in heaven, so this Mount Zion must be identified otherwise. Indeed! It is Jerusalem, David's city as described in 2 Samuel 5:7, "Yet David did capture the stronghold of Zion, that is, the city of Jerusalem." Zion is the city of Jerusalem from whence, in the end, the Lamb will rule from the throne of David.

With Him are the 144,000. Recall that in Revelation 7:3 they are described as "slaves of our God" from every tribe of the Israelites. While scholars do not agree with respect to their identity, I believe that there is sufficient commonality between the two images in chapter seven and chapter 14 to identify them as one and the same. They are Jewish evangelists who are proclaiming the Gospel of Jesus Christ to the Jews of the Tribulation. The 144,000 are pure, undefiled followers of the Christ. They are described as "virgins," meaning either that they truly were unmarried and sexually pure, or they were morally and religiously pure. They were liberated from the contamination and idolatrous practices of harlotry for which Rome was known. They refused to bow to the claims of the Beast and the religious system established by the False Prophet. Because of their devotion to Jesus as the Messiah, they have the special task of evangelizing their Jewish brethren during the last half of the Tribulation.

They are, indeed, a select group that has been sealed with the name of both the Father and the Son and who have dedicated their lives to the propagation of the Gospel among their own people. They have already lived through the first half of the Tribulation but, because of the mark of God, they cannot be killed. They are the "firstfruits"[116] of God, and they will be the first to look upon the face of Christ in the Eternal Kingdom.

John continues his drama by observing the sounds of "cascading waters" and "rumbling of loud thunder." From the portals of heaven came the loud, thunderous sound of music, rising in crescendo. The sound, the singing of the Tribulations saints, possessed the rhythm of waterfalls and the intensity and sharpness of thunder and is presented in the presence of the angels ("beasts" from 4:6) and "elders," representing the church, the body of Christ. The song being sung is a "new song," a song of redemption, understood only by the 144,000, those Jewish believers who have been "redeemed" from the earth. They understand the song because, like the Tribulation saints who are singing, they know what it means to go through the Tribulation. After all, they have already experienced the first half of the Tribulation. They are spiritual kinsmen from the Tribulation, so they can relate, and they alone are capable of recognizing, understanding and learning the "new song."

Ever since that fateful day when Jesus cried, "It is finished," angels have been chomping at the bit to be a part of world evangelization.[117] Now, in the last days, notice the appearance of four angels, each offering a different proclamation. The first angel in verses 6-7 proclaims the "eternal gospel" to the earth's inhabitants. The "gospel" here is the Greek word εὐαγγέλιον, *euanggelion*, meaning "good news." It is a gospel that always has been and always will be. It appears to be a gospel of the kingdom declared before the news of Jesus ever came. It is a gospel that says one must repent in order to get ready to meet God. Then the gospel of Jesus declares that, having repented, one can be saved by faith in Jesus Christ. It is a gospel of grace, a gospel of peace, a gospel of Jesus Christ.

This "eternal gospel" also seems to be the embodiment of the single truth that righteousness will be rewarded, godliness will be judged and, at last, the good news that everything is set right. It is the same gospel entrusted to the saints and preached today. It is a gospel admonishing people to change their sinful ways and receive Christ by faith. It is a gospel that cautions the people to stand in awe of Christ rather than the Antichrist, to offer all glory to the One who loves them and has provided a way of salvation for them. It is a gospel "urging the people of the world to change their allegiance from the beast to the Lamb."[118]

Once more, keep in mind the idea that the Book of Revelation is not written in chronological order. There is no specific historical sequence to its narrative. Events occur as John the Apocalyptist saw them. A good example is that of the second angel in verse 8. Here the second angel announces the fall of Babylon. This verse typically represents a "cliff notes" version of chapter 18.[119] Two times the angel declares that Babylon has fallen. The first reference to Babylon is not to a literal city. It refers, however, to the world religious system established by the Antichrist. Its purpose is to destroy Christianity through evil means and its final fate is obliteration at the mid-point of the Tribulation.

The second reference to the fall of Babylon does denote a specific city, Rome. Rome will become the capital city of a one-world government. But it will also be designated as the nerve center for false religion based entirely on astrology, sorcery and necromancy. According to chapter 18, this city will be "burned up with fire," perhaps referring to a nuclear disaster.

Enter the third angel in verse 9. The final judgment of God is announced to all who insist on taking the mark of the Beast and worshiping Evil and the Antichrist. They are doomed to destruction. They shall "drink of God's wrath," a reference to God's righteous anger which will be poured out undiluted. The word used here is ἄκρατος, *akratos*, meaning "undiluted," "unmixed," "full strength." Some scholars translate it as "unmixed" and interpret it to refer to the mixture of wine and gall offered to Jesus on the cross. A study of the crucifixion shows that two drinks were offered to Jesus as He was dying. One He accepted; the other, wine mixed with gall which would have served as a pain killer, He refused. The more accurate translation is "undiluted" or "full strength," indicating that God's torment upon those with the mark of the Beast will come upon them in all its full fury.

Their doom will be sealed; it is fire and brimstone resulting in chronic torment.[120] Such torment will be so unbearable that the smoke of it shall "go up" eternally, without end. Not the smoke that caused their torment, but the smoke of their personal torment will rise like the smoke of a chimney fire. There shall be no mercy for the unbelievers. While those who have accepted the mark of the Father and the Son rest eternally in peace with God, unbelievers suffer the "cup of His anger," not just today, not just tomorrow, but forever and ever.[121] Such is the outcome of unbelief.

In the midst of all the wrath and judgment, John hears a voice from heaven declaring, "Write: The dead who die in the Lord from now on are blessed. 'Yes,' says the Spirit, 'let them rest from their labors, for their works follow them'!" What a contrast to what he has just written! Who is this voice? It is none other than the voice of Christ. Here the "dead who die in the Lord" refers to the Great Tribulation martyrs, those who die during the Tribulation because they are unwilling to accept the mark of the beast, those who have persevered in spite of the opposition of Evil. They are the ones who, when man's environment, man's social order, man's universe and man's world system of religion have all militated against God and Christ in all the outpouring of the devastation of evil, these saints still stand.[122]

With respect to these glorious saints, Jesus offers a twofold beatitude.[123] First, these martyrs shall "rest from their labors." The voice of Christ recalls His words in Matthew 11:28, when He said, "Come to Me, all of you who are weary and burdened, and I will give you rest." The word for "rest" is ἀναπαήσονται, *anapaēsontai*, which literally means "refreshed." The word for "labors" is κόπων, *kopōn*, which literally translates as "laborious toil involving weariness and fatigue." For the faithful follower of the Father and His Son, the end only brings an unequalled restfulness from the labors of this life. No longer will the specter of death hang over those who have been sealed with the name of the Father and the Son. They will also experience the privilege of being raised and reigning with Christ during the Millennium to follow.

The second beatitude, "their works follow them," reflects God's knowledge of their ministry efforts on His behalf. Recall the words of Hebrews 6:10, "For God is not unjust; He will not forget your work and the love you showed for His name when you served the saints." God is a God of His word. Their obedience will result in great reward.

The believer who dies in Christ is ushered into the presence of God with all his own works attesting to his life of faithful service. His works are not what allows him entrance into the heavenly realm, but his works bear witness to his faithfulness in the Lord's service. Oh, may we be found faithful so that when we enter the portals of heaven, our spiritual achievements number many.

The final thrust of this pause in thought is written in verses 14-20. Here the Seer of Patmos describes in detail the punishment that sinners can expect as the judgment of God is poured out on them. He envisions "One like the Son of Man," which appears to be a way of underplaying the real identity of this personage.[124] This "Son of Man," who is Jesus in all His consummate glory, has returned in judgment on a cloud just like the angels in Acts 1:9-11 declared. He is adorned with the golden crown of a conqueror, indicating that the final victory is already realized, and He holds in His hand a sharp sickle or scythe, not unlike that used by ancient farmers to gather wheat and other grains. He is prepared to supervise the separation of believers from unbelievers.[125]

In verse 15 the fourth angel appears from out of the Temple in heaven, declaring to Him who sat on the cloud, "Use your sickle and reap, for the time to reap has come." The perversion of sin and the godlessness of the earth have escalated to the point of no return. John writes, "The harvest of the earth is ripe." The word he uses for "ripe" here is the Greek word ἐξηράνθη, *exēranthē*, which means ripe to the point of wasting away, overly ripe to the point of becoming dried fruit. Here we are approaching the very end of time, and at every point, God has offered mercy, love and patience in giving man every possible chance to repent. Now, those who have rejected the gospel have become overly ripe and receive their just reward. And so the earth is reaped, the grain gathered and the judgment of God's wrath is poured out upon all who have turned their backs on Him. It is "the saddest day in all of human history."[126]

But God is not finished! Two more angels appear on the scene in preparation for a second harvest. One from the "sanctuary in heaven" and one from the "altar." The first angel holds in his hand a sickle not unlike that being held by the "One like the Son of Man." He awaits the harvest to come. But unlike the grain harvest, this harvest will be reaped by the angels who represent the Messiah.

The second angel, who is associated with fire on the altar, represents the answer to the prayers of the Tribulation saints who have been martyred for the sake of Christ.[127] That angel appears to assure those saints that their prayers for judgment and the coming of the kingdom are about to be answered. Then the order is given! "Use your sharp sickle and gather the clusters of grapes from earth's vineyard because its grapes have ripened."

The vineyard is the earth, and the grapes are the individual unbelievers. These grapes are also ripe and ready for harvest, but the word "ripened" used by John here is not the same word as in verse 15. Here he describes the grapes as ἤκμασαν, *ēkmasan*, meaning beyond ripe, ripe to the point of bursting. It is as though the grapes (read, unrepentant man) are begging God to judge them. The world has marched on, parading against God and mocking God to the point that the stench of sin so fills His nostrils that judgment is demanded. No separation this time, however; just the reaping of a harvest of unrepentant sinners whose doom is hell and whose torment will rise like smoke as they suffer eternally for their rejection of Jesus Christ.

Once gathered, the grapes are thrown into a winepress "outside the city." The winepress pictures a mass slaughter, a bloodbath as it were of the enemies of God. Many believe that it represents Armageddon, that final battle against the enemies of the Father and Son. Whether it is the Battle of Armageddon or a battle preceding the "great war," it is a scene of carnage unlike anything seen in history.

Notice that the winepress of judgment is "outside the city." The city is Jerusalem, the city of David. In speaking of the last great war, Zechariah prophesies, "I will gather all the nations against Jerusalem for battle. The city will be captured, the houses looted, and the women raped. Half of the city will go into exile, but the rest of the people will not be removed from the city. Then the Lord will go out to fight against those nations as He fights on a day of battle." (Zechariah 14:2-3) Such will be the first strike of Jesus in preparation for the final battle.

Then He will execute His second strike against the armies gathered in Armageddon. But blood will not be shed in the holy city; the city remains clean; the city remains secure; the city is spared because it is the king's city where Jesus will reign as king of kings and lord of lords. Dr. John Bisagno preached, "I do not believe that a first-class king will rule over and reign from a second-class city."[128]

But oh, the ferocity, intensity and carnage of this battle. As God's judgment is rendered in the winepress, the blood flows, and the grim reality of the battle is revealed. As the juice from the winepress flows out, it is reminiscent of the bloodshed in this battle. With the bodies of millions stacked high and damaged battle armament strewn throughout the region, the blood flowing from the battle is deep enough to reach the bridles of horses. And it runs for more than 187 miles. A cursory calculation on maps will show that from the northern limits of the Valley of Armageddon along the Jordan River southward past the Dead Sea to the port of Elath on the Gulf of Aqabah is close enough to this precise measurement to make this description a reality. This whole valley will be filled with the consequences of war.

So, be warned! God's judgment IS coming. And anyone rejecting the grace and mercy of God will have no one to blame but himself or herself for the judgment that shall befall them.

APPLICATION TO OUR POST-CHRISTIAN WORLD

I sat one day with an unsaved friend discussing my work on this book. I told him that I was concerned that he had never accepted Christ as his Saviour, and I worried that he might be one of these described by John in this section of Revelation. He respectfully responded that he appreciated my disquietude but that I should not worry about his future life. He quickly countered that he does not believe in life after death, and my apprehension about him is unfounded.

I reminded him that the Bible, while a book of morals and ethics (his words), is also a book of prophecy. I also reminded him that many of the prophecies that were declared by the prophets of old had actually been fulfilled in history. So, the

Bible should not be discounted lightly. His response: coincidence.

I reminded him also that the Bible is more than a book of morals and ethics, yea, even more than a book of prophecies. It is a playbook. Like the game plan that every coach prepares before his team takes the field, God has a plan that He prepared from before the foundation of the world. Knowing that His creation would sin—after all, He is omniscient—He set a plan in motion so that sinful man would have an escape from the consequences of his iniquity.

And finally, I reminded him that God also had a plan for those who steadfastly refuse to accept His redemptive work in Jesus, and that plan is seen in the words of The Revelation. God is righteous and just. And like any civil society calls for justice to be meted out in judgment for law-breaking, so His righteousness and justice demand judgment, and that judgment, as harsh as it can possibly be, will be visited upon those who refuse, and continue to refuse, God's offer of forgiveness.

Look around. What do you see? I am observing the infiltration of a Godless culture that has developed into a religion of its own making. The self-aggrandizement of segments of our population has reached epic proportions. Whether that means adhering to identity politics, whether declaring a sinful lifestyle to be normal and healthy, whether calling the murder of innocent lives "choice," whether living for self over the welfare of others or simply whether adopting an attitude of "me first and always," these doctrines are being espoused by a 21st century culture and religion known as the "new age" or "the new world order."

It is this new world order that has already laid the groundwork for Satan to establish his world system of religion that John calls "Babylon." It is also this same world system of religion that will be smashed, destroyed and obliterated from the face of the earth. Like grapes so over-ripe that they burst from their own juices, so the world religious system of Satan will be trampled so completely that its "juices," the blood of its adherents, will literally fill the valley of Armageddon.

In the 21st century, it is probably difficult to imagine a battle so intense and gruesome that the blood of its vanquished would be deep enough to reach the bridles of horses for more than 187 miles. But, even if this imagery is only symbolic and is not intended to depict reality, the result remains the same. God will be victorious, and the enemy—Satan and his forces of evil—will be crushed, conquered and annihilated to the point of non-recognition. The new world order will never achieve maturity. The Lamb will reign, and God will still be on the throne! TODAY IS THE DAY OF SALVATION!

CHAPTER 10
UNREPENTANT EARTH CONDEMNED
15:1-8

INTRODUCTION TO THE BOWL JUDGMENTS

In this great drama of eschatology, the stage is now set for the final judgments of God to be poured out upon the earth. Recall that judgments have been pronounced before with the seven seals in chapter 6 followed by the seven trumpets in chapters 8, 9 and 11. Now God will finish the job by pouring out His worst wrath yet on an unrepentant world before the return of Christ. This timeframe is a part of the last three and one-half years of the Tribulation that will be described in chapter 16. Our invincible Lord, absent emotion and without graphic description, pauses with harsh but sensible wisdom to present justifiable reasons for what is about to happen.

Before detailing the account of God's wrath, the Apocalyptist writes a parenthesis in which he offers three reasons for the pending outpouring of God's judgment on unrepentant man. In this introductory chapter he provides a glimpse of the future. The purpose for the Seer of Patmos to write this brief chapter is to help man understand that God is a just God, justified, fair and equitable in what He will do. The scene takes place in heaven; the "sea of glass" is still visible; the beasts (angels) remain present; and God is still on the throne.

Notice once more, as John did in chapter 12, that he classifies what he is seeing as a "sign," a "great and awe-inspiring sign." John is not simply offering a picture or dramatization by writing what he saw, he declares it to have meaning, spiritual meaning beyond the actual event. It points to a greater truth; it possesses genuine and authentic symbolism intended to encourage Christians of the current times and the future to hold fast; Christ will win in the end.

God's patience has now been exhausted. He has taken all He can of Man's rebellion, and He sends His angels to finish the job. John observes these seven angels with the seven "last plagues." In fact, he writes, "for with them (the plagues), God's wrath is completed." The word translated "completed" is the word ἐτελέσθη, *etelesthē* from the root word τελέω, *teleō*, meaning "finished" or "accomplished." It is the same word, "it is finished," spoken by Jesus on the cross in John 19:30. Those who have continued to reject this finished work of Jesus now find that God's forbearance is ended. God is done. There is now no chance to repent. It is, in every way, the beginning of the Hell experience.

Of all the judgments so far faced by sinful man, this last judgment will be the worst of all. The word John uses is the Greek word θυμός, *thumos*, meaning "rage," "intense anger." God is fed up. Now everything that God has to throw at them will be poured from these bowls. Throughout the history of the world, God has exercised a succession of judgments on mankind. He judged the antediluvian flood; He judged Sodom and Gomorrah; He judged Egypt; He judged the Roman Empire; He judged Hitler's Germany; He judged the Japanese Empire; and He will judge America and our modern, reprobate world. He will act neither judicially nor emotionally. He will not exercise the powers of His office as a lawgiver but as the moral ruler of the universe. God is angry!

The first reason John suggested for the coming judgment is the retribution of God. John observed "something like a sea of glass mixed with fire" reminiscent of the sea of glass of chapter 4. Here, however, the sea of glass does not surround the throne but is mixed with fire representing God's judgment. Further, there are figures with the appearance of people standing on the sea of glass. David Smith sees the crystal sea here turned red by the reflection of the lurid conflagration of persecution which was raging down on earth.[129] Another line of thought, advocated by William Milligan, sees the sea as reflecting either the fire of God's judgment or the trials by which God purifies his people.[130] Then there is a third possibility. It is, I believe, an illusion of glass (Greek, ὡς, *hōs*, "as it were") upon which stand the Tribulation saints that have been victorious over the beast.[131] They have been through the fiery trials of evil and martyrdom and have emerged victorious. They suffered the most horrible of deaths, and now they stand as winners before the tabernacle in heaven as a testimony to their faithfulness.

They are playing harps, symbolic of praise. They praise the One who has brought them through the trials and who has avenged the death of His saints. They stand by the words of Jesus in Matthew 16:26: "What will it benefit a man if he gains the whole world yet loses his life?" I recall those words being echoed by Jim Elliot in his journal shortly before his martyrdom, "He is no fool who gives up what he cannot keep to gain that which he cannot lose."[132]

God says, "I'm going to avenge my saints. I shall bring vengeance on those who hate My church, despise My beloved, killed My saints, martyred My children, detested My word. I'm going to set things right. Sin will be out of business, and righteousness will rain down and cover the earth as the waters cover the sea."[133]

You may ask the question, Why is God determined to judge and punish sinners? The answer is simple. God is a truthful and faithful Father of all. If He is not righteous and faithful to prosecute evil, how can I as a Christian be assured that He will keep His word by forgiving the penitent sinner? He must bring order to the chaos; He must set right all that is wrong.

The second reason given by John for pouring out these bowls of judgment is the nature of God Himself. God is great and marvelous; He is just, authentic and holy. He prefers freedom over servitude. To illustrate this principle, God presents a picture of these saints singing the "song of God's servant Moses and the song of the Lamb." These songs speak of the faithfulness of a dependable and changeless God. The "song of Moses" is a reminder of freedom from Egyptian bondage symbolized by the blood on the lintels. The "song of the Lamb" recalls freedom from sinful bondage for which Jesus paid the price on the cross. These two significant acts celebrate two great redemptive events and show God's faithfulness to Himself, to man and to His Word with respect to His changeless nature.

As John observed the goings on in heaven, he saw the "tabernacle of testimony," the third reason for the judgments. What he saw was the Word of God. In order for God to keep His word, He must effect retribution on those who steadfastly refuse to acknowledge Him as Lord.

In this heavenly sanctuary John sees the tabernacle. The tabernacle, the earthly symbol of God's presence, contained the Ark of the Covenant. You may recall that, inside the Ark was placed Aaron's budding rod, a pot of the manna provided by God in the wilderness wanderings, and the tablets of the Law. But John did not see the rod or the manna; all he could see was the Law, the Word of God. The breaking of God's law demands punishment, therefore, in order for God to honor His eternal word; He must bring judgment on evil.

The angels bearing the plagues were attired in clean, bright linen, a stark contrast to the sinners He will judge. They were adorned with sashes of gold representing God's glory and purity. One of the creatures (angels) gives the seven angels from the sanctuary the bowls from which will be poured the wrath of God. Smoke is now seen rising from the heavenly sanctuary as the angels accept the bowls and go forth to execute their mission. "Smoke" here represents glory, God's glory, a glory that is revealed when He sets all matters straight. His glory is manifested when His changeless nature is disclosed; His glory is made known when the faithfulness of His Word is authenticated. "The power that explodes evil is such that the whole temple is filled with glory, and man could not even see God until the smoke of that power and glory settled."[134]

Read again the words of verse 4: "Because You alone are holy, for all the nations will come and worship before You because Your righteous acts have been revealed." What a reminder of the admonition in Philippians 2:9-10: "For this reason God highly exalted Him and gave Him the name that is above every name, so that at the name of Jesus every knee will bow—of those who are in heaven and on earth and under the earth—and every tongue should confess that Jesus Christ is Lord, to the glory of God the Father."

God will keep His word, not because of vengeance but because, as promised, retribution shall come upon those who persist in their sin and refuse to repent. God will set all things straight. So "How will we escape if we neglect such a great salvation?"[135]

THE BOWL JUDGMENTS—CHAPTER 16

You may recall from our discussion regarding methods of interpretation, an analysis of the word τάχος, *tachos* was provided as a part of the examination of Preterism. Holding that the word should be translated as "soon," Preterists believe that it refers to events that would soon occur with respect to the fall of the Roman Empire. The other side of that coin is the idea that the word actually is best translated as "quickly" and most likely refers to the trumpet judgments but most especially the bowl judgments which are, in fact, to be poured out in rapid succession over a short three-and-one-half-year period.

So where are we with respect to man's relationship with God and why are these judgments being poured out? We find throughout time that man has habitually violated the first two commandments of Scripture. In Exodus 20:2-3 God declared that man was to put no other god before Jehovah Himself. Furthermore, man was not to make an image or idol of any god. In John's vision man has violated, even persisted in violating these fundamental laws of Jehovah. The world is worshipping the Devil incarnated in one man and bowing to the image of the beast as demanded in Revelation 13:14. Man has committed the greatest personal affront against God, and society has turned its back on Him and thrown its collective sins in the face of the Eternal One. Jesus warned of these bowls in Matthew 24:21 as events of "great distress" (NIV). It is now time for such worldwide rebellion to be met with worldwide judgment and wrath. Little wonder that the period is designated the Great Tribulation.

From the portals of heaven a loud voice, like unto the voice of God, shouts to the seven angels from chapter 15, commanding them to pour out the seven bowls of God's wrath on the earth. These bowls are reminiscent of the plagues that God inflicted upon Egypt at the time of the Exodus, except that time is now accelerated. The plagues of Egypt occurred slowly; then the plagues from the seven trumpet judgments came a bit more quickly, compressed in time. Now the seven bowls of God's wrath will bring to life that word "quickly" from Revelation 1:1. They will seem to be poured out all at once.

These plagues also have a similarity in scope. In Exodus, the plagues were quite localized, limited to the region of Egypt. In the trumpet judgments, the plagues affected one-third of the world—one-third of the earth, one-third of the waters, one-third of the stars, one-third of the grass and trees and one-third of the human race. In these bowls the wrath of God will be felt by the whole world. There will be an increase in swiftness, an increase in intensity and an increase in enormity until God has given all He has against a rebellious world. The clock of time has struck midnight, and the opportunity for repentance is now past. For those unrepentant sinners remaining on the earth, time has run out, and the wrath of God will be poured out in indescribable suffering and untold misery. Truly a Hell on earth.

As John views the Temple in his vision, he sees, as described in verse 8, "a sanctuary filled with smoke from God's glory and power." This smoke, reminiscent of the pillar of fire and its accompanying smoke, represents the presence of God in the Temple. The wrath of God also fills the Temple to the point that no one—no human being, repentant or unrepentant—can enter the sanctuary until the angels have poured out the bowls of the wrath of God's displeasure upon the earth. This cloud of God's glory will remain within the sanctuary until the earth is purified—cleansed of all sin and unrepentant souls—and prepared for the coming of the King and His kingdom. For the time is at hand for God's retribution to bring ultimate judgment on His impenitent world.

APPLICATION TO OUR POST-CHRISTIAN WORLD

As a parent, have you ever become so exasperated with the behavior of your child that you resorted to corporal punishment to get that child in line? As a youngster, I remember my sweet and compassionate mother taking a "switch" to my backside, reminding me that she was in charge, and I would behave in a civilized manner. Such is where God finds Himself at the middle of the Tribulation. He has provided every opportunity for man to repent and turn to Him; He has been faithful to His Word; He has been patient in His dealings with sinful humanity; He has offered "signs" in the previous judgments that He is serious to appease His just character.

Today's world can almost be characterized by sin. One needs only to read the newspaper or watch the news to observe man's inhumanity to man; or watch television to hear jokes made of Christians or derisive comments voiced about a Christian's beliefs that are counter to the culture. Man has strayed so far from God's ideal that God must be ashamed that He ever created mankind. God is pure and holy and just and cannot look upon sin. Remember the words of Jesus on the cross: "My God, My God, why have You forsaken Me?" The Father could not look upon His own Son because He had become sin incarnate, bearing the transgressions of all mankind in His body.

But man has increasingly chosen to reject all of God's efforts to redeem him. And because God is pure and holy, He cannot tolerate sin. He must purge the world of sin before He can reclaim it. So, the time has passed, and God's patience has been expended. God has had it with a world that is so intent on rejecting His salvation. And because God is a God of justice and righteousness, retribution is required. God will now act! TODAY IS THE DAY OF SALVATION!

THE FIRST BOWL, 16:1-2

The order comes down from the sanctuary to the seven angels. It is time. The midnight hour has struck, and the angels are commanded to pour out the bowls of God's wrath upon the earth.

The first angel pours out a bowl of "severely painful sores." These sores afflict only those who worship the Antichrist and have taken the mark of the beast. Comparable to the boils in the sixth plague of Egypt,[136] the same Greek word written here is identical to the Greek word used in the Septuagint to characterize the boils of Egypt. This same word is used in Luke to describe the sores of the beggar Lazarus.

Could these open, running abscesses be a form of melanoma? Could they be caused by radioactive pollution triggered by some atomic device designed to poison the atmosphere?[137] Could they simply be painful, boils caused by infected hair follicles? Whatever they actually are, all the people of the world will be afflicted with these untreatable, incurable, oozing pustules of pain. No one will be exempt.

APPLICATION TO OUR POST-CHRISTIAN WORLD

We live in a world where, in almost an instant, life can change from healthy to sick. In 2020, within weeks the world went from health to a pandemic. Could this be a foretaste of the first bowl judgment? Perhaps. It certainly forecasts the reasonable possibility that the health of the world can change in the snap of a finger. Whether real boils and abscesses or burns and pustules caused by nuclear radiation or the rise of a skin disease pandemic, it will be God's wrath being poured out on the world, and it will produce unbearable pain and suffering. It has occurred more than once in the history of the world already, do not discount it happening again. TODAY IS THE DAY OF SALVATION!

THE SECOND BOWL, 16:3

Reminiscent of the first plague of Egypt,[138] this bowl represents the first of several in which God turns the tables on mankind. In the beginning God planned to create a utopia in which man would be drawn to Him in relationship. Even Paul, in Romans, made it clear that there was enough in creation to make man aware of a sense of a higher power, but man has refused to acknowledge God and divine creation.[139] Man has not responded to God's overture to have a relationship, and now God takes all creation and turns it against man for his rebellion. He does so by polluting and destroying man through his own environment.

This bowl of wrath is poured into the seas (salt seas), and they are turned to blood. Not just any blood, not living blood, not life-sustaining blood but blood like that of a dead man. The blood is coagulating and rotting, putrefied, causing all life in the oceans to die and wash onto the shores of the world. The death and decay of billions of sea creatures add insult to the misery of this judgment. With life in the oceans depleted, a major nutritional source is destroyed, and man and animal life lose a valuable food resource. The prospect of disease now looms heavily over all life.

APPLICATION TO OUR POST-CHRISTIAN WORLD

One of the loudest voices in today's culture is the call for environmental responsibility. Several years ago, the environmentalists ceased focusing on improving the environment and moved on to making it a political issue. However they wish to portray the environmental movement, it should not be politicized, but rather it should become an educational objective dedicated to keeping our air and water clean and the earth's resources plentiful and healthy.

But man has chosen to ignore the environment. One need only observe the water in China to recognize that no effort is being made in that country to curtail water pollution from industries. In fact, half of China's population cannot access drinkable water and two-thirds of China's rural population depends solely on defiled water. Yet, as awful as the water quality is in China, it is nothing compared to the global catastrophe that will encompass the world when God turns the salt seas into blood. Could John be describing a form of red tide or some other super algae bloom event? Perhaps, but whether the phenomenon is explainable, whether the result is real blood or whether this is simply an ancient explanation for an oceanic disaster, all resources of the seas will be destroyed. The result will be disease caused by the rotting carcasses of untold numbers of sea creatures. Livelihoods will disappear, food sources will die away, commerce will no longer be viable on the high seas. Many will take notice of the clarity and purity of the remaining lakes, rivers and streams (fresh water) which will now become the primary source for seafood and drinking water. For this they will offer thanksgiving to whatever deity they serve, including the Antichrist. Because of their continued disobedience, such thanksgiving will not be directed to the God of the universe. But even then, God will only be in the first stages of His plan to avenge His justice. Do you wish to be here? TODAY IS THE DAY OF SALVATION!

THE THIRD BOWL, 16:4-7

Thanksgiving for the fresh waters is short-lived. Retribution is now rendered upon the worshippers of Antichrist and the followers of the Beast because, together, they have tortured and killed God's saints and shed their blood for refusing to accept the mark of the Beast.[140] To avenge[141] the death of His saints, God's wrath is now poured out on the fresh waters of the earth—the rivers, the fountains, the springs—have turned to blood. Satan has shed the blood of saints; it is now time for his followers to have only blood to drink, and not just any blood but blood that causes disease and brings pestilence. Humankind no longer has life-giving, fresh water to drink. No longer can one bath in impure, undefiled water.

What the world has done to God and to His people, He now does to the world. He evens the score, He sets right the wrongs that have been committed against Him and His own; righteousness prevails, wickedness and unrighteousness are crushed and punished.

In verse 5 the angel declares that God is justified in rendering such harsh judgment on the people. Because this eternal God is holy and righteous, He alone has the power and authority to bring retribution and justice upon those who have indiscriminately tortured and murdered His saints. Even the angel exonerates God from any indictment that He is too harsh on the unrepentant. Rather, God's judgment is fair and appropriate. A voice from the altar of 6:9-10 acknowledges this reinforcing truth that God is justified in His judgment, and a day will come when God will have had enough and will fairly render His verdict upon the entire sinful world.

APPLICATION TO OUR POST-CHRISTIAN WORLD

Lo, the third bowl removes the sole source for quenching the thirst of every man, woman and child remaining on the earth. For now, even the fresh waters of the lakes, rivers and streams have turned to blood. Once more, could this be the result of a naturally occurring event? It certainly could. After all, nature has experienced its share of fish kills in tributaries and rivers over time, and this could simply be a global form of these events. Or it could yet be an occurrence the likes of which the world has never experienced. Whatever form it takes, the result will be the eradication of all sources of potable drinking water. Can you imagine the agony of going days without suitable water to drink. And in spite of modern technology that can filter putrefied liquid to a potable state, technology will be useless to provide such a life-sustaining necessity as drinking water. How do you think you will feel in such circumstances? TODAY IS THE DAY OF SALVATION!

THE FOURTH BOWL, 16:8-9

The bowls of God's wrath continue to bring more and more misery. The fourth angel pours out his bowl on the sun. With today's environmental movement proclaiming that man is destroying the ozone layer—our protective cover—this occurrence is entirely possible. Rather than man bringing on his own suffering, however, it will be God who will touch the sun and command it to shine more brightly. After all, God created the sun, and He can tell it what to do.

Interpreted literally, the results of increased solar intensity will multiply the travail of mankind. Man will already be suffering from extreme thirst caused by the fresh waters turned to blood. Now, with additional exposure to the rays of the sun, surely conditions such as melanoma will proliferate in geometrical progression. The polar ice caps are certain to melt, raising the levels of the bloodied oceans, inundating land masses. All life will suffer extreme pain from sunburn caused by exposure to the ever-increasing intensity of the scorching rays of the sun. There will be no escape!

Another possibility could be the almost simultaneous nuclear exchange by the powers of the world resulting in a nuclear holocaust. One is reminded of the heat produced from atomic testing during World War II and the ultimate dropping of atomic bombs on Japan.

Many people suffered severe burns and chronic pain for years as a result of those weapons. Could John be describing such an exchange? Could he be explaining unknown occurrences of the future by the known experiences of the present? Such is, of course, possible. In whatever form this bowl takes, the suffering will be interminable and severe.

APPLICATION TO OUR POST-CHRISTIAN WORLD

Have you ever experienced a serious, blistering sunburn? I have, and it is no fun. I even remember passing out in the bathroom of my home as a teenager following a long day at the beach. Lying on the sand without sunscreen, my skin literally blistered to the point of a third-degree burn.

Now think what it will be like when the intensity of the sun is increased multiple hundreds of times, and there is no escape from its heat and burning effects. Shade will be totally ineffective. Skin will be seared, pain will be deep and severe, and yet death will not come. What has been predicted will now be fulfilled in the melting regions of ice throughout the world; the sea levels, already a bloody mess with unimaginable stench, will rise dramatically; thirst will be exacerbated by the nonexistence of drinkable water. Whether a natural phenomenon, the result of a manmade nuclear catastrophe or an occurrence currently unknown to man, the results will be the same—indescribable agony, pain and suffering by those who have abjectly refuse to acknowledge the sovereignty of God. And yet it is too late to repent. What a day when the outpouring of the fourth bowl rains its distress on an unrepentant human race. TODAY IS THE DAY OF SALVATION!

THE FIFTH BOWL, 16:10-11

What a place to start! Notice that this fifth bowl is not poured out on some obscure, out-of-the-way people or place but at the very seat of authority for the Antichrist, the False Prophet and the Beast. The bowl is poured out on the core, the crux, the heart of their authority. The result—their kingdom was full of darkness. Not a darkness of local effect but a darkness that covers the entirety of Antichrist's dominion. In so many ways, the physical darkness is a manifestation of the spiritual darkness in which the world finds itself.

The results are devastating to the people. Suicide, despair, and all kinds of evil attacks on the mind occur.

Darkness has often been expressed as a means of describing one's spiritual condition or as a punishment on spiritual lethargy.[142] The answer has always been a cry for forgiveness and a God who freely provides it. But why darkness at this particular moment? Could it be that, under the cover of this darkness, the 200 million-man Oriental army from the sixth trumpet judgment in chapter 9 can now move into the battle area of the Middle East? Such timing would be perfect.

But these people are already in misery resulting from the sores, the drought and the heat. And repentance now is not possible. The time for repentance has past, and they gnaw at their tongues from the pain of thirst and the searing severity of the heat. With no water to drink and no way to alleviate their suffering, all that is left is to blame and blaspheme God. Yet God is not the cause of their suffering. They are.

APPLICATION TO OUR POST-CHRISTIAN WORLD

Have you ever been in a place where you literally could not see your hand in front of your face? I recall a visit with my wife and young grandson to Mammoth Cave in Kentucky one year. As we wandered through the cave, the guide took us to a room with a very low ceiling. The room appeared to be about 30 x 30, illuminated with lights for the visitors to find their way through. Stopping there, he asked everyone to stand still for a moment. Then he warned us that the lights would be extinguished to give us an idea of how dark it might be there. As the lights were turned off, the darkness seemed overwhelming. My grandson grabbed my legs and held on for dear life. For him, it was a fearful experience, so he sought refuge in the grasp of his grandfather.

The surroundings of that dark cave, even in the company of others, was frightening. The darkness was so deep that, as I lifted my hand to within an inch of my face, I could not see it. I could not make out the silhouette of my own hand. At that moment I thought how frightening it might be to get caught in that place alone. The darkness was depressing, disarming and disheartening. One tends to ask, "Where do I go from here?"

As if the earlier suffering were not enough, God now adds darkness to the misery of the moment. What a way for God to reveal the soul status of mankind at that moment than to bring physical darkness to a world shrouded in spiritual darkness. Such an act only intensifies one's sense of fear and dread. TODAY IS THE DAY OF SALVATION!

THE SIXTH BOWL, 16:12-16

Be careful not to confuse this bowl with the actual Battle of Armageddon in chapter 19. This bowl represents the preparation for the battle to follow. Satan is determined to foil the second coming of Christ, and this is his final attempt to do so. The great army, which has been stalled by the waters of the "Great River," is now on the move.

The Euphrates River is the eastern boundary of the land God promised and ultimately gave to Abraham. Historically it was also the eastern border of the Holy Roman Empire. Near Ramadi, Iraq, in 2015, ISIS closed the gates of the dam at Ramadi and lowered the level of the Euphrates River, making strategic military actions easier. It also produced a humanitarian crisis by limiting the amount of water available to the major cities for consumption. Aoun Dhiyab, a former head of the Iraqi water resources department said "the goal of (ISIS) is not to cut the water, but to reduce the level, to take advantage of it for military purposes. When the water level is reduced, it allows them to infiltrate from Ramadi to Khaldiyah and then easily move to other areas."[143]

From this incident, we know that, even in our modern times, it is possible to dry the Euphrates for military purposes. Here in Revelation we read that the riverbed of the Euphrates will be dried up by the sixth bowl poured out by God's angel, making it possible for the kings from the East to enter the battlefield called by Napoleon as "the most natural battleground of the whole world."[144]

Who are these "kings from the east"? The Greek text of Revelation identifies them as the "kings from the rising of the sun," thus the east. Some scholars have identified them as the Father and the Son. Others believe it to refer to the Parthian army, the archenemy of Rome. The context not only of this passage but also the entirety of the Book of Revelation argues against these positions and for the fact that this army is an enemy of Israel that will be amassing forces against it and preparing to do battle. While the general message of the Book of Revelation is the second coming of Jesus and the establishment of His kingdom, these bowls of wrath speak to judgment and preparation for the second coming. To "prepare" the way for the "kings" implies a strategic move rather than a preemptive effort at describing the coming of the Lord.

These bowls of wrath are a proactive plan for God to march toward the inevitable conflict that is ultimately played out in chapter 19. To consider this bowl anything else but an explanation of the coming conflict does not do justice to the original text. The forces of the "kings from the East" will ford the dry riverbed and join with a massive coalition of armies from eastern countries to make one final assault on God's chosen people.

John now sees, emerging from the very pits of hell, "three unclean spirits" proceeding from the mouths of Satan, the Beast and the False Prophet. These "spirits" are like frogs, indicating their uncleanliness,[145] their vile, repulsive and repugnant character and confirming their association with evil and the devil. They are demons who support all the efforts of the Unholy Trinity and have the power to perform "signs" and wonders. These miraculous happenings are so deceitful and powerful that they draw the kings of the east to invade Palestine in spite of their sores, the intense heat, drought, and darkness.[146] Further, their signs and wonders attract the powers of the west toward Palestine as the two sides begin to gather for the final battle of earth.

As with the scroll and trumpet judgments, John takes a breather in verse 15 and pauses before he presents the last plague. As preparation continues to mount in intensity for the battle to come, we are reminded that Christ will come "like a thief." Here John is urging the surviving believers to remain faithful to the end regardless of the consequences of the battle, to walk in righteousness and to remember that they have been washed in the blood of the Lamb of God. They are to walk in their robes of righteousness, proudly displaying their preparedness for the coming of Christ.

In verse 16 John introduces the identity of the place where the ultimate battle between good and evil will occur. "So they assembled them at the place called in Hebrew, Armageddon." Now that the identity of the battlefield is known, perhaps this is a good place to review a bit of the history of Armageddon.

Armageddon as a name is mentioned only here in Revelation 16:16. Meaning "Mount of Megiddo," it refers to the valley to the east of Mount Megiddo where as many as thirty-four battles have been fought throughout history. With respect to Israel and Christianity, the foundational event that defined this valley in Jezreel is described in Judges 4 and 5. It is the battle between the Israelites and the Canaanites. Outnumbered and outgunned, the Israelites, led by Barak, go into battle with the help of Jehovah and rout and defeat a much more powerful army. This battle became a "type" for Armageddon.

In 2 Kings 19 and 2 Chronicles 32 another battle in the Valley of Jezreel occurred. At this time in history, Sennacherib demanded that Hezekiah and his people pay taxes to the sovereign and his Assyrian kingdom. At the time the Assyrians were the most powerful empire in the world, so when Sennacherib quartered 185,000 troops outside Jerusalem, then Hezekiah knew his people were doomed. Isaiah, under the inspiration of Jehovah, prophesied that the angel of the Lord would slay them all, and in one night all 185,000 troops were killed. Sennacherib is defeated and withdraws. Like the battle with the Canaanites, Megiddo and the Valley of Jezreel once more became types for the victory of good over evil.

So it seems appropriate now, when the final battle of good and evil is to occur, that it take place in the Mount of Megiddo on the Plains of Jezreel, the site described by Napoleon as the "perfect battlefield."[147] Like so many battles before, the outcome is known because the Lord is leading the charge. Confidence is high, and victory is assured.

APPLICATION TO OUR POST-CHRISTIAN WORLD

This bowl is God's strategy move consistent with the release of the four angels in the sixth trumpet judgment. The drying of the Euphrates riverbed will make it possible for the 200 million-man army from the East to traverse that great river and enter into the land prepared for the great battle of the end times. The stage is now set for a battle that has already been decided. Unsaved man is doomed. TODAY IS THE DAY OF SALVATION!

THE SEVENTH BOWL, 16:17-21

The same author who wrote The Revelation also observed and wrote the last words Jesus spoke from the cross, "It is finished." The Greek form of this verb is in the perfect tense, an incredibly meaningful point. The perfect tense in the *Koine* Greek language is a tense that indicates the continuing effects of a past action. When Jesus spoke these words, He was telling the world that His mission on the earth was complete, but the results of His actions would continue.

As we read the words of Revelation 16:17, we are once more reminded of the perfect tense. John hears a voice from the heavenly sanctuary, likely the voice of God Himself, declaring, "It is done!" These English words translate the Greek γεγονεν, *gegonen*, a perfect tense verb meaning "it has happened" or "it is done." The idea here is the same as when Jesus spoke His words from the cross. The declaration means that "I have now judged the world, effected the sentence and avenged the persistent unrighteousness of a stubborn world that insists on rejecting Me by pouring out My wrath. My mission is done!" Yet, although the mission is complete, the lingering effects of that mission will continue until Jesus Christ has made His final appearance on the earth.

This bowl completes God's indignation on an unrepentant world. It is the consummation of the period of Tribulation and the end of the time of trouble.[148] It will be marked by natural calamities that include thunders and lightnings and the most devastating earthquake ever experienced on the earth. The word employed here to describe the earthquake is σεισμος, *seismos*, which, while it can mean "earthquake," can also mean generally a "shaking of the earth." Hal Lindsey writes that such shaking might be the result of a nuclear exchange among the great powers of the world. He states that "when these powers lock forces here, there will be a full-scale exchange of nuclear weapons, and it's at this time that 'the cities of the nation will fall'."[149] In whatever form it takes, the destructive power of this shaking will affect the entire globe and every city of the world will be leveled to dust.

The "great city," Babylon, will be split into three parts representing the Unholy Trinity, all of whom, in the person of Satan, the Beast and the False prophet, will fall. But Jerusalem will emerge as an improved city, a spiritually defined city. It will become the center of Christ's rule during the Millennial Kingdom and shall remain so until the Great White Throne judgment and the establishment of His eternal reign.

This final outpouring of God's wrath on the earth will result in the destruction of Babylon, the capital city of the Antichrist.[150] The city, that has so long sullenly resisted the efforts of believers, will taste the bitterness of God's "cup filled with the wine of His fierce anger." The enormity of this disaster, whether natural or manmade, will be unprecedented. The islands of the oceans and seas will disappear, submerged beneath the growing water levels due to the heating of the earth. The mountains, once so majestic and beautiful will be reduced to unsightly chasms in the earth. The earth, as known before, will be unrecognizable.

To add insult to injury, all life on earth will suffer the indignity of being pounded relentlessly by hailstones, some weighing as much as 100 pounds. Not only do the hailstones destroy buildings and cities and farms and crops, but they also kill all life on whom they fall. The suffering is agonizing. Death becomes a pleasant companion.

And yet, unbelievers continue to "hate on" God. They continue to blaspheme His name, blaming Him for all that has encompassed them and destroyed their lives. They take no responsibility for their own actions, no accountability for the martyrdom of the Tribulation saints, no fault for not accepting the grace and mercy God offered to them again and again.

But now, "it is done!" With the pouring out of the final bowl of judgment, the third "woe" is concluded.

APPLICATION TO OUR POST-CHRISTIAN WORLD

Modern culture lives as though these words of Jesus are simply myth. Through every season of life mankind is presented the Gospel and an opportunity to respond affirmatively and obediently to it. Yet where are we today?

Like the parent whose patience will endure just so long, so God's patience and His mercy, while longsuffering, are not eternal. In a world where thoughts concerning God are a consolidation of all thoughts about God, the idea of a genuine relationship with the Triune God seems inconsistent with modern ideology. How blasphemous it is for people to worship the creature and creation rather than the Creator!

Yet our modern age people have turned a blind eye to the One behind the Plan for creation and salvation. And like ignorance of the law is no excuse for violating the law, so ignorance cannot be blamed for not recognizing God in all that He has created and sustained.

Over the last few years, our world has seen its share of calamities, resulting in the deaths of thousands of people. I'm reminded of the words of Romans 1:18-19 where Paul wrote, "For God's wrath is revealed from heaven against all godlessness and unrighteousness of people who by their unrighteousness suppress the truth, since what can be known about God is evident among them, because God has shown it to them." Could God's patience be wearing thin? Could God be displaying His power and greatness in the many disasters that have befallen earth in the last few years? In the words of C. Bouwman from a sermon delivered on March 25, 2011, " Let our eyes be open, dear readers, to the reality of God's wrath as it presses down day by day on today's ... society! God is terribly displeased with man's original sin as well as our actual sins, and so He punishes them by a just judgment both now and eternally. A godless society receives from God's hand a foretaste of the eternal weeping and gnashing of teeth that characterizes hell. For God would have people repent while it is called Today."[151] TODAY IS THE DAY OF SALVATION!

CHAPTER 11
GOD'S JUDGMENT OF THE TWO BABYLONS
17:1-18:24

JUDGMENT PERICOPE, 17:1-18:24

At this point in the Revelation narrative the Tribulation is ended. John now pauses from the weariness of delivering his primary message to offer a glimpse into the destruction of Babylon the Harlot and the future of the Antichrist. Even though, chronologically, the Tribulation is over, he describes the vision in detail and reveals what will happen to the kingdom of Satan and the earth both before and during the final seven years of world history. So, just a reminder: this is a pericope, a pause in the narrative that does not occur in any chronological order with the remainder of the book.

MYSTERY BABYLON, THE HARLOT, 17:1-18

John sees and hears the seventh bowl angel, who introduces us to the great harlot of the end times. It seems that God wanted John to see the end result of power and self-aggrandizement, and to illustrate that message, God offered yet another vision. In verses 1-7 he presents the vision as he observed it.

John's vision once more takes a grotesque turn. He is entranced ("astonished," verse 7) with what he sees and hears. He sees a "notorious prostitute who sits on many waters." This same prostitute of John's vision had committed all kinds of "sexual" sins with the "kings of the earth."

At this point John is transported to the wilderness where he sees a woman sitting on a "scarlet beast" with seven heads and ten horns. This woman is arrayed in purple and scarlet and "adorned with gold, precious stones, and pearls." In her hands is a gold cup filled with the abominable impurities of her life. She is identified by a name written on her forehead.

Now that we have read a description of the vision itself, verses 8-18 offer an explanation of the vision. The woman observed by John both in verses 1 and 3 is singularly the same person; she is neither a literal nor a physical person. She represents Babylon the Great as explained in verses 5 and 18. She is people, the human race, besotted by the harlot, enticed by the seduction of the world—its false pleasure and attractions, its worldly culture and tempting indulgence. She is a harlot who represents fake love, pretentious affection. She is "mystery Babylon" embodied in the counterfeit church, the apostate church, the copycat church. She is a woman married to the world who represents a system of religion marked by union with the world.

She is the woman of the letters in chapters 2 and 3. She is the influence of such churches as Pergamum where Christ said, "You have some who hold to the teachings of Balaam." Or the church in Thyatira to whom Christ said, "You tolerate the woman Jezebel who . . . deceives My slaves to commit sexual immorality." Or the church at Smyrna when Jesus spoke: "Those who say they are Jews and are not, but are a synagogue of Satan." Or the church at Sardis when Jesus said, "You have a reputation for being alive, but you are dead." Or the church at Laodicea when Jesus declared them to be "lukewarm, and neither cold nor hot." All of these churches masqueraded as Christianity but preached only an apostate gospel as Jesus had warned his disciples in Matthew 24:3.

But why call this harlot Babylon? We know from archaeological evidence that Babylon was the cradle of civilization. It was famous for its religious fervor and its development of a successful governmental structure. In chapter 17 the spiritual vacuum of Babylon takes center stage. Recall that it was in Babylon that Nimrod lead the building of the Tower of Babel designed to reach heaven and, therefore, prove that there is no God. But its construction was in defiance of God's command to Noah and his family to "be fruitful and multiply and fill the earth." From these beginnings Satan began to establish Babylon as the capital city of his evil empire. Babylon became synonymous with a religious system based upon two premises: (1) we do not have to obey God, and (2) there is no God anyway. It represented godlessness at its very core.

From then until now, from the seat of that empire, Satan's great malevolence has doomed the souls of millions of people by counterfeiting God's work and claiming it as legitimate. More than simply a geographical city, this "great city" is symbolic of the concept, the philosophy and the ideology of Babylonianism because she is called "mystery Babylon." The word used here is μυστήριον (*mustērion*), meaning a mystery revealed. She is not just a locale, but she is the spirit of Babylon in its most perverse, religious state. She is a place and time in history, but she is also a philosophical attitude that is the "mother of all harlotry religion, all works religion, all do-it-yourself religion, all non-deity of Jesus religion,"[152] which describes all liberal theology and apostate religion.

Note here that the Babylon of chapter 17 and the Babylon of chapter 18 are two different entities. The Babylon mentioned here is "mystery Babylon," the great harlot that represents a false religious system which the Beast will ultimately bring under his subjection. In fact, the word "prostitutes" in verse 5 is a plural form indicating that she is the mother of many false religions.

In chapter 18 the scene will change to Babylon that represents the political and governmental system over and through which the Beast will rule and will bring the entire world to its knees. Both Babylons will be destroyed but at different times and by different means.

The identity of the woman is confirmed in 17:18 as the "great city," a religious city in which a kind of religious blending will emerge. She stands on "many waters," a term also identified in 17:15 as representing the unrest of the nations of the world. By "standing," she dominates and controls all who dwell on the earth. So great is her influence that her power is over all the world's people; it is universal; it covers the whole earth. This city, before whom royalty, despots and lands have been forced to give homage, this same city is no more than a metropolis of idolatry. And so this woman represents a united, evil religious system of idolatry. Just as Apple is synonymous with technology and Wall Street with investment, so Babylon is tantamount to false religion at its basest.

But she is not alone. When John is transported to the wilderness, he sees her astride a scarlet colored beast from which her authority is derived. This beast is the Antichrist who represents the other Babylon, the governmental and political Babylon. The scarlet attire is a color of indulgence, grandeur and royalty representing one with power and authority. This picture indicates, then, that at some point, in the Tribulation perhaps, the religious system will be so powerful that it will take control of the political system. Ultimately, the "woman," Babylon, will unite all of the religions of the world into one global religion headed by the False Prophet and merge all of the governments of the earth into a one-world government.

In order to accomplish such a feat as consolidating all the religions of the world, the woman must be attractive, exude the power of wealth. The woman whom John sees is dressed in purple and scarlet, both colors of royalty and rule. She is adorned with "gold, precious stones, and pearls," all accouterments of prostitutes of her day. She pursued her trade quite successfully and even drank from cups of pure gold. But the contents of those cups are nothing but filth and all life activities that are abominable to God.

The depth of her rottenness is seen in verse 6 where she is depicted as "drunk on the blood of the saints and the blood of the witnesses to Jesus." As a false religion she is responsible for the deaths of ten of millions of believers for the past two millennia around the world. And yet what the world has experienced to date is no comparison to what is yet to be. Her deadly rampage will continue unabated, and even the apostate church, which Chuck Missler declares to be the Roman Catholic Church, will have the blood of the saints on its hands.[153]

APPLICATION TO OUR POST-CHRISTIAN WORLD

The "Woman." Ah, the Woman. As I look around me, I observe a spiritual space unlike any spiritual space I have seen before. I view true spirituality as reading and understanding the Word of God in its truest form. I see the true church consisting of genuinely born-again, saved people who have been joined by Christ and the Holy Spirit. No attempt to make the Gospel weak or watered down. Sin is sin, and any attempt to call it "sin but" is giving Scripture the message rather than allowing the Scripture to deliver its own message.

Too often, in today's post-Christian world, man is going about his business and "doing his thing" completely independent from God. Many churches have succumbed to the idea that Scripture is too strict. Living the Christian life is too difficult for humans to attain. Churches and preachers are too often declaring a "truth" that is not truth. In order to make the church more palatable and acceptable to an ever-increasingly world-focused society, the proclamation of God's Word has been diluted to make it appealing to attract a more secularized church membership. In too many churches theological truth as epitomized in Jesus Christ has been altered for the sake of convenience and "fitting in" to the cultural and social distortion that the world has forced upon us. By such action many churches have fallen into apostasy.

These words from the Apocalyptist declare that the apostate church will thrive in the last days. This woman of Revelation represents that apostate church, a one-world-view church; a church that has turned from the truth of God; a church that allows sin to invade without being called out; a church that permits the ways of the world to adulterate the Gospel message; a church that looks upon sin as simply a human weakness; a church that looks inward rather than outward in missions and evangelism; a church that focuses on activity and busyness rather than spiritual enrichment.

Three simple characteristics identify the apostate church. (1) The apostate church will accept ecumenism by declaring that there is more than one way to get to heaven. A one-world church will be the standard and all religions will be the same.

(2) The apostate church does not profess the virgin birth, that Jesus was the Son of God, that He did not provide a vicarious atonement for the sins of mankind, that He was not resurrected on the third day and that He did not ascend to the Father to await His return. These are considered to be beyond the capability of man.

(3) The apostate church conforms to the constant cultural changes of the new age. When the ideas about moral wrong and faith change, so does the church. It is a church that allows the culture of the world to dictate its doctrines and practices.

Modern culture, the New World Age, the New Enlightenment have all edged their noses under the tent of the modern church. Powerful and spiritually discerning is the church that recognizes these heresies and takes action to combat them. Such action means declaring the Gospel in all its true form, telling it like it is, not sugar-coating the truth but offering a message that can find refuge deep in the soul of the transgressor and change a person's heart and manner of life—a message that begets repentance.

Real religion and faith thrive on possessing the truth. When Jesus is removed, when the truth is extracted, when the Holy Spirit is eliminated, then we will see the Laodicean church prosper. Many leaders are calling for a push toward ecumenism. This cry for unity is unprecedented in the history of Protestantism—a call to "get together." Too often today's religious mantra is "It really doesn't matter what we all believe as long as we all come together. After all, aren't we trying to go to the same place?" But Jesus declares unequivocally, "I am the way , the truth and the life." Unanimity on doctrines, ecumenism, social action or philosophical existentialism will not produce the truth.

The best guidance I can provide to you, the reader, in this moment is: If you attend a church and hear a message that emphasizes a social lesson above the truth of the Gospel, then seek another church. Within the Gospel there is definitely a social component, but the true church must allow the Gospel itself to effect social change, not the other way around. Hear the words of the "Good News" and heed them. TODAY IS THE DAY OF SALVATION!

HER STEED, 17:7-18

The beast upon which she sits is blasphemy incarnate and, because he so deifies himself to the world, he proudly wears on his forehead the profane names he so proudly claims. His grotesque appearance—the seven heads and ten horns—are explained in verse 9. The seven heads are "seven mountains." This presents an interesting word study that might offer clarification or even additional confusion to what has long been an issue in theological scholarship. Many scholars believe that the "seven mountains" refers to the seven hills of Rome, and therefore, the Roman Catholic Church. But a cursory glance at the language does not seem to support such a position. The word used here for "mountain" is the Greek ὄρη (*orē*), which actually does means "mountain." The other word used in the New Testament is the Greek word βουνός (*bounos*), which means "hill or hillock." Both words are used in Luke 3:5 and are employed to distinguish between the two geographical features. The picture, then, would be the absolute supremacy of Babylon over wide swaths of the earth, including whole continents.

Throughout Scripture, the term "mountains" has often referred to governments or ruling powers. Therefore, as much as I would like to think that words alone would explain the seven "heads/mountains" question, reason and Scripture lead me to the conclusion that the words here refer to Rome and the Roman Empire. The description in verses 8 and 11 refers to ancient Rome and its supremacy as a nation. But Rome did not last. It was defeated as an empire in the fifth century and has not existed as a kingdom since. And it will not exist again until the Antichrist revives it during the Tribulation. In this kingdom to come, the Antichrist, the counterfeiter of all counterfeiters of the true Christ will reign as the eighth king, the "little horn" of Daniel, the final king whose kingdom, a New Rome—a globally united Rome—will dwarf that of Babylon. His rule will be worldwide, and the peoples of the earth will be amazed at his incredible feats and his power of persuasion.

John then glimpses seven kings who are a reminder of the "ten toes" of Nebuchadnezzar's image, and the "ten horns" of the fourth beast or kingdom in Daniel.[154] The seven kingdoms include five that "have fallen," one that "is" and one "not yet come." The five fallen kingdoms are Egypt, Assyria, Babylonia, Medo-Persia and Greece. The one that "is" would be Rome, the major ruling power at the time of the writing of Revelation. The one "not yet come" is Babylon, the kingdom prophesied as the last political power in the world represented by the woman on the beast. Because the seventh king represents ten "kings who have not yet received a kingdom," it does not embody a single personage but rather symbolizes a confederation of ten nations not unlike the original European Common Market.

Although today the Common Market, formally designated as the European Economic Community, consists of 27 nations, its number will eventually be reduced once more to ten nations and become the world's last great empire. Its purpose will be to exercise financial control over the world, and it will have the appearance and character of a revived Roman Empire. Out of these kings and nations will arise an eighth king, the Antichrist. The ten nations then will hold a one-hour conference with the beast (the Antichrist) during which the Beast will give them transitory power. The "kings" of the ten nations are so wonder struck with him that once the conference is concluded, the nations, single-mindedly and unanimously, return power and authority to the Beast. It is a kind of mutual respect that ends with mutual allegiance.

Let me pause here to elaborate on the term Antichrist. This word is never used in the Book of Revelation; it is only used by John in his first two letters.[155] Unlike the beliefs of most people,

"Antichrist" does not mean "against Christ." It actually means "one who puts himself in the place of Christ," or the "enemy of Christ." Interestingly, the word "vicar" as in the official title of the pope, the "Vicar of Christ," means to be in the person of or a substitute for Christ. Little wonder that many believe the harlot of chapter 17 to be a Pope of the Roman Catholic Church.

Sometime during the last half of the Tribulation, this eighth king, the Beast, the Antichrist, representing governmental and political Babylon, will come forward from his alliance with the ten nations. He will wield great authority and power. He will possess such personal charisma and will rule with such mystical power that the world will bow down and worship him. No longer will he require the support of the harlot to gain the acceptance of the people of the world. He proclaims himself to be God, establishes the abomination of desolation in the Temple in Jerusalem and brings his evil rule once more to the entire world.

What is this abomination of desolation? It is none other than the Antichrist himself. He sits in the Temple upon the throne of David demanding that all the world worship him as God.[156] By doing so, he will desecrate the Temple of Yahweh. He will take this opportunity to prove his designation as "deceiver." Because he derives his authority from Satan, he will exercise dominion and power and will command an army of great power to oppress the people of God. He will use his authority to create a legal system that will oppose Christianity, even outlaw it. And he will persecute, even execute any Christians who resist his efforts.

Praise God, the rule of this seventh king will be brief and will ultimately be entirely obliterated by fire. Before its annihilation, those who are subjects of this seventh king, including the ten nations, will receive power from the Beast, but only for a short period of one hour. "Hour" probably does not refer to sixty minutes but more to the short time they are with him.

The nations, then, have one purpose and that is to return supreme power and authority to the Beast, after which time, all will go to war against the Lamb in the Battle of Armageddon. There they will be conquered, and Jesus Christ will begin His thousand-year reign.

APPLICATION TO OUR POST-CHRISTIAN WORLD

What we know today as the European Common Market was originally created by the Treaty of Rome in 1957 by the European Economic Community (EEC). In 1993, when the European Union was established, it was redesignated simply the European Community (EC). Its goal was to create economic unity among the six participating nations (Belgium, Italy, France, Luxembourg, West Germany and the Netherlands). By adding other communities to its charter under the European Economic Agreement, by 1994, it had achieved its ultimate goal of allowing for the free movement of goods, capital, services, and people within the organization's states. With the formalization of this agreement, an additional fifteen member states became active participants in this economic strategy.

In today's post-Christian world society, the European Common Market only exists through the European Union. The goals remain the same for its twenty-seven member states. To date, the only country to leave the European Union is Great Britain who exited the Agreement in January 2020.

While I am confident that the Antichrist will emerge from within Europe, it seems entirely plausible, if not likely, that the ten nations of this Scripture would or could be a remnant of today's European Union. While there remain more than ten states in the Union at the present time, like Great Britain, others might be expected to depart the Union upon disagreement with actions taken by the Union. Regardless, at some point in history, ten nations will unite in a historic confederation of states with the aim to control the economic power of the entire world. Out of this confederation will emerge the Antichrist who will demand complete allegiance and the taking of the "mark" that will designate such allegiance. For the non-believer, the unrepentant sinner, be alert lest you be caught up in the maelstrom of the Antichrist's power. TODAY IS THE DAY OF SALVATION!

POLITICAL AND GOVERNMENTAL BABYLON—18:1-24

In chapter 17 we have observed the efforts of the harlot and the Great Beast and, by the close of the first three and a half years of the Tribulation, we have seen the collapse and destruction of spiritual Babylon. Now the Spirit turns its attention to revealing to John the work and judgment of the commercial and political Babylon.

In chapter 17 Babylon was not a real geographical location on the map but rather the designation of a spiritual condition that had penetrated the cultures of many cities. Scholars of Revelation differ widely with respect to chapter 18, however. Many reputable interpreters of Revelation believe Babylon of chapter 18 to be a specific city, to be physically rebuilt on the Plains of Shinar. Other scholars, equally as reputable, hold that it is a place where man has supremely rebelled against God, a place characterized by successful commerce, industry, wealth, indulgence and moral profligacy, but a figurative locale nonetheless. Let's take a look at both of these positions.

One of the leading proponents of the physical Babylon is Chuck Missler. In fact, he maintains that the Babylon of chapter 17 and the Babylon of chapter 18 are one and the same. There is no dichotomy. He bases his viewpoint on three provisos: (1) Babylon is never used of the Beast or the heads or horns, 17:5, 18; (2) The context before and after chapter 18, namely, 16:19; 17:1, 18; 18:2-3; 19:2; (3) Statements in Revelation itself, 18:3, 24 in conjunction with 6:9-11. Based upon these considerations, he accepts the idea of a physically rebuilt Babylon being depicted in both chapters 17 and 18.[157]

On the other side of the issue is Dr. John Bisagno who held that Babylon would not be a physically rebuilt city. Rather as it is presented in chapter 18, it is a symbol, an image describing a false political system, the other half of Satan's kingdom, that will arise and ultimately be destroyed.

Is one interpretation correct and the other incorrect? Yes, but only from the perspective of God's intent, which we cannot know. It is my belief that these words continue the symbolic picture of Babylon. She is first described as a woman, and now she is illustrated as a city. Whether a physically rebuilt Babylon or simply a symbol of evil Babylon, the end result is clearly the same. Both the false religious system established by Satan and personified in the apostate church and the corrupt commercial, political, social and governmental system created by him will be entirely destroyed.

Observe the text. In verse 1 we once more encounter the Greek words Μετὰ ταῦτα (*meta tauta*), "after these things." What things? The things you just heard. Then the angel announces God's judgment on Babylon. "It has fallen, Babylon the Great has fallen!" The Greek of this phrase is in the aorist tense designating an action already completed. The city's fall is so certain and impending that it is described as having already been accomplished.

Notice here the double use of "fallen." Anytime, in the Bible, that words or ideas are repeated, an emphasis is added. Such doubling means that what will happen will be sudden and soon, but it will also be with authority and finality. In Isaiah 21:9 these words are echoed with respect to the fall of Babel.

In Genesis 41, Joseph interprets two dreams of the Pharaoh as possessing the same meaning. For Pharaoh these dreams would certainly and soon be fulfilled. Then again, in Daniel 5:25-26, Belshazzar read the writing on the wall, "*Mene, mene, tekel parsin.*" "Mene" means that God has numbered the days of your kingdom. With the repeat of these two words, Daniel was telling Belshazzar that with absolute certainty, his rule would not last. Not only certain, but also soon it would be destroyed. So, to read here that Babylon "is fallen, is fallen" indicates, with surety, finality and brevity of time, the false religion of the woman and the fraudulent social and political system of the Beast will both meet certain destruction.

Such destruction would be expected as a result of Babylon's influence upon and fornication with the nations and kings of the earth. She has been the source of estrangement from God, and nations and kings have followed her lead into sin, idolatry and false religion. She is, in every sense, married to the world.

Another angel declares, "Come out of her, my people so that you will not share in her sins or receive any of her plagues." Through the angel God is calling his people, the elect of God, to desert the world system, to abandon the apostate church of which they are a part and to come to faith in Jesus Christ, to resist the world system and to be the true church.[158] Do not bow to the pressures of the system to become what the church was intended not to become. Be who you are called to be.

That world system is walking a path of destruction; there is to be no forgiveness. God's judgment is inevitable because God memory is exact and unmistakable. He remembers the sins of the apostate church, but even now, offers an opportunity to be redeemed. For the unredeemed, recompense will be double judgment, the precise quantity of judgment and punishment that has been earned.

This Babylon, this world system of religion and commerce possesses three characteristics. First, she considers herself a queen, glorified as a ruling monarch deserving of adoration and submission. She is arrogant, prideful and wants for nothing. She lives in the lap of luxury and is dependent upon no one.

Second, she claims to be "no widow." She does not need a husband to complete her. She is totally independent. She maintains an air of arrogant self-indulgence and self-sufficiency because she can "go it alone." She is even proud to make such a claim.[159]

Her third characteristic is her lack of "grief." This entire verse is an echo of Isaiah 47:8 where Babylon is described. This loss of sorrow or "lack of grief" refers to a loss of children, either at birth or later. What a mistake she makes by such a declaration.

But her end is near, and it shall come with haste. The judgments of God will be swift, over a very brief period of time.[160] Her destruction will not be a protracted obliteration but a swift, decisive annihilation that will bring "death and grief and famine." It will be instantaneous, in the blink of an eye, and its certainty is guaranteed by God Himself.

Notice that it is not Babylon's sin that affects the lamentation rather it is Babylon's total destruction with fire. Unlike the ruin of spiritual Babylon for which there were no mourners present, three groups of people "stand far off" and observe the intensity of the fires that destroy "blessed Babylon." These groups of mourners represent the leadership with the most to lose from the extinction of an evil, world economic system.

The first group includes kings who have been Babylon's allies and who have committed fornication with her, have worked against God in an effort to win the souls of the nations. The political leaders who have lived in luxury now mourn the loss of their empire lead by the Antichrist. They weep over the forfeiture of their power and the failure of the evil world system. Once more the double "woe" is sounded indicating the suddenness and certainty of the calamity.

The second group comprises the "merchants of the earth" who mourn because of the loss of their commercial enterprises. No longer are their wares demanded or needed. Where they are going, their goods will not be needed.

Notice that the list of goods and merchandise includes 28 items. Considering the symbolism of numbers, this would represent a quadrupling of the number 7. Whenever we see multiples of numbers, especially 7 and 10, we recognize ultimate completeness. The totality and finality of the destruction is so described by this multiple of 7. God does not exercise judgment half-heartedly; His judgment is complete, and here it will be both swift and total.

Recall at this point that the only way to buy or sell is to have the mark of the Beast. And what a materialistic world it is! But once God begins to exercise His destructive powers, His judgments on a sinful and unrepentant world, buying and selling becomes nil, worthless. In fact, it will not even be possible to buy and sell because the entire financial system upon which the world has depended so long will now be in shambles. Even food will become scarce or near impossible to afford, causing many people to die of starvation and hunger. Commerce will cease to exist; business will die and the fatal blow of God's hand of judgment will bring down the system that Satan not only put in place but also sustained by way of his evil and malicious strategies.

Once more they will cry out, "Woe, woe, the great city." But weeping and mourning over the circumstances will be useless for those unwilling to repent and accept Jesus Christ as their Lord and Redeemer. But weep they will, if only for the short time that the earth will last; for their weeping and mourning shall last for an eternity.

The third group observing the burning of the Great Lady is the "shipmaster, seafarer and sailors." If one ponders life on earth today, one will conclude that shipping is big business. Without sea lanes and shipping companies, many commodities, especially food, would not find their way to the nations of the world. In fact, shipping is probably the biggest business on earth.

Now God introduces His final judgment on the sea. In chapter 16 John described the first of the sea-related judgments when God turned the sea to blood. Everything in it died causing excessive foul odors and the swollen and bloated bodies of dead sea life. Now God turns His attention to commerce. While the words of 18:17-20 specifically denote sea-going personnel, there is no reason to believe that today it could not refer to all forms of commerce, including planes, trucks, trains and any other means of delivering goods. After all, earthquakes will have already destroyed roads, and the skies will have turned dark, the sun has refused to shine, all of which makes it impossible for planes to fly or trucks and trains to move from place to place. Commerce is done!

When it is over, it is over! And when it is over, then the angel will call on all the saints, those in heaven and those who have been gloriously redeemed during the Tribulation, to "rejoice over her . . . because God has executed your judgment on her." Her burning will spell the end, not because God seeks revenge, for God loves sinners, but to avenge the sins of unrepentant man.

When materialism is gone, when power is gone, when spiritual lethargy and indifference are gone, God will still be on the throne. Music and mirth will cease to exist; even the sounds of church bells and organs will no longer be heard in the streets; utter decay will characterize the culture because the artisans, craftsmen, all who plied everyday trades will disappear; the sounds of trumpets at festivals and joyous jubilees will be silent; and work shall cease and the millstone shall no longer grind out its products. Time shall be no more.

Light shall cease, and the light of the Gospel shall be heard no more. There shall be no more witnesses to Jesus, and the proclamation of Christ's bride, the church, shall never pour forth from pulpit or platform. Literally, everything that has been considered to be normal will end after all the scroll, trumpet and bowl judgments have been exhausted. Life will not just be disrupted, but it will be at an end.

Then the angel will "perform a spiritual autopsy" on Babylon, that great city.[161] There the angel will find unspeakable atrocities that have been perpetrated against God's people, and God will have avenged their slaughter. Inside the world religious system will be found the blood of the righteous. Babylon's best days are behind, and an eternity of judgment and punishment is ahead.

APPLICATION TO OUR POST-CHRISTIAN WORLD

The political system of the world has always and continues to rest on a single entity—money. Control the world's money, and you control the world. And the best way to control money is not to exchange money—go cashless.

A quick glance at history will reveal that as far back as 8,000 years ago, society exchanged goods and services without the benefit of cash. In Mesopotamia bartering or exchanging goods and services for equivalent goods and services was a common practice. About 3,500 years ago, ancient man began to forge rings of precious metals and cut them into thin caps and exchange them as money. By the 14th century checks appeared and by the 17th century handwritten checks were commonplace. Then in the 19th century wire transfers were initiated through Western Union, and by the 20th century plastic cards were in use. Today, with credit and debit cards, checks and digital currency, the world is on its way to a completely cashless society. In point of fact, Sweden and India are today moving toward a totally cashless economy. In a July 5, 2020, Facebook post, Kevin Monroe stated, "Cashless means fully digital, fully traceable, fully controlled. I think those who support a cashless society aren't fully aware of what they are asking for."[162] Add to this idea the technology behind bar codes and RFID chips, and one has the making of a world completely controllable by an outside force.

To rule the world financially is to control the world politically. In Daniel's vision of the ten toes I believe we see the reconstitution of the Common Market which will produce a man who manipulates the world by controlling the Common Market. This financial union will form the basis for dominating the world in the last days.

And yet, it will all be for naught. In a world gone mad with materialism, both commerce and finance will utterly be destroyed. Those who have need for anything, who have become owned by their possessions and who believe only in their own independence will find themselves destitute. God has declared that one must seek first the kingdom of God before seeking material possessions. If one seeks possessions first, then one must sacrifice God, and in the end, possessions will be taken away and God will be lost as well. You can be a double winner or a double loser—your choice.

When the world's money is gone, it is gone! When the resources of our materialistic society have disappeared, all will be lost. The light of the candle will shine no more. There will be no more light from the church; no more witness of Jesus; the voice of the bride shall be quieted; believers will no longer testify. This is the end of the world as we know it. How will you stand? TODAY IS THE DAY OF SALVATION!

CHAPTER 12
THE FINAL RETURN OF CHRIST
19:1-21

This chapter resumes the chronological picture of the future that we pick up from chapter 16. From that chapter where the final acts of a godless world come to a roaring crescendo, what is pictured here, especially in verses 1-10, shows the preparation in heaven of the events that are yet to happen.

THE GREAT HALLELUJAHS—19:1-6

Following the final fall of Babylon, the Harlot, there is great rejoicing in heaven. In fact, five choruses of praise can be heard from the portals of heaven. Those declaring such praise are described as a "vast multitude," whose voices raise in "Hallelujah" to the Lord Jesus Christ, the Triune God whose salvation these voices enjoy. Literally meaning "Praise Jehovah," they declare praise for His glory and power and His vindication of their righteousness. These are the redeemed who now delight in the presence of Jesus and offer adoration to Him. He has rendered judgment on Babylon the Harlot, for she has the blood of the saints on her hands. By doing so, He has avenged the sinfulness of the unrepentant.

They are not satisfied to proclaim praise just once, they continue to praise Him. With this second "Hallelujah," the Tribulation ends. The most powerful empire in the history of the world is gone; the smoke from that destruction, symbolizing a perpetual ruin, continues eternally. There is no more weeping, no more death, no more fear. Just praise forever in the presence of the Lord Jesus Christ.

The earth was God's even before its foundation was laid. Now Christ is returning to claim the title deed for what already belongs to Him by creation. The prospect of His return is so overwhelming that those surrounding the throne where God is seated must get in on the act and sing the third chorus. They cry, "Amen! Hallelujah!" The group includes the 24 elders who are believed to be the twelve prophets of the Old Testament and the twelve disciples of the New Testament, all representing the church. It also includes the creatures of Revelation 4:6, who are the cherubim, representing all the cherubim. With these words they express a song of joy at the triumph of righteousness and truth.

Now John detects a fourth chorus from a single voice, which appears to come from the very throne area where God is seated. Perhaps it is one of cherubim declaring to all who could hear, "Praise our God all His slaves, who fear Him, both small and great." Notice here that this angel refers to God as "our God." He calls on all of the redeemed of all ages, here referred to as "slaves," to praise God. Notice also that all distinctions of class are gone. From the poorest to the grandest, all are admonished to "praise our God."

The fifth chorus emanates from a "vast multitude." This multitude, probably made up of angels and all the redeemed of history, declare once more, "Hallelujah." Notice the sound of the chorus. It is like "cascading waters" and "rumbling of loud thunder." They are not ashamed; this multitude is not timid; these people rejoice with great gusto and feeling; they want to be heard.

APPLICATION TO OUR POST-CHRISTIAN WORLD

What a glorious day that will be when we stand with the saints of all the ages and sing "Hallelujah!" to our Saviour. Eternally we will praise Him and revel in the splendor of His glory and presence. With voices of adoration and worship, we shall forever delight in the presence of our Lord and sing "Amen! Hallelujah!" TODAY IS THE DAY OF SALVATION!

THE BRIDE AND THE MARRIAGE FEAST—19:7-10

The second coming of Christ is the central event of all history. It is the event toward which history has been moving for millennia. In this coming, the bridegroom Jesus leaves His Father's house and returns to His earthly house that He created in order to establish His kingdom with His bride and reign for a thousand years.

God has now revealed Himself in all His full glory and majesty and is prepared to initiate His reign and once more claim the title for His creation. But before this event occurs, Christ is ready to receive His bride. He is prepared to take His wife who has prepared herself with "fine linen to wear, bright and pure." This fine linen represents the blamelessness of the church, what John calls the "righteous acts of the saints." The church has been purified through tribulation and suffering and, spotless before God, is ready to be joined to Christ at the final marriage ceremony.

In order to understand the imagery of the marriage supper of the Lamb, one must be familiar with the ancient marriage customs of the day in which The Revelation was written. Marriage, in ancient times, possessed several progressive elements. The initial element was the betrothal. In our modern culture this would be the equivalent of engagement. But in ancient times, it was much more than that. Usually betrothal involved the arrangement of marriage by families of the bride and groom with a contract prepared and signed that "sealed the deal." It involved a much stronger commitment than we generally consider when thinking about engagement.

It was much more binding than simple engagement. Consideration was given to all aspects of the relationship, and the terms of the union would be specified. Sometimes occurring when the children were young or up to a year prior to the marriage, the contract would be negotiated, and a dowry established.

As the second element, the bridegroom would bring his bride home. The bride is adorned in her finest clothes and prepares herself with perfume and jewels. The groom, attired in his best, is accompanied by his friends as they go to the home of the bride and accompany her to a house which the groom will have prepared for them as a couple. At this point the dowry, determined at the first stage, is paid, and the groom presents his gifts to his new bride.

The final element in the marriage process is the wedding feast. Lasting seven days, many guests would be invited to this gala event as, together, they all celebrate the joining of the bride and groom as one and revel in their happiness.

Today, in history, the church has already become "betrothed" to Christ. Even now, when a new believer enters the kingdom of God, a kind of "betrothal" occurs that binds that new believer to Christ in a relationship that cannot be broken. As the new believer grows in the faith, the bond becomes stronger and spiritual maturity develops. The dowry for His bride has been determined and has already been paid by Jesus' death on the cross. Only time is needed now as we wait for His return.

Today we also stand in the interim between betrothal and the coming of Christ to remove His faithful from this world. When Christ ascended to the Father, this period of separation began. It will continue until that day when Christ calls home all who believe in Him and have faithfully borne His name in their lives. But in God's timetable, this interval is a single moment in time. In the meantime, we, the church, must make ourselves ready for that return. Attire ourselves, purify ourselves, sanctify ourselves and make ready for the return of our Bridegroom. Our imputed righteousness, made possible by the grace of God, makes us worthy to receive and offer ourselves to the Bridegroom.

In 19:9 John introduces us to the final chapter of the marriage process, the marriage feast. At the close of this interim period between the betrothal and the coming of the Bridegroom He, the Bridegroom, will come with His band of holy angels, to receive His Bride. But unlike the wedding feasts of ancient times, this one will not last for only seven days but for all eternity.[163]

Notice carefully the wording of verse 9. John writes: "Those invited to the marriage feast of the Lamb…" Who are these that are invited? Are they Christians? Are they the church personified? He cannot be referring to Christians because Christians comprise the church, the Bride of Christ. And as with any wedding, the Bride is not an invitee; she does the inviting. The context here points rather to those declaring faith in God before the resurrection, all of the faithful who have experienced the grace of God up to the birth of the church.[164] The invitees are the glorified ones who, along with the Bride, will reign with Christ in the millennial kingdom. They also represent the Tribulation saints, who experienced the grace of God through Christ during the Tribulation, both Jew and Gentile, especially those martyrs who were beheaded for their faith.

Where will this feast be celebrated? One line of thought is that it will certainly take place on the earth after it has been restored to its original beauty.[165] However, given the appearance of Christ beginning in verse 11, it would appear that the feast will actually be celebrated in heaven at the close of the Tribulation and immediately preceding the millennial reign of Christ on earth.

Next, John did what came naturally, he worshipped this being who brought a message from the One who sits on the throne. But who is this messenger? None other than the angel, described in 18:1, who possesses "great authority" and "illuminates the earth by his splendor." He is a "fellow slave" who has the "testimony about Jesus." He is a part of the congregation of those who have either pointed forward to the coming of Jesus or preached Jesus as the crucified Lamb of God. Though an angel, yet being a fellow slave to the Good News, he ordered John to remember the truth of the Gospel, arise and worship the One True God, the Bridegroom, the Peace-Bringer, the King of Kings.

APPLICATION TO OUR POST-CHRISTIAN WORLD

Unlike the marriage process of our post-Christian world, the marriage of Jesus to His Bride, the Church, is an eternal relationship. All too often in today's world, marriage is seen as an experiment in relationships rather than a union of two souls. Though the word "soulmate" is thrown around in today's society, it can never fully communicate our relationship with our loving Lord. Ours is truly a bond of eternal import. TODAY IS THE DAY OF SALVATION!

CHRIST RETURNS, HALLELUJAH!—19:11-16

The Tribulation is over! All that has been prophesied has been fulfilled in the scroll, trumpet and bowl judgments, and the only event left is to declare victory. But before victory can be declared, Satan and his armies must be defeated in a final onslaught. "We need only to remember three things: We come back with Christ; He fights; they lose."[166]

Now before we observe that final victory, let's take a 10,000-foot view of these last days. We have read in Revelation 16:14, "For they are the spirits of demons performing signs, who travel to the kings of the whole world to assemble them for the battle of the great day of God, the Almighty." Many perceive this battle to be the Battle of Armageddon prophesied in Zechariah 14:1-5. But "battle" is not what the word itself means. It refers to a war in general or an armed conflict. When we view other Scripture, we find that the reference here in chapter 16 is not to a single battle (after all, a war is not won with one single battle) but a series of conflicts that climax with the battle in the Valley of Megiddo. While the exact sequence of these conflicts cannot be pinpointed, they have been prophesied with certainty and will occur in whatever sequence God chooses.

The first conflict is found in Isaiah 63:1-6. Here the Lord sought vindication and wished for help from the "nations," but He rescued Israel alone from the hand of the Antichrist. As a result, His clothes were stained with the blood of His enemies.

The second conflict occurs in Jerusalem and can be found in Zechariah 12:1-10 and Revelation 16:17-21. Here the Antichrist has deployed a scout team or tactical guard whose sole goal is to destroy the city of Jerusalem. They are to "take out" the Holy City. But the Lord comes in all His glory, defeats this tactical force and leaves Jerusalem intact. As a result of this conflict, Israel will be redeemed, and the covenant of God with Abraham restored.

The third conflict will occur in the Valley of Jehoshaphat, with a description found in Joel 3 and Revelation 14:14-20. This is the only battle whose occurrence can be determined. In verse 1 of Joel 3, the writer states, "when I restore the fortunes of Judah and Jerusalem." This statement would indicate that the battle will occur at some point after the Battle of Jerusalem, and God even names the adversaries, Israel and the region of "Tyre, Sidon, and all the territories of Philistia." All of these areas comprise the ancient, ancestral lands of today's Palestinian population. And while this battle is not the final battle of the war, it plays its role in returning the Jews to their rightful and God-appointed home. Joel 3:7 concludes the role of the Jews in this battle: "I am about to rouse them up from the place where you sold them; I will bring retribution on your heads."

When the final battle begins, the armies of the world will converge from every direction to attack Israel. Such has been prophesied in Zechariah 14:1-5. There they will fight each other first before seeing the heavens open. Suddenly they see a horseman riding down through its portals, along its streets of gold, "through Heaven's pearly gates, past suns and moons and stars; leaving the lightning's flash behind; straight on down."[167] This rider of the white stallion is none other than "Faithful and True." Recall how He was described in 1:5 as the "faithful witness"; or in 3:7 as "the True One"; or again in 3:14 as "the faithful and true witness." This rider is none other than the warrior Christ Himself. CHRIST HAS ARRIVED!

Just as He promised, He has returned for the second time, in His physical body, to wage war against the Antichrist and his forces and to make a final claim to His world. His first appearance as a babe in a Bethlehem manger was to show God's love for His world and to offer grace, forgiveness and imputed righteousness to all who repented of sin and accepted Him as God's Son. Now He comes as a warrior in holiness, justice and judgment to wage war against the forces of evil and to settle up with those who continue in their unrepentant state, resisting Christ and refusing His offer of redemption. When the armies observe this rider of the white horse, they will then join together in a last-ditch effort at victory but will come up short. With Jerusalem as the prize, Jesus will now rule from the same throne in Jerusalem upon which the Antichrist has sat for three and a half years, because who rules Jerusalem rules the world.

The description of Christ in His appearance is picturesque, to say the least, and overwhelming at best. He is astride a "white horse," the ancient symbol of conquest and victory. But what a contrast to His first coming (Mark 11; Luke 19:28f) when He strode into Jerusalem on the back of a humble donkey. Now the hooves of the victory horse clatter down the streets of heaven as "Faithful and True" rides down to earth prepared for a final struggle between good and evil. Hear these words regarding "Faithful and True": "The first time He came to a cross; the second time He will come to a crown. The first time He stood before Pilate and was judged; the second time Pilate will stand judged before Him."[168]

Christ comes with "eyes like a fiery flame," indicating wisdom to penetrate even to the very soul of man. Nothing escapes His vision. The fire of His eyes defines His virtue and judgment. On His head are many crowns, representing complete authority and total sovereignty, not the crowns of a victorious athlete. In antiquity, tradition called for a war victor to remove the crown from a defeated sovereign and placed it on his own head. In this battle Christ will conquer the kingdoms of this world—kingdoms of knowledge and science, kingdoms of education, kingdoms of entertainment, kingdoms wealth and influence, kingdoms of politics and government and kingdoms of the devil—and in the end He will wear the crowns of all these kingdoms. He is truly the Son whose coronation is lauded in Psalm 1.

He is wearing a robe stained with the blood of His enemies,[169] after all this is not His first battle. In His most important battle He went to the cross and fought with His enemies whose blood was mixed with His own blood. He is a blood-soaked victim who offers the victor's cry.

He bears three names. In 19:12 He has a "name written that no one knows except Himself." It is a mysterious name. In 19:13 His name is the "Word of God," the *Logos*, that which was from the beginning, is now and forever shall be. It is a name that reveals the

One and True God—who He is and what He is. He is, indeed, the Word made flesh—the visible manifestation of the invisible God. And in 19:16 He is King of Kings and Lord of Lords, a name that bespeaks His eternal nature.

But, hark, Christ is not alone. Seven years before, Christ appeared in the air and raptured His saints to the heavenlies, but now, after seven years of Tribulation, the "armies that were in heaven" join Him as Christ leads them through the clouds of heaven to earth. But who are these armies? They are none other than the church that was Raptured before the Tribulation (Revelation 19:8), the Tribulation saints (Revelation 7:13), Old Testament believers (Jude 4; Daniel 12:12; Revelation 19:9) and even angels (Matthew 25:31). Are these armies there to assist Christ in battle? Not at all! They are there to rejoice over His pending victory and to reign with Him. They will have the privilege to share the glory of victory.

In His mouth is a "sharp sword," powerful enough not simply to kill His enemies but to annihilate them. This sword is artfully placed in His mouth to indicate that only His words are necessary to defeat the enemy. In this bitter struggle, Christ will destroy His enemies and bring all nations in subjection to Him. He will rule with a "rod of iron" under which His law is absolute and resolute.

He will "trample the winepress," a symbol of God's wrath and judgment. The winepress is a graphic and familiar symbol of judgment.[170] So its employment in this context is appropriate. Christ comes in judgment to execute, upon the persistently unrighteous, the sentence that has been imposed by God Himself.

You can't miss this rider. As the battle winds down, He appears wearing a banner across His robe and down His thigh which declares His ultimate victory and authority. He is "KING OF KINGS AND LORD OF LORDS."

THE FINAL DEFEAT—19:17-21

So ghastly and unspeakable have been the results of this final conflict in the Valley of Megiddo (Battle of Armageddon), that the final call of the angel is an invitation to the birds of the air to come and feast on the bodies of the fallen. Whether animals that have been forced into the battle or men whose struggle was futile against the might of God, the birds may now come and gorge themselves on the flesh of the fallen. Whether a general or a private, alike they lie dead amidst the blood and water that has now filled the valley. And the birds do not care either, because they wish only to fill their bellies with the carrion of war. What an indignity!

The "beast" (Daniel 7 and Revelation 13), the "kings of the earth" (Revelation 17:12-17) and "their armies" (Revelation 16:13-14) have made their appearance in the Valley of Megiddo, faced the army of the Lord as prophesied in Zechariah 14:5 and suffered appalling defeat. The rider of the white stallion and His host have prevailed—have emerged victorious as prophesied. It is now time for the Antichrist and his henchman, the False Prophet, to be taken into custody by the Lord of the universe. Judgment is swift, and the fates of these two are pre-determined. The Lord then executes that judgment immediately by throwing them, conscious and kicking, into the lake of fire.

While this is the first mention of the "lake of fire" in the New Testament, it is not the first mention of eternal punishment. Unrepentant beings are doomed to an eternity of suffering. Whether you are human or an unrepentant angelic being, eternal punishment awaits you. Scripture often speaks of such punishment in sadistic terms. One needs only to read Revelation 14:10-11, Matthew 13:40-42, Mark 9:43-48 and Luke 3:17 to find just a few references to the eternal damnation of the unsaved. It is truly a hell for the unbelieving dead. In this case, however, it becomes the abiding place for the Antichrist and the False Prophet, who will suffer there alone throughout the millennial reign of Christ.

The final verse of this chapter sounds the final call for the remainder of the armies. With the sword which the rider has clenched between His teeth (Revelation 19:15), the armies are dispatched with swiftness, and the birds of the air, as invited to do so, feast on the flesh of the dead and dying. Now all of those who have opposed Jesus Christ, those who ridiculed His saints, those who persecuted believers and even those who persecuted the 144,000 during the Tribulation now find themselves judged by Christ and thrown into a fire that is never extinguished. For the next one thousand years, they will suffer torment from the heat and sulfur of that hideous place.

So, now the voice of the Beast is silent; the wranglings, manipulation and sorcery of the False Prophet have been stilled; the entire battlefield is filled with the dead of battle and is silent except for the sound of the birds devouring the flesh of the dead. What a tragedy! But there is yet one mighty foe to be defeated.

APPLICATION TO OUR POST-CHRISTIAN WORLD

The second coming of Christ is the central event of history. It is the event toward which all of history has been moving since creation and without which history makes no sense whatsoever. Christ is the Creator of all that is or ever has been, and He will return to take back what rightfully belongs to Him. Just like the bridegroom, Jesus leaves the heavenly home of Hs Father and returns to His earthly house to establish His Kingdom and reign with His Bride for a thousand years. To get to that point, however, He must defeat the one personage who stands in His way, Satan and his forces of evil.

By this time in the eschatological chronology, the entire world, both religion and politics, is under the control and power of the Antichrist. The apostate church is thriving under the influence of Satan, and devil worship is the order of the day. All that God has created is now against God, and He returns to take it back.[171]

We live in a post-Christian world where trust is at a premium. People do not trust the media to report the truth anymore; people do not trust the government to be honest with the voters; people do not trust local government to protect them or act judiciously on their behalf; and even some people have little trust in their pastors or spiritual leaders. Skepticism in today's society is not only on the rise, it is also epidemic.

Perhaps you are reading this book as a skeptic. Perchance you consider the words of The Revelation and this explanation of the Second Coming of Christ to be claptrap, rubbish. Let me offer an oversimplified example. You are sitting in your living room one night when your home is invaded by thugs who steal your most prized possession. Maybe it is an object that has been handed down in your family for generations; maybe it is an item for which you worked many hours to earn enough money to obtain. Whatever it is, you cherish it beyond all other possessions. But now it is gone because of the selfishness and thievery of others. Do you sit by and do nothing? No, you declare that every effort will be made to take it back, and you will not stop until you once more possess it. You will go to the ends of the earth to get it back.

Such is the attitude of God. The Holy Trinity created a perfect world which was tainted by the sin of Adam, and now, even that has been stolen by Satan and his forces and turned into an idol-worshipping, God-hating, materialistic, unrepentant world. God is determined to avenge such action. He wants His world back; He wants to make it over; He wants to restore His world to its former glory, because not only is it the nature of man to wish to get back what has been lost, it is also a part of the divine nature. If you happen to be thinking that what has been written is nothing more than fiction, you might think again. Just as you would seek the return of your lost property or loved one, so God seeks the return of His creation and His people.

But He will not come alone. He will be accompanied by all of those who have previously been Raptured to Heaven prior to the Tribulation. They will not be there to fight, however, only to observe the victory of Him who will put one foot on the Mount of Olives and declare Jerusalem as His headquarters.

Just as logic dictates that our universe is not the result of an accidental explosion millions of years ago, so logic must also dictate that an end will eventually come to all that is. Just as logic demands intelligence and rationality for our world to exist, so that same intelligence must exercise rationality in bringing it to a conclusion. Nothing material lasts forever. Only the Kingdom of Him who provides the intelligence and rationality for our world to exist will survive.

The clock of history is approaching the midnight hour. You will not always have time to respond. TODAY IS THE DAY OF SALVATION!

CHAPTER 13
THE MILLENNIAL REIGN AND THE GREAT WHITE THRONE JUDGMENT
20:1-15

The 20th chapter of Revelation forms the basis for more controversy than almost any other chapter in the book. For it is here that the millennial interpretations find their roots. Depending upon how one interprets the millennium—who participates in it and when and where it occurs—determines one's position with respect to end times.

You may recall from our introduction that two interpretations generally dominate the scholarly world of Revelation. First are the plenarists who generally believe that there will be no literal thousand years of peace on the earth, making them, in most cases, A-Millennialists. They believe that there will be no thousand-year reign of Christ on the earth or no thousand years of peace. There will be no literal earthly kingdom of God; the reign of Christ is simply here portrayed as a picture, a drama that, when Christ returns to earth, He will remove all of the believers and condemn all of the unbelievers. Once that has been accomplished, the Rapture occurs.

From this point on the plenarists consider the Scripture not to be true, not an historical foretelling. To the plenarist, Revelation is nothing more than a metaphor in which all prophecies about the promised kingdom are simply allegorized. They teach that Israel forfeited God's promises because of her unbelief; the church has since inherited the promises that were originally intended for Israel and that the church, in many ways, has discouraged and disappointed God in the manner in which it has lived out its beliefs. But because the church has inherited the original promises intended for Israel, the church will realize the results of those promises and thus be issued into the great Kingdom of God at the end of the age.

The second mainline interpretation, the prophetics, believe strongly in the coming Millennium. They believe that Christ will literally and bodily return to earth before the thousand-year reign will begin. Christ will eventually set up his kingdom, and He will reign from the throne of David from a rebuilt city of Jerusalem. A Jerusalem instead of Rome—Rome being the headquarters of the

Antichrist. Jerusalem then will be the headquarters of Christ during his thousand-year reign.

What, then, do we know about the Millennium? Several points seem clear from the text or at least can be inferred from other Scriptural references. (1) The Millennium will last for 1,000 years (Revelation 20:4). Such is the translation of the word itself. (2) The Millennium will be a time of peace and tranquility (Isaiah 2 and 11; Micah 4); (3) No one will enter the Millennium unless he/she is a believer (Revelation 20:4, 6); (4) Most people will live the entire 1,000 years and will have children who possess the same will to accept or reject Christ (Isaiah 65:20). It will be a time when Christ shall reign with His saints, but the power of Satan (not to be confused with the personage of Satan) will remain present and accounted for. Perhaps "influence" would be a better term. After all, man will retain his sinful nature, and many will fall prey to that nature and rebel against God. For those who insist on rebelling, death will be a real possibility.

The Binding of Satan, 20:1-3

Suddenly John sees a personage descend from heaven with a key in his hand. Could this be the same key about which John wrote in 9:1? Perhaps. He also sees a chain in the angel's hand. Obviously, the chain is not to be used to pull someone out of a ditch but to bind someone. Suddenly the "dragon" appears, Satan himself. He is immediately seized by the angel, bound for what will be 1,000 years, the same 1,000 years of the Millennium. He is thrown down the shaft (9:1-2) of the abyss, the door or lid to the abyss is closed, and the lid is sealed for 1,000 years. The words of verse 3, "so that he would no longer deceive the nations," offer the reason for the sealing. The person of Satan is now out of the picture, at least momentarily.

An interesting play on words can be found here in chapter 20. The word translated "bound" is ἔδησεν (*edēsen*) which means "to bind or tie up." It is the same word employed by Jesus in Matthew 12:29 when He spoke about a robber binding a homeowner in order to rob him. William Hendriksen believes that this binding of Satan started when Jesus resisted the Devil in the wilderness temptations and triumphed over his attempts to make Jesus less than what He was.[172]

But Satan's work will not be concluded—not yet. Following the 1,000 years, he will be loosed for a brief period. During this time he will seek many of the progeny of those who have lived through the Millennium, and he will attempt to deceive them one final time, seeking to bring together, for one last time, a successful rebellion against God.

The Messianic Reign, 20:4-7

John then observes "thrones," multiple thrones. These are the seats of those who are administering the messianic kingdom, who are judging other souls. But who sits upon these thrones? John tells us that, seated thereon, are the those who have been Raptured to the heavenlies to be with Christ. But from verse 4 we learn that he also sees the Tribulation saints, those who have faced an enemy of sin and, according to the world, lost the battle because they were beheaded for their faith. While the world thought they lost the battle with sin, they, in fact, had won the battle because now they are with the Raptured saints. They now sit in judgment of those who beheaded them as well as those who declared to the world that they had lost the battle. Now they will rule (reign) with Christ for 1,000 years.

But, praise God, they will not be alone. In addition to the Tribulation saints, Christ will reign for 1,000 years also with the Old Testament saints (Daniel 7:18, 27); the apostolic saints (Matthew 19:28); the saints of the church age (1 Corinthians 6:2; 2 Timothy 2:12); and Messianic Israel (Jeremiah 31:33). All will participate in this reign of Christ and will enjoy the fellowship of each other throughout the 1,000 years.

Given that John experiences a vision, the question naturally arises: Did John see "souls" or " bodies" in his vision of the Millennium? We cannot be certain, but two streams of thought can be identified. The first believes in a bodily resurrection with the 1,000-year reign to occur here on earth. Such a belief is based upon both Old and New Testament writings that declare a bodily resurrection, specifically, Job 19:25-26.

Linguistically the word resurrection occurs exactly forty times in the New Testament where it either means directly or strictly implies a bodily resurrection. In this line of belief one is directed to John 5:28 where the Gospel writer turned Apocalyptist writes: "Do not be amazed at this, because a time is coming when all who are in the graves will hear His voice and come out—those who have done good things, to the resurrection of life."[173]

On the other side of this question is a belief that strongly suggests that the resurrection will only involve the souls of man and the 1,000-year reign will occur exclusively in heaven. Three reasons are offered for consideration: (1) The 1,000-year reign occurs where the thrones are, namely, in heaven. The key reference is to Revelation 1:4, 3:21, 4:2. (2) The 1,000-year reign will occur where the disembodied souls of martyrs are found. Here mention is made of the use, by John, of the word "souls" not "bodies." (3) The 1,000-year reign occurs where Jesus lives, namely, in heaven. For evidence reference is directed to Revelation chapters 5 and 12 where Christ is declared to dwell.[174]

So, will it be souls or bodies? Allow me to offer another bit of evidence. In verse 4 John writes, "they came to life and reigned with the Messiah for 1,000 years." The word translated "came to life" ("lived," KJV; "came back to life," ISV) is the Greek word ἔζησαν (*edzēsan*), a form of the word ζάω (*zaō*), meaning "to live." This is the root word also for ζωή (*zōē*) which means "life, living, existence."

Zaō possesses several meanings depending upon its context. First it can mean "physical existence in contrast to death." Examples of this usage can be found in Romans 7:1, 1 Corinthians 15:45, 2 Corinthians 1:8, Hebrews 2:15, Matthew 27:63, and 2 Corinthians 4:11. Second, it can refer to a dead person who has returned to life or become physically alive again. Biblical examples include Matthew 9:18, Acts 9:41, Mark 16:11 (relating to Christ), Acts 1:3, and 2 Corinthians 13:4a.

Third, it can imply sick persons who have recovered from a lethal illness, thus meaning to "recover" or "be well." Examples can be found in Mark 5:23, John 4:50, 51, 53. Fourth, it can suggest a healthy person as in "remain alive" or "live on." Writings using this meaning can be located in Acts 25:24, Acts 28:4, and James 4:15.[175]

In none of these references do we find its usage to refer to souls, only physical bodies. It is my consideration, then, that John saw physical bodies, resurrected bodies, who lived and reigned with Christ during the Millennium.

Although there are scholars who propose that the first resurrection is actually the Rapture, such is not my conclusion. When we are Raptured, only believers who are alive at the time on the earth will be Raptured with Christ. The believing dead will have already met Christ face to face and require no resurrection.

With respect to where the Millennium occurs, we simply are not told. There is not sufficient evidence—factual or linguistic—to make a rational judgment. What we do know, however, is that Christ will reign for 1,000 years with those mentioned above in peace and harmony, praise and joy, glory and celebration.

Now, just to be certain that the reader understands, John writes in verse 5 (which follows chronologically with verse 11) that "the rest of the dead did not come to life until the 1,000 years were completed." The phrase rendered "rest of the dead" refers specifically to the unbelieving dead of all ages whose bodies will not be resurrected and rejoined to his/her tormented soul until the time of the Great White Throne Judgment following the 1,000-year reign of Christ. This resurrection, then, is the single, general, first resurrection to life as described in John 5:28-29.

At this point, John seems so overwhelmed that he issues a magnificent beatitude for deceased believers. They are "blessed and holy" because of their trust and faith in the Lord Jesus Christ and are privileged to be resurrected at the time of the Great White Throne Judgment.

Satan's Final Reward, 20:7-10

Remember the words of verse 3 where Satan "must be released for a short time"? That time has now arrived. The world is emerging from the Millennial days and people are living their lives. Remember, now, during the Millennium, life will go on and people will be born. They will thus possess the Adamic nature, the propensity for sin and rebellion against God. As they reach the age of accountability, that Adamic nature will wish to find expression against all authority, physical and spiritual. Satan will provide the leadership required to release and expose this latent sin and rebellion. Some people may even appear loyal to Christ, offer outward obedience to His law, but with the cheering and incitement of Satan, they will seethe in their hearts with a deep-seated desire to live in sin.

But why would God wish this on the world? Why would He loose Satan to execute his dastardly deeds on the peoples of the earth? John Bisagno preached that reason on August 10, 1980, when he proclaimed: "It is essential that God vindicate Himself. After all, it is only under the reign of Christ that true peace is achieved. God wished to show that, one last time after 1,000 years of a perfect environment, human personality has to be drastically changed by the new birth before there can be peace."[176] Once Satan has been loosed and the real nature of man exposed, then God can execute His plan so that peace can, indeed, rule.

God is not done! The final battle to expose Satan and destroy him once and for all is about to occur. Verses 8-9 describe this battle. Those who have been saved during the Millennium will fall under intense persecution during this period. From the four corners of the earth, meaning from the entire world, Satan gathers his forces once more, including those from Gog and Magog, ancient enemies of Israel. The force will be overpowering, innumerable, an almost uncountable multitude.

With weapons in hand and determination in their hearts, they will lay siege to "the beloved city," Jerusalem, God's city, the seat of His authority. But almost before they can unsheathe their swords, they are struck down by "fire from heaven." Representing divine judgment, God rains fire upon them and devours them instantaneously. It is all God, not man, victory from heaven and not earth. They are quickly and completely exterminated. However, their physical death is only a part of the story; their spiritual destiny is also determined immediately and forever.

And now Satan is to learn his final destiny. Once and for all, forever, eternally he is cast into the same lake of fire and brimstone into which the Beast and the False Prophet were thrown earlier in 19:20. There he will feel the tormenting pain "day and night forever and ever." Now God's creation can breathe easy, for he who has caused so much pain and suffering is now the object of pain and suffering, not for an hour or a day, but forever. Man is at peace, and Satan is in his rightful place.

The Great White Throne Judgment, 20:11-15

God has dropped the curtain on the drama of human history, and everyone has been accounted for. Born again Christians are with Christ on earth. The angels are also here with their ministry to God the Father and Christ the Son. Satan, the Antichrist and the False Prophet have been thrown into the lake of fire and brimstone. False angels who have been cast into the abyss now await judgment and ultimate banishment to the lake of fire. Fallen men have been defeated and destroyed at Armageddon. Angels and saints have accompanied Christ in His return. Everyone has been accounted for except the lost, the unsaved. It is now time for them to be called before God to give an accounting.[177]

John sees a throne. Is this the throne of chapter 4? Perhaps, even probably, but notably absent from the scene are the four living creatures, the twenty-four elders, and the angelic hosts. Even though Christ is not mentioned by name as sitting on the throne, He is implied by the masculine noun employed here. Details are really unimportant at this point, so whether this is the same throne or not, the day of judgment has arrived.

Immediately the earth and the sky ("heaven," HCSB) "fled from His presence," yet also evidence that the One on the throne is Jesus. The implication from these words is that the earth and heaven that had existed from creation were dissolved; even evidence of the renovated creation prior to the Millennium could not be found. All that man had known during his lifetime has now vanished into nothingness.

And then the first great resurrection. All the dead, great and small, those "rest of the dead" from verse 5 have now come to life and stand before God with body and soul reunited. Verse 13 adds that the sea as well as Death and Hades gave up their dead. All who have died in all the ages past are now accounted for and stand before Christ at the Great White Throne. Whether you were immensely wealthy, politically powerful, intellectually astute or simply an ordinary person on the street, you now stand before your final Judge.

From the archives of heaven the accounting records are brought forth, and the books are opened. It's now time to give an accounting. Three books find their way before the Great Judge of Heaven. One is the "book of works." This book contains an account of all the activities and responses of every human being who has ever lived. And it is upon these activities and responses that each person will be judged. Will there be degrees of punishment for the unsaved? That is not clear from the text, but certainly their rejection of Christ as Saviour will condemn them to eternal punishment.

The second book will be the "book of life" in verse 12. This book contains the names of every person who has ever been born.[178] It is a record of every thought, word and deed of every person and is an unabridged account of all men throughout all history.

The third book is the "Lamb's Book of Life." It is the book of verse 15 and contains the names of every person throughout history who has accepted the claims of Christ, believed on Him and followed Him. All of their names are in the "book." They will not be judged here because their judgment was decided at the cross when Jesus sacrificed His life for their sins. And now they will have their reward.

To this point the body and soul have been separated. Now in the resurrection, body and soul are reunited, so death and hell ("Hades") are no longer required. "Death cannot forever exist if God is to reign, for eternal death would be a denial of the *living* God. Death must die if eternal life is real; death must die if the gateway to the New Jerusalem is open!"[179] In verse 14 both Death and Hades are cast into the lake of fire where all sin and sinners will ultimately become inhabitants.[180] Never again will there be a separation of body and soul. This is the second death, far more important than the first physical death.

To press home his point, John adds in verse 15 the fateful words of judgment. I like so much the way Hal Lindsey has dramatically portrayed this moment. "He (God) solemnly opens the 'Book of Life' and begins to scan the pages for the man's name. Those nail-scarred hands turn first one page, and then another, all the time wishing the man's name could be found there. Tragically, it can't be found on any page, and God slowly closes this final book of judgment and says with great reluctance: 'Depart from Me, you who are cursed, into the eternal fire prepared for the Devil and his angels!'"[181]

The rebellion of the earth is done. The horrors of the Great Tribulation are an experience of the past. The books are now closed. The judgment of God has been pronounced. Separation from God is now eternally complete. The clock of human history has struck midnight, and the victory belongs to Christ.

APPLICATION TO OUR POST-CHRISTIAN WORLD

It is difficult for me to understand how, in our post-Christian world where people believe in the paranormal, ghosts, the occult, apparitions, an evil spirit world, hauntings and time slips, so many in our intelligent populace do not accept the writings of Revelation 20 regarding a Day of Judgment. Why is our world becoming increasingly indifferent to the idea that God will one day judge mankind for rejecting Him?

Let's go back to the beginning. When God created man and placed him and his wife on the earth, He intended for them to live forever. The Bible clearly states, "The Lord God took the man and placed him in the garden of Eden to work it and watch over it. And the LORD God commanded the man, 'You are free to eat from any tree of the garden, but you must not eat from the tree of the knowledge of good and evil, for on the day you eat from it, you will certainly die'" (Genesis 2:15-17). Yet, in spite of being handed paradise "on a silver platter," in spite of being unadulterated, both physically and mentally, God's supreme creation rebelled against Him. In so doing, eternal existence was lost, and sin and death for them and their descendants now hung over their heads. By introducing sin into the world, judgment became an inescapable response from God.

Even in a world where skepticism rules the belief of a judgment day, the Bible is clear about its inevitability. Even during His earthly ministry, Jesus declared, "The Father, in fact, judges no one, but has given all judgment to the Son" (John 5:22). It is the final judgment of God upon humankind; never again will God sit in judgment.

The very nature of the everlasting Gospel is to set right the wrongs that have been committed. If, indeed, God is a righteous God, then evil must be judged so that His righteousness can prevail. God determines, therefore, to restore the world to what He intended. Vindicating righteousness will ultimately showcase what God had in mind at the beginning—one world under the control of Christ who created it.

A word of caution! To you who hear the Gospel, who know the Truth that will set you free, who can change your eternal destiny, TODAY IS THE DAY OF SALVATION! God keeps His word as He has since time began. Your acceptance or rejection of Jesus is tantamount to passing judgment on Him. In the end, the Great White Throne Judgment underscores the fact that God's justice will be ultimately be passed on you and, outside of Christ, that justice will be terrifying, sure and final.

CHAPTER 14
ETERNITY BEGINS
21:1-22:5

Remember the words of Jesus in John 14: "In My Father's house are many dwelling places; if not, I would have told you. I am going away to prepare a place for you. . . I will come back and receive you to Myself, so that where I am you may be also." These words find their fulfilment beginning in chapter 21.

John saw a new heaven and a new earth just as predicted by Isaiah.[182] Isaiah prophesied that the end time would be carefully planned by God, just as was creation and redemption. Eternity will end the way it began. It is not a passing after-thought of God.

But how does John begin to describe the indescribable? How does he give expression to the inexpressible? John's words here are one man's attempt to describe in vision mode what eternity will be like.

John sees a "new heaven and a new earth." The old heaven and the old earth have "passed away," that is they have been refined by the fire of God's retribution. John probably views this new heaven and new earth as a fulfilment of the prophecy of Isaiah in 65:17. The word "new" here is the Greek καινός meaning "new in quality" (innovation), "fresh in development" or "opportunity." This new heaven and new earth are a completely new kind of heaven and earth that emerges from the rubble and ashes of an old heaven and earth that are totally and completely destroyed.[183] Patterned after the Garden of Eden, it is not like anything that has existed before.

Even the sea will no longer exist. Remember that, on the earth, the sea was vital to life, for from it originated food and water, both so essential for life. But in the new heaven and the new earth, the sea is not needed because God is the water of life, and that water flows from the very throne of God. The sea will not be needed for food because we will have the tree of life. The sea and its life-sustaining provisions are no longer required.

Some scholars[184] view the "sea" as the same as that described in chapter 4 that separated people from God, so that when it is "no more," John is saying that man is no longer separated from God. Man is now in intimate fellowship because God dwells with His people as demonstrated by the appearance of the tabernacle.

John was also privileged to see the "Holy City, new Jerusalem, coming down out of heaven." Not the Jerusalem of Palestine but a new city—a holy city—because, as the capital city of the new heaven, it is bereft of sin and unrighteousness and dedicated to God. Did this city exist before now? Probably, but now it is revealed to take its place as the capital city of our eternal abode. It is the city from which God will rule in His eternal kingdom. The city is called the "bride," meaning that it is surely the church of the living God. It is so called because it takes on the very character of its inhabitants—the redeemed in Christ from all the ages, the martyred, the Tribulation saints and the saved of the house of Israel, those pre-Christian era believers in Jehovah. All will live forever in the eternal city which the Father has prepared for His saints.

Ah! But the unveiling of the unique essence and distinctive character of our everlasting abode is not yet complete. John hears the voice of God who delivers a declaration of doxology in which God reveals the true nature of His Kingdom and our home and declares the effects of the curse of Genesis 3:16-19 as null and void. In this doxology He makes known four exciting but unique characteristics of our forever home.

First, it will be the dwelling place of the God. We first encounter this idea when Jehovah led His people out of Egypt and visibly manifest Himself in the pillar of cloud by day and the pillar of fire by night. From the root word שָׁכַן, (*sheken*), meaning to dwell, God's *Shekinah* revealed that He was always present and dwelled among His people. The idea is translated into the Greek with σκηνὴ (*skēnē*) which means a "tent or tabernacle." Just as the original Tabernacle was a symbol of the dwelling place of God during the wilderness days, so God will dwell (tabernacle, pitch a tent) with His people. The word used here in verse 3 is the same word employed by John in 1:14 in which John wrote: "The Word became flesh and took up residence among us." Just as He dwelled in the Tabernacle, then dwelled among us in the form of Jesus Christ, so He will dwell with us in our forever home.

Not only will He dwell among us, but we will be His people and He will be our God. For eternity we believers will see God face to face and praise and glorify not just His name but also His person. We will enjoy fellowship like we've never known before because the Father is present. We will walk with Him and talk with Him,[185] not as we do today, but in reality, in fact. We will be His, and we shall never again know what broken relationship means.

Second, "He will wipe away every tear from their eyes." Because negativism will not exist in heaven, there will be no sadness about which to cry. There will be no disappointment or disillusionment, no sin or wrongdoing. Tears will not be needed and will not be shed.

Third, "death will no longer exist." The only death that the believer will ever experience will have already been experienced on earth. Remember from 20:14 that the second death is the lake of fire, and Christians do not experience it. Rather, death is an event of the past having been conquered by our Saviour who nailed it to the cross so that we would never know the pain of eternal death.

Fourth, there will be no "grief, crying, and pain." They simply will no longer exist because there is no reason for grief or crying. With victory over death, our sin character will vanish, and there will be no pain, whether it is of spirit or body.[186] Cancer and heart disease will be forgotten, death will be no more, and the pain of broken relationships will be history. There will be no difference of opinion because the only opinion that will count is that of the Father, and we will be worshipping Him. Heaven will be a place where only love and tranquility are the order of the day.

Now God speaks once more declaring that He has made "everything new." Then after ordering John to write, God declares "It is done!" What is done? The end of redemptive history is done. The consummation of the plan of God from the beginning is done. God has accomplished the eternal purpose He planned from before time, namely, to assemble to Himself a righteous, sacred and faithful people. In so declaring, He asserts that He is "Alpha and Omega, the Beginning and the End," the sum of everything. These two letters, which mark the beginning and end of the Greek alphabet aptly illustrate His eternal position. He is the "Beginning," the starter, the originator, the source of everything that is. He is also the "End," the completer, the goal, the finish line as well. As such He can provide, from the river that runs through the eternal city, thirst-quenching, life-giving water that shall never run dry.

In verse 7 God grants to every believer the inheritance promised.[187] "To the victor belongs the spoils of victory."[188] "Victor" here is the word ὁ νικῶν (*ho nikōn*) from a root that means to "conquer, overcome or vanquish." Who is this "victor," this "overcomer"? It is none other than he who willingly accepts Jesus' sacrificial death on the cross in faith believing that salvation is in none other than the Lord Jesus Christ. He is the "victor" addressed in each of the letters to the seven churches; it is he who will inherit "all things."[189] Not only shall the "victor" inherit "all things" that belong to God, but his relationship with God will now be direct, no intermediary needed. He shall enjoy a personal love relationship that is indescribable.

Ah! But what a contrast in verse 8—these who are not victorious, these who have rejected Christ, these who are unregenerate—they shall inherit only pain and suffering in the eternal lake of fire. What an age-old dichotomy! Right vs. wrong. Good vs. evil. Believers vs. unbelievers. For the believer, the future is bright with the glory of the Father shining eternally on a New Jerusalem. For the unbeliever, the future is only torment and travail in an ever-burning lake of fire for which there is no extinguishing. We are urged to remember that there is truly a "definite relationship between the life to come and the life that now is."[190]

New Jerusalem, 21:9-27

Beginning in verse 9, John is introduced to the "bride, the wife of the Lamb." He is carried away in spirit to a "great and high mountain" where he sees the "holy city, Jerusalem, coming down out of heaven from God, arrayed with God's glory." What is this New Jerusalem? It is a city that has so taken on the character of its inhabitants that it has become identified with them. It is none other than the Bride of Christ, the redeemed of all the ages who occupy this holy city and enjoy the presence of God and His *Shekinah* for eternity.[191]

It is important to note that John did not witness the creation of a new city or a new heaven. He observed the descent of a heaven that had already existed from eternity and now has been made visible. It is a city "not made with hands,"[192] but created from before time by the hand of God. It is a creation of God, not man. God is there, and we now see Him face-to-face as promised by Paul.

Oh, my, what a city! Possessing twelve foundations, it also has a "massive high wall, with 12 gates." Each gate has inscribed upon it the names of the twelve tribes of Israel, a commemoration of and tribute to the covenant relationship between Jehovah and His people, Israel. Thus, heaven becomes the abode of the one true Israel, the church redeemed. Each cardinal direction has three gates offering ample opportunity to enter gates that are never shut. Each gate is monitored by an angel who ensures entry only to those who have been redeemed by the blood of the Lamb and whose names are in the Lamb's Book of Life.

The "massive high wall" sits on twelve foundations on which are inscribed the names of Jesus' twelve apostles. So fundamental to the spread of the Gospel early on, God celebrates these men by inscribing their names on the foundations, the very stones upon which the dissemination of the Gospel depended. Just as the gates celebrate the covenant relationship with Israel, so the apostles' names on the foundations celebrate God's covenant relationship with the church.

Have you often wondered how the redeemed of all the ages could fit into one heavenly dwelling place? An understanding of verses 15-17 will set aside all wonderment. The angel who has been addressing John now holds a "gold measuring rod to measure the city." The description provided by John indicates that the city is a perfect cube. It measures 12,000 *stadia* in every direction,[193] making the city almost two million square miles, quite sufficient to accommodate all of the glorified redeemed from every age of history. William Hendriksen says: "Twelve thousand is the product of three (for the Trinity) times four (for the universe) times ten times ten times ten (for reduplicated, ultimate completeness and perfection). This number expresses the complete and perfect result of the saving power of the Triune God operating in the universe. That complete and perfect result is the Church of God enjoying fellowship with God in the new universe."[194]

Then the angel measured the wall and found it to be "144 cubits" high,[195] making it 216 feet across. Compare that to the Great Wall of China which is only 13-16 feet across, or the walls of Babylon which were just wide enough for two chariots to pass. Notice that the walls are made of "jasper." This is the same jasper about which we read in 21:11; it resembles a diamond, clear like a crystal. It will lack opaqueness but, because it is clear, it will allow the light of the glory of God to shine down every corridor of heaven and into every corner. The city itself will be pure gold, not solid like earthly gold, but it will be clear gold, once more designed to radiate and refract throughout the city the glory of its designer and chief inhabitant.

Notice also in verse 17 the use of "human measurement" or the Greek "measurement of man." Could this indicate that the angel is measuring, and John is describing a real city? Or is it just a spiritual heaven not reality-based? It is my judgment that these words are employed intentionally to demonstrate that the city being observed is real, not simply a figment of John's imagination. It is real; it can be measured; it is a definite, specifically proscribed place.

Once more John glories in the spectacular beauty of heaven. He returns to the foundations to offer a more detailed description. Each is constructed using a different type of stone. Eight of the twelve stones listed also appear in the breastplate worn by the High Priest as described in Exodus, chapters 28 and 29. The remaining four may also be related to the breastplate, but there is no certainty that such is the case. The significance of the stones lies in the witness of the Twelve Apostles whose faithfulness in proclaiming the Gospel is unparalleled in human history, and that faithfulness is celebrated in these foundations of precious gems.

In completing the physical description of the city, John tells us that the twelve gates mentioned earlier were made of pearl. We have often heard of the "pearly gates" to portray entry into heaven, but these massive gates are beyond comprehension. Standing 1,400 miles tall and made of a single pearl, they overwhelm and remind the redeemed of the enormity of God's grace and the significance of Christ's suffering. Just as a pearl results from the suffering of the oyster, so the heavenly gates of pearl are produced by the life, agony and ultimate death of the Lord Jesus Christ.

These magnificent gates are opened onto a street that is pure gold, yet translucent and clear like glass. For eternity, we shall walk along a street that reflects the glory of our Father. It will be a street constructed of material which, on earth, is considered to be highly prized, yet in heaven will be humdrum and commonplace.

Remember, we are looking at the New, Heavenly Jerusalem. What was the central feature of the old, earthly Jerusalem. Was it not the Temple? So where is the Temple in the New Jerusalem?

John tells us that he sought the Temple but saw none. Why? Because God Himself is the Temple; He is the sanctuary. The Temple has always represented the presence of God; now God's presence need not be represented. He does not indwell a structure, He IS the structure. He IS always present, and fellowship with God is direct and immediate. God dwells ("tabernacles") with His people, and they are eternally in His overwhelming, overpowering and consuming presence.

John seems overwhelmed by the brightness that radiates throughout the portals of heaven. No need for the sun; no need for the moon. Only the need for the glory of God to provide light and brilliance to the heavenly abode. There will be no night and day, only one eternal day ruled over by the God of Heaven. He will illuminate this New Jerusalem; all darkness will be dispelled by the true Light of the World, the Lamb of God, Jesus. Everlasting day and gates that never close—all of this forever.

When we've been there ten thousand years
Bright shining as the sun,
We've no less days to sing God's praise
Than when we first begun.[196]

In two locations, 21:24 and 21:26, John emphasizes that the redeemed of the world will inhabit the New Jerusalem. Christ will take control of all the peoples and nations of the earth and so fulfil the prophecy of Daniel 7:14. As the Prince of Peace he will cause enemies to "beat their swords into plows, and their spears into pruning knives. Nation will not take up the sword against nation, and they will never again train for war."[197]

John says it like this, "The nations will walk in its light…" referring to the grace loving people from every nation and ethnic group. All will dwell in the light of heaven. There will be no more divisive barriers, whether philosophical, racial, political or ideological. We all will meld into the people of God, moving about the city. The word translated "nations" here can mean "peoples," referring to all nationalities. No longer will there be national distinctions, rather, we shall all live as one people under the banner of God. Every tongue will be represented, every tribe will be represented and every country will be represented. Our common denominator will be the Lord God Almighty and the Lamb.

Praise God, this will be a holy place, a sacred place. Nothing unholy will tarnish the holiness of that abode because it is the place where God dwells. It is a place inhabited by those who have been redeemed by the blood of the Lamb and whose names have been found in the Lamb's Book of Life.

Paradise Restored, 22:1-5

Recall from Genesis 2 that God "planted" a Garden into which he introduced Adam and Eve. From that Garden flowed a river whose sole function was to provide water to the Garden. God designed that river to be the river of life. But once man sinned, he was expelled from the Garden of Eden (Genesis 3:23) and could no longer enjoy the purity and life-giving qualities of this river of life. While we read references to its water in John 4:14 and John 19:34, we see no mention of it elsewhere in the Bible until we come to Revelation 22.

Now the angel shows John a river, not just water but a river. It is not still water like that of the Good Shepherd in Psalm 23, but it is living water, flowing from the throne of God. Divine in its origin, it is life-giving water, offering eternal life to all who drink it. Like an artesian well, this river flows continuously symbolizing the uninterrupted outpouring of eternal life to the inhabitants of this heavenly dwelling place. This river, like all of heaven, is crystal clear so as to reflect the glory of the One who rules and reigns over this celestial city.

As John stands transfixed by the dazzling glory of this majestic city, he sees the main boulevard, a thoroughfare through the median of which flows the River of Life. Along both banks, between the river and one side of the boulevard is planted the Tree of Life. Since the tree was found on both sides of the river and along the boulevard, there must have been many of these Trees of Life, each bearing a different fruit for each month. Such is a symbol of the abundant provisions not simply to offer minimal nourishment but abundant supply for both nourishment and general health.

Ray Summers writes an interesting perspective with respect to these verses. He says, "There are three basic things necessary to the sustaining of life: water, food, and health. This picture symbolizes the provision of all three. The water of life and the perpetual fruit of the tree of life furnish the food and drink; the leaves with their healing powers furnish health. Together they symbolize God's nurture and care for his own . . . God has all that is needed to sustain eternal life in man."[198]

Could this river be an expression of the Holy Spirit? We already know from 21:22 and here in 22:1 that God the Father and Jesus the Lamb occupy the throne. So where might the Holy Spirit be? In John 3:5, John 4:13-14, and John 7:37-39 water is used to symbolize the Holy Spirit. Could this river be the final person of the Triune God or an outpouring of the Holy Spirit? Hal Lindsey believes so.[199] Whether it is the person of the Holy Spirit who provides nourishment and health or whether what John saw is a real river, we can be assured that the abundance of sustenance and good health will never diminish.

Verses 3-5 bring to a triumphal conclusion John's description of the heavenly city. The curse of humanity caused by the disobedience of Adam and Eve in the Garden of Eden is done. All that is left is for the slaves of God, the Redeemed of all time, to serve the God of glory. Even His name will be on our foreheads. The word "serve" is from the Greek word λατρεύω (*latreuō*), which means to "offer spiritual service," sometimes, to "worship." Throughout eternity we will be serving (read, worshipping) the God on the throne and the Lamb.

But most important of all, we will see His "face." As humans we could never look on the face of God. Recall Moses' encounter with God in Exodus 33:22. He was not allowed to look upon the face of God because of His divine glory.[200] But through all eternity we will see the face of the Father, touch Him, know Him as we have never known our closest friend or relative. We will look on His face without the possibility of harm or hurt, for He will be our constant companion.

I'm reminded of the poem entitled "The Sands of Time Are Sinking," authored by Anne Ross Cousin in 1857:

The Bride eyes not her garment, but her dear Bridegroom's face;

I will not gaze at glory but on my king of grace;

Not at the crown He giveth but on His nail pierced hand:

The Lamb is all the glory in Immanuel's land.[201]

Finally, heaven will be bright with the brilliance of God's glory. Night will no longer exist, and there will be no need for sunlight or artificial light of any kind. Our light will be the continuous light of Him who is, even today, the Light of the world. His spectacular light will be all that is necessary to provide illumination for the heavenly city and its inhabitants.

John declares, “they will reign forever and ever.” The redeemed of all time will share in the reign of the heavenly kingdom. But over whom or what will we reign? The message is not clear. Paul declared in 1 Corinthians 6:3, “Don’t you know that we will judge angels—not to mention ordinary matters?” So, could we rule over the angels? Whatever the form of our reign, we will rule like kings once more.

APPLICATION TO OUR POST-CHRISTIAN WORLD

How could I ever create commentary on Scripture that is so powerful and descriptive. While we certainly cannot know the exact details of our new home, it will be far different from the alternative. I am thankful to my Father in heaven for His promise of an eternal abode that is more beautiful and joyful than the most beautiful and inspiring earthly mansion. And we will not only live there, but we shall also rule there. It will be a place of peace, and all that we need will be provided.

God promises a new kind of world, unlike anything we have ever seen before. It is not an after-thought of God. It has been planned just as creation and redemption were planned. It will be a paradise. And we can live with the assurance that it will never again be messed up. TODAY IS THE DAY OF SALVATION!

CHAPTER 15
"I AM COMING."
22:6-21

In this climax to the Book of Revelation, the final Hallelujah is sounded. The second hand on the clock of eternity is about to go past midnight. The time for the seal judgments has passed; the time for the trumpet judgments has passed; the time for the bowl judgments has passed; Christ has reigned for a thousand years, and the Great White Throne Judgment has put all of the unrepentant, unredeemed sinners in their place for eternity. The final chapter has been written and, for believers, it is not only faithful and true, but it also offers an infinite future in the presence of the Lord Jesus Christ.

The angel, who has been John's companion throughout much of this journey, assures John that what he has written is true, authentic, genuine. He declares that the same God who inspired the prophets of old—men like Daniel, Ezekiel and Isaiah—sent the angel to give the message to John so that he could write it down for the churches of the time. It is not a book of man, but it is a book of God.

Could this also contain a special plea to the Jews? Probably. By mentioning the "spirits of the prophets," he may have been reminding the readers of the Jewishness of the book.

Once more the word "quickly" is mentioned by the angel. The same root word, τάχος, *tachos*, meaning "speed," "quickness" or "haste," is the same as that also employed by John in 1:1. Here he emphasizes that, when events start to occur, they will happen with speed, quickness. Be assured the events *will* happen, and when they begin, they will hit with a force and thrust that is inconceivable.

And now Jesus speaks! He echoes once more the words of the angel, "Look, I am coming quickly!" Same word, same meaning. Could He mean that His return is imminent? Of course, but recall the words of 2 Peter 3:8 where Peter writes, "with the Lord one day is as a thousand years, and a thousand years like one day." Here Peter simply reminds the church that God's view of time is far different from ours. We live a relatively short life, and time—every minute—is important to us. But God is eternal, and for Him, time does not exist.

Jesus tops off this verse by offering yet another of the beatitudes that can be found in Revelation. He declares blessing upon him who reads this prophecy and "keeps" it. This word is a form of the verb τηρέω (*tēreō*) meaning to "keep, guard, heed or watch over." Since this word is in the present tense, Jesus does not want us merely to heed its admonitions sporadically or on occasion or when we feel like it. But we are to guard its message and heed its message continually, as a lifestyle. He is saying, "Now that you know what you know, act upon what you know, and I will bless you."

While it is not necessary to do so, John inserts his "two cents worth" by declaring that what he has seen and heard is true. Now put yourself in John's place. How do you think you would feel, especially if no one believed you?

John was astounded! He could not believe what he had seen and experienced. He probably sat with his head in his hands, shaking his head and marveling at what he has witnessed. He takes this moment to write, "I, John, am the one who saw and heard these things." So overwhelmed, much as he was in 19:10, he falls down to worship the angel-messenger. And just as in 19:10 the angel tells him, "Don't do that." He reminds John that he too is a being just like the prophets and John. He may be an angel, but he is still a created being who should not be worshipped by any other created being. He admonishes John to be like all who keep the words of this book, Worship God!

John is now ordered not to seal the prophecy. Recall from 10:4 that John heard the voice of seven thunders and was commanded to seal the message of the seven thunders and not write it down. He probably carried the burden of that message in his heart for the remainder of his life. However, here he is directed *not* to seal what he has written. Why?

He explains to us, "because the time is near." Recall how the prophecies of Daniel were ordered sealed "until the time of the end." Unlike the prophecies of Daniel,[202] proclaimed centuries before the death and resurrection of Christ, the prophecies of John were closer at hand. The message included an element of urgency. In fact, the message possessed such urgency that it must remain unsealed so that it may be preached with vigor, vitality and without vacillation. Nothing was more important. The Word is opened (not sealed), taught, preached and believed.

Verse 11 offers some interesting grammatical structure. The original Greek verbs of each of the four phrases here is an aorist imperative form, meaning "let them continue." It is God's words through the voice of the angel saying, "their fate is sealed." Whether unrighteous, filthy, righteous or holy, each, by virtue of personal choice, has determined his destiny. Reject God, and your eternal future is in hell where you will continue in your unrighteous and filthy ways apart from God. Once death has occurred, there shall be no second chance. Accept the sacrifice of the Saviour, and remain righteous and holy, and your eternity shall be forever be in a place of holiness. In a real sense, these phrases could be summed up by the angel simply saying, "Let them be who they are."

Now Jesus speaks once more. For the fifth time we encounter the Greek word ταχύ
(*tachu*), meaning "quickly." Recall that the context of this word each time it has been employed refers to a rapid, instantaneous appearance. Reminiscent of the words of Paul in 1 Thessalonians 4:13-18 and Peter in 2 Peter 3:10, Jesus declares that He will "come quickly," as a thief in the night, unexpected and sudden. And He will bring with Him the rewards due every believer for the works of eternal value which each believer has stored up.

When the time on God's calendar has reached the day and hour, Christ will return to take us to our final home where we will abide with Him and worship Him eternally. As with all matters of faith, there are doubters, questioners who believe either that there is no God or that God is not coming. But from Genesis to Revelation, God has developed and implemented a plan, and He will not abandon that plan. He *will* come, and His coming will be so sudden and so unexpected that we are all commanded to "be ready!" Hear His words in Revelation 16:15: "Look, I am coming like a thief. The one who is alert and remains clothed so that he may not go around naked and people see his shame is blessed." You can take that assurance to the bank.

Once more Christ emphasizes that He is God. He is the "Alpha and the Omega, the First and the Last, the Beginning and the End." You see, Jesus is the brackets of life because he is the Alpha, the first ray of hope, given to fallen man in the Garden of Eden. Here in the last book of the Bible he is Omega, that final champion who has defeated the enemy in combat and sits astride the great white horse of victory. The universe around him is victorious and alive in his triumph. He possesses infinite, eternal equality with God. He wants to offer a final assurance that He is God, and no one will snatch from His hand the final victory.

In a final beatitude, verses 14-15 offer details of those who will be allowed in heaven and those who will not. An assumption derived from reading these verses is that every person who has ever lived has been clothed spiritually in a robe that has been sullied and defiled by the filth of a sinful world. And every effort to clean that robe using worldly methods is ineffective. Spiritual grime is cleaned only by the cleansing blood of the Saviour, Jesus Christ. In order to purify our robes and make them stainless in the sight of God, we must wash them in the "fountain of blood drawn from Immanuel's veins."[203] So heaven will be populated by those who have willingly accepted the salvation of the Saviour and have washed their robes in His blood.

In contrast, outside the city gates will remain those whose robes remain dirt-filled, worldly-stained and evil soaked. Unrighteous men and women will never eat of the tree of life or enter the city gates because of their sinful state.

In a final statement Jesus reverts to a time when impenitent man still had a chance to turn from sin and accept the imputed righteousness of Christ. For the only time in the Scripture, He refers to Himself with the personal pronoun "I." He emphasizes that He is both the source of David's life as well as his descendant. He may be an ancestor of David, but He was also before David. Just as He is an ancestor of Abraham, He was also before Abraham. As Creator, He always has been; as the "Bright Morning Star," the last star seen just before sunrise, He shall always be, sovereign over glorious heaven and all its inhabitants.

"Come, come, come!" The Holy Spirit says "come"; the bride, the church, issues an invitation to "come." He who is thirsty is invited to "come" and taste the water that offers life. Jesus offers himself as the thirst-quenching water of life which, when a man drinks from this fountain, he never again thirsts in the depths of his soul. But he lives forever in eternity with the satiated palate of one who never, ever thirsts. In fact, whoever desires to enjoy life eternal should "come" and accept the gift of living water. St. Augustine of Hippo once wrote in his *Confessions*: "You have made us for yourself, O Lord, and our heart is restless until it rests in you."[204] If you look very closely at the outstretched hands of this one who says,

"Come," you'll notice something very interesting. There are nail prints in those hands. They are hands that suffered for us so that every awful judgment described in this book may never come upon us. Our imperative, therefore, is to preach the Gospel with boldness so that the atoning death of Jesus Christ and the salvation made possible by that atoning death can be enjoyed and appreciated by every single person on the face of God's earth. As God's children, we must be obedient to God's command and invite all sinners to "come and taste."

Verses 18-19 sometimes present a dilemma with respect to the security of the believer. How does this Scripture complement the idea of "once saved, always saved"? My first advice is not to read into these verses elements that are not there. A good Scripture with which to start is 1 John 3:9, the Scripture upon which that principle is based: "Everyone who has been born of God does not sin, because His seed remains in him; he is not able to sin, because he has been born of God." Sounds fairly straightforward, doesn't it? But let's take a closer look at it.

The phrase "does not sin" (HCSB) is more literally translated "is not practicing sin." The verb in this phrase is in the present tense, meaning that one does not make a habit of practicing sin. In the same sense, the following phrase "is not able to sin" is also in the present indicative, possessing the same kind of meaning. Does this mean, then, that a man who has been born of God will not sin? No! John is simply saying that a man who has been truly born of God will make a lifestyle change and will no longer make it habit to sin. He cannot turn his back on God totally and return to the old lifestyle from which he was freed. The Spirit of God remains in him, and his changed nature will not allow him to do that.

Now returning to 22:18-19 with these thoughts in mind, the idea becomes much clearer. One whose life has been changed will not turn his back on God. One who "adds to" or "takes away from" the message of The Revelation will be a person who has never truly been freed from a lifestyle of unrighteousness. If he takes away from this message, then he assuredly disbelieves the written Word of God and is a phony to the world. To say "I love Jesus, I believe the written Word of God and I am saved" yet discredit and deny the message of this Scripture is living a lie. These words are the living Word of God, and to deny them is to deny Christ and never to share in "the tree of life and the holy city."

Jesus declares, "Yes, I am coming quickly." We do not know the day or the hour, but His coming will be sudden and impactful. Until that day, we must be watchful and eager with anticipation that the day of our final salvation is drawing near.

John is so filled with joy and expectancy that he can only get out the words, "Amen! Come, Lord Jesus." These should be the words of all of us as Christians as we await the fulfilment of His promise to return and "save us at last in heaven."

APPLICATION TO OUR POST-CHRISTIAN WORLD

God is a God of His Word even if our 21st century, post-Christian world does not believe it to be true. He not only tells the truth, He IS the truth. He has declared that He will return to reclaim His creation. You can count on that as fact. But how can we know when He is coming?

Matthew 24:36 clearly reminds us that no one knows the time or the season for Christ's return. But those who possess the spirit of Christ can observe natural changes all around them and in their hearts can discern the spiritual importance of these changes based upon Scripture. In summary, let's look at the six signs of Christ's imminent return.

WIDESPREAD DECEPTION BY FALSE CHRISTS

Matthew 24:5 declares, "Watch out that no one deceives you. For many will come in My name, saying, 'I am the Messiah,' and they will deceive many." Even today, false Messiahs have arisen in several Eastern nations. People are being deceived by those who claim to be the "anointed one," preaching a false doctrine. The world is being blinded to the truth; cults are thriving; Islam, that great deceiver of men and destroyer of anyone who does not believe as they do, is on the rise throughout the world; and Satan is joyful that his strategy is working. But the deception extends beyond the spiritual. These false Christ's also deceive through the use of the media, including radio, television, internet, cellphones and other electronic and technological means. Daniel prophesied (12:4) that "knowledge will increase."

In an article published in 2013, David Russell Schilling wrote: "By the end of World War II knowledge was doubling every 25 years. Today things are not as simple as different types of knowledge have different rates of growth. For example, nanotechnology knowledge is doubling every two years and clinical knowledge every 18 months. But on average human knowledge is doubling every 13 months."[205] So, perhaps we are approaching or may be in the end times with this explosion of knowledge and increase in the rapidity of information exchange.

No better example exists of this element of the end times than in Revelation 11 where John describes the killing of the two witnesses whose dead bodies lay in the streets for three and a half days with the entire world engrossed in watching the violence. Only in a technological world with satellite television and internet could such an event be observed by the whole world simultaneously.

In a world where false Messiahs are proclaiming "truth," the natural outcome would be false believers. At the beginning of the end many people will be teaching the truths of Scripture, but they will be comingling other teachings that are completely inconsistent with the Bible and therefore, will deceive many. There are many Christian Bible teachers and pastors today who have deviated from sound Biblical doctrines and have added culturally inclusive ideas as a means to be more accepted by an increasingly worldly society. Some of these ideas and doctrines are quite subtle; others are utterly deliberate and flagrant. It is important, therefore, to be vigilant and aware that such teaching may point toward the end.

We also live in a world where the focus of most people is on being entertained or informed but not spiritually so. As a result, the apostate church is on the rise. Simply observe the churches that now view abortion as acceptable; or premarital sex, or adultery, or homosexuality as normal and conventional lifestyles. The ultimate goal of these false teachers is to preoccupy humanity with ideas that make no difference in life so that spiritual matters become irrelevant. Once deception has flourished, Satan will cause to arise a charismatic leader who will successfully amalgamate all of the religions of the world under his direction. Because the deception of humankind will be so deep, he will promise to bring peace, justice and unity to the world's faiths. Be aware of false Christs and deception, for they are a sign that the end is approaching.

DISPUTES, CONFLICT AND WARFARE

In Revelation 12, God reveals that Satan will "come down to you with great fury, because he knows he has a short time." During this time there will be an increase of conflict in the world unlike any faced before in history.

In Zechariah 14:12 the prophet proclaimed the advent of nuclear war when he wrote, "their flesh will rot as they stand on their feet, their eyes will rot in their sockets, and their tongues will rot in their mouths." Today, the threat of nuclear war is greater than ever before with states like Iran and North Korea advancing rapidly toward the development of nuclear weaponry. With China, India and Pakistan joining an ever-increasing number of nuclear capable countries like Russia against the United States, nuclear war, at some future point, is almost inevitable.

Add the most current threat to the world—terrorism—and one may be led to interpret the threat of warfare as real and present. Constant conflict in the Middle East, 9/11, the rise of ISIS and its war on Christians, small skirmishes like the "lone wolf" attacks in Paris, Las Vegas, Sandy Hook and throughout the world and the constant threat of cyber-attacks may suggest that the "beginnings of sorrows" may be imminent.

In the United States race relations have deteriorated to the point that peaceful protests for racial equality now quickly turn to violent attacks on people and property. Could these escalating events lead to an all-out race war in our nation? Let's hope and pray not. But race wars could certainly be one type of war in the end times.

Could our country become ground zero for a war between the "haves" and "have-nots"? Economically, the gap between the poor and the rich is ever widening. Will the poor rise up in violent protest against the rich and ultimately wage war? While possible, perhaps even likely, pray that mankind will not reach a point of such escalating anger that war actually breaks out over a widening wealth inequality.

VAST DEVASTATION OF THE WORLD

Matthew 24:8 describes how the frequency of disaster will befall the world in the "beginnings of sorrows" just as birth pangs increase in frequency and intensity. Natural disasters can be expected to affect every living being on the earth as they increase in number and power.

Wildfires, pestilence, floods, hurricanes, tsunamis can all be seen throughout the world. Recall the forest fires in Australia in 2019; a plague of locusts destroyed crops in East Africa causing famine not only there but also in many other countries. In 2011 Japan suffered a life-changing earthquake with a resulting tsunami that killed almost 16,000 people, injured thousands more and destroyed homes and crops. It triggered one of the worst nuclear disasters in history when the Fukushima nuclear plant exploded, sending tons of radioactivity into both the air and the sea. Earthquakes have occurred regularly throughout the world, and even here in the United States in locales like Tennessee and northern Florida where earthquakes are extremely rare. As a result of these phenomena, world food supplies are dwindling. A reasonable expectation would be famines in many areas of the world resulting in a global food shortage.

Even as I write this, reports on the national newscasts are describing the rising food shortages that are occurring in the United States. Some restaurants and grocery stores are unable to purchase certain food items, especially vegetables and meat supplies. And if this is happening in the United States, it most certainly can and will spread to the remainder of the world.

Pestilence will also take its toll in the end times. Recall the effects of swine flu which infected more than 60 million people in 2009-2010. Add Ebola, a deadly disease that is easily transmitted, AIDS and the crisis it created throughout the 1980s and 1990s and now COVID-19 which has caused a complete shutdown of the entire world in 2020. Unprecedented! Perhaps these events could be a part of the "beginning of sorrows" mentioned by Jesus in Matthew 24.

In Luke 21:11 Jesus said, "There will be violent earthquakes, and famines and plagues in various places, and there will be terrifying sights and great signs from heaven." As one observes the happenings in the world of the 21st century, one cannot question Jesus' words because the signs of His coming are all around us.

PROLIFERATING EVIL AND WICKEDNESS

In Matthew Jesus declares that His coming will be marked by unparalleled wickedness and an increasing lack of love. "Because lawlessness will multiply, the love of many will grow cold" (Matthew 24:12). We live in a world where selfishness is the cultural norm—all in the name of "me." All around us is encouragement to satisfy my needs, find happiness in buying and living for myself, engaging in activities that bring joy to me.

And then there is an even deeper self-satisfaction derived from accepting a moral perspective that is counter to God's moral law. Couples living together without the benefit of a marriage relationship; so many children being born out of wedlock; abortions for the sake of convenience; divorce caused by selfish ambition or desires, forcing children to become confused triggering psychological issues and sometimes mental illness; child abuse and the sex trafficking of children; and children being born into unhealthy homes and not receiving the kind of love and training from their parents that children deserve. All of these cultural changes are becoming not only more and more accepted as normal but also offer signs of a growing evil influence in the world and the ultimate of coming of Christ.

Jesus declared in Matthew 24:37, "As the days of Noah were, so the coming of the Son of Man will be." We know from Genesis 6:5-7 that man's "wickedness was widespread," so much so that God said, "I will wipe off from the face of the earth mankind." In Matthew Jesus is reiterating God's message from Genesis. He avows that His second coming will be at a time when mankind and the earth have degenerated to the same point as in Noah's day. As I look around me today, I wonder, *Have we arrived at that point yet? How close are we to the same wicked state of mankind as in the days of Noah?*

Paul describes, in words from the first century, a world that looks a bit like today's global society. Paul wrote, "But know this: Difficult times will come in the last days. For people will be lovers of self, lovers of money, boastful, proud, blasphemers, disobedient to parents, ungrateful, unholy, unloving, irreconcilable, slanderers, without self-control, brutal, without love for what is good, traitors, reckless, conceited, lovers of pleasure rather than lovers of God, holding to the form of godliness but denying its power. Avoid these people!"[206] We are admonished to shun those whose lives reflect an egomaniacal perspective. We are not to be influenced by them but rather avoid them altogether.

Observe today's post-Christian culture. What do you see? Do you find examples of these people around you—at work, at leisure, at home, even at church? Society is teeming with people whose lives are motivated solely for self. It is little surprise that we observe lawlessness, disrespect for parents, hedonism, money mongers, liars, contempt for authority and thanklessness. If these are signs of the end times, then we MUST be approaching or are already in the last days before Christ's return.

RESTORATION OF ISRAEL AS A NATION

For centuries Israel has alternately been independent or conquered and enslaved. From bondage in Egypt to independence and establishment as a wandering nation to its claim upon the Promised Land of Canaan, Israel's history has been storied. After experiencing a succession of good and evil rulers and even a division into two nation-states, its final blow in AD 70 removed Israel's independence as a nation. Over the next centuries Israel was attacked and conquered by several groups including Greeks, Romans, Egyptians and Islamists. But true to the words of Matthew 24:32-33, like the fig tree points to the nearness of summer, so the restoration of Israel points to the nearness of the second coming of the Messiah. And that restoration occurred on May 14, 1948, when, once more, Israel became a modern, independent nation.

Other prophecies also point to the return of Israel as a watershed event in the end times chronology. Amos 9:13-15 declares, “The days are coming—this is the Lord’s declaration… when I will restore the fortunes of My people Israel. They will rebuild and occupy ruined cities, plant vineyards and drink their wine, make gardens and eat their produce. I will plant them on their land, and they will never be uprooted from the land I have given them. Yahweh your God has spoken.”

Today the greening of the desert lands comprising the southern half of Israel is nothing less than spectacular. In this “uninhabitable “ land, the people of Israel have developed a lush, productive and covetous environment where they grow all kinds of vegetables, grapes for wine and other forms of food production that are the envy of the world. Crops, livestock, fishing and aquaculture, fruits and vegetables and flowers comprise a litany of success stories for the people of Israel today. They have truly “come back” to their land not only as a nation but also as a people.

In Ezekiel 37:21-22, the prophet says, “”This is what the Lord God says: I am going to take the Israelites out of the nations where they have gone. I will gather them from all around and bring them into their own land. I will make them one nation in the land, on the mountains of Israel.” History indicates that as early as 1882, significant immigration to Israel from other nations had begun in earnest. Between 1882 and 1903 more than 35,000 Jews immigrated to Israel, settling mostly in the southwestern area of Syria. Between 1904 and 1914 about 40,000 Jews immigrated from Russia, settling in the same area and establishing the first kibbutz. From 1919 to 1923 approximately 40,000 more Jews arrived from Eastern Europe as a consequence of World War I. Between 1924 and 1929 almost 82,000 Jews arrived from an unsettled Poland that was experiencing extreme anti-Semitism. Then between 1929 and 1939 more than 250,000 Jews fled Nazi Germany seeking protection from Arian dominance and growing anti-Semitism.

These waves of immigration continue to today. Over the years beginning in 1882, more than 3.8 million Jews have left their homes and immigrated to their beloved homeland of Israel. Today, Israel's population is over 7 million. In 2018, Israel celebrated its 70th anniversary. It is still mostly a secular state, but it has a growing percentage of Orthodox Jews and Christians. It is safe to say that the prophecy so clearly proclaimed in the prophets has truly been fulfilled.

UNIVERSAL PROCLAMATION OF THE GOSPEL TO THE WHOLE WORLD

Once more the words of Matthew become a prophetic message for us. Probably the single most important sign of the end of the age and the return of Jesus is the worldwide preaching of the Gospel. Hear the words of Matthew 24:14, "This good news of the kingdom will be proclaimed in all the world as a testimony to all nations. And then the end will come." In the first century, such a statement would never have been believed. Not possible! But we live in the 21st century where internet and satellite television can reach almost every blade of grass in the entire world. As a result, the preaching of the Gospel to all the nations is now within reach.

Note that Jesus is not saying that every single individual in the world will hear the Gospel but only that the Gospel will be preached throughout the whole world. And that is possible right now!

I have always been amazed that Jesus began with twelve disciples and within a lifetime the Gospel had spread throughout the known world. Little wonder that today's technology makes it possible for all the nations to hear and heed the Word of God. Jesus' words in Matthew have been fulfilled even as you read this book. Perhaps every individual in the world has not been reached, but every nation has experienced the preaching of the Word. For any person who has heard the Word, it remains his discretion to decide to be obedient to what is heard or persist in his disobedience. TODAY IS THE DAY OF SALVATION!

EPILOGUE

As we conclude this study of the Book of Revelation, I would like to use this last chapter to summarize a bit of what we have learned from this wonderful prophecy. Allow its message to reach deep into your heart as you face the culture and persecution from a post-Christian world that does not share a belief in Jesus as Messiah.

Eternal Rest

Allow me to begin with helping all of us to understand the status of the dead who have gone before, the Rapture and the resurrection to come. I have been asked numerous times, where do our souls go when we die? Let me first try to answer this fundamental question.

When we depart this earthly realm, our bodies and souls are immediately separated. With our last breath, our souls take flight, leaving the shell of our body to be laid to rest. That body, as we are told in Genesis 3:19, Ecclesiastes 3:20, Genesis 18:27 and Psalm 104:29—our bodies—are but "ashes and dust." And to dust we shall return. Our bodies are expendable, biodegradable. They shall return to the earth from which they have been formed.

Ah, but not so with the soul! At death the soul lives on in a conscious state only to take up abode either with Jesus or eternally apart from Him. And, of course, that determination is made during life when the individual decides to repent and accept Jesus as Saviour or not.

Now let's take a quick look at these places of abode. Two words are used in the Bible to refer to the place of the dead. In the Old Testament the word is שְׁאוֹל (*Sheol*); in the New Testament the word is ᾍδης (*haidēs*). While often translated as "hell," they both refer to the same place, to the place of the dead. When *Sheol* is used, it never is employed in the plural, and nowhere can be found a reference to the body going to *Sheol*.

It was considered to be the abode of the dead, both good and evil, prior to the resurrection of Jesus. As such, it contained two compartments, "Paradise," sometimes called "Abraham's Bosom" and "Torments."[207] Torments was where all unbelievers lived following the resurrection of Christ.

Clearly taught in Luke 16:19-31, the rich man died, his body was buried, and he went to hell (*Sheol/ Hades*).[208] In *Sheol/Hades* he was tormented (tortured) by a flame (verses 23, 24, 25, 28). Conclusion? It can only be considered to be a literal "place" (verse 28), this place where the souls of the unsaved go when they die. But *Sheol/Hades* also has another compartment occupied by the saints of the Old Testament like Abraham and pre-resurrection believers like New Testament Lazarus (verse 23). It was the place where the righteous dead would live, "Paradise." This compartment is a place of well-being, solace, relief (verse 25). It is called "Abraham's bosom" (Luke 16:23). "Abraham's bosom" is the place where the righteous dead can enjoy mutual fellowship, enjoying the company of Abraham, the father of the faithful. *Sheol/Hades* is also called "paradise" where the thief on the cross and Christ abode together (Luke 23:43).

Between these two compartments communication was possible (verses 24-31). However, passing from one compartment to the other was not possible (verse 26). The destiny of the occupants in each compartment was fixed and could not be altered. The only way to avoid the "Torments" compartment and the way to enter "Paradise" with Abraham was to hear and heed the Word of God while one is still alive (verses 27-31). For pre-resurrection man it meant a faith in the God of the Old Testament and a hope in the future appearance of a Messiah.

We know, from Acts 2:27f that, between His death and resurrection, the soul of Christ went to Hades, but He was there only briefly. In Acts 2:31 Peter gives further explanation by quoting King David: "(David) seeing this in advance, he spoke concerning the resurrection of the Messiah: He was not left in Hades, and his flesh did experience decay."[209] Between His death and resurrection, Christ's soul was in *Sheol/Hades*, the place called "Paradise" (Luke 23:43). Recall how He promised the thief on the cross that on that very day that he would be with Him in "Paradise."

Now, since the resurrection of Jesus, when a believer dies, his soul is ushered immediately into the presence of Jesus in heaven where he/she enjoys fellowship with the Father and contentment in worship. The body may deteriorate, but the soul lives on forever. And one day, the soul will be reunited with a glorified body, never to experience the pain and suffering, sorrow and disappointment that mortal life has inflicted.

But the soul of the unbeliever who dies unrepentant, who refuses to accept Christ's sacrifice for sin, will be led into the anguish of "Torments" where he/she shall remain until the body is resurrected after the Millennium, rejoined with a tormented soul, face the Great Judge at the Great White Throne Judgment and ultimately live eternally in the lake of fire.

God's Redemptive Plan

Clearly God had a plan for His world from before the beginning of time itself. In His Divine Wisdom, He revealed His plan to us through His Word. So unmistakably divine is His idea, He even book-ended it in Genesis and Revelation. In Genesis we read that God created this perfect world where evil did not exist, and man was free to live life in freedom and plenty, naked but unashamed. God even provided a "tree of life" as written in Genesis 2:9: "The Lord caused to grow out of the ground every tree pleasing in appearance and good for food, including the tree of life in the middle of the garden." This tree was a sign for Adam: as long as Adam maintained his dependency upon God and obeyed the commands of God, his life would result in a state of happiness. And according to Genesis 3:22, the fruit of this tree would produce immortality. He would live forever!

But man yielded to a baser nature, sinned and "the Lord God sent him away from the garden of Eden to work the ground from which he was taken" (Genesis 3:23). Furthermore, the eternal life that God had made available to man in his sinless state now slipped through his fingers.

But in His omniscience, God had a plan. In His omnipotence, He implemented that plan through the working of His will in history. During the Age of Noah, man continued in his rebellious ways, even to the point where God said, "I will wipe off from the face of the earth mankind." But in Noah, God found an upright man, and Noah "found favor in the sight of the Lord." Obeying God's command, Noah began work on an ark even as God promised to "establish My covenant with you." But Noah's friends and neighbors ridiculed him, mocking him and calling him a fool. But God was faithful to His covenant with Noah, offering grace, saving a remnant, salvaging mankind, and from that remnant, from the line of righteous Noah, came the Son of Man, Jesus Christ our Lord.

Through Noah's son, Shem, was born Abram, later to be called Abraham. During the time that Abraham lived in Haran, God recognized him to be an honorable and principled man.

During the Age of Abraham, God acknowledged his righteousness and, commanding him to leave Haran and go to "the land that I will show you," recognized him as the "father of the faithful." He had confidence in God and was willing to conform his life to a standard of unconditional and unstained righteousness. He believed in God, but he also believed God and felt assured that God's ways and God's standards were upright and fair and good. In turn God was so assured of Abraham's faithfulness that he made him the father of a great nation through which would come the Saviour of the world.[210]

The line of Shem ultimately produced Jacob, later named Israel. The father of Joseph, Israel, traveled at the command of Joseph, Pharaoh's second in command, to the land of Egypt, settling in the land of Goshen. His line as well as that of Joseph prospered until Joseph's death at age 110 years.

By this time a new king "who had not known Joseph," came to power in Egypt. Because of the proliferation of the Israelite population, the new pharaoh enslaved the Israelite nation. But God raised up another leader after an encounter with a burning bush. There he met God.

During the Age of Moses, God enlisted this ordinary, yet privileged man, to lead His people out of bondage in Egypt. Tongue-tied and nervous, Moses resisted the efforts of God to exercise his leadership abilities and guide His people through the next forty years. But through it all, he remained faithful, loyal and true to his God. Finally, Moses relented, badgering Pharaoh to the point that the children of Israel were released from their 400 years of slavery in a foreign land. During this Age, the Tabernacle was built, Jehovah was formally worshipped and ritual sacrifice was instituted to forgive sin.

As a part of His redemptive plan, God chose to use a woman whose character and reputation were not untarnished. Rahab had been a sinful woman, yet she had a remarkable understanding of the work and sovereign will of God. Her faith was simple, but so strong was her faith that she was willing to risk her own life in order to save two

Israelites, trusting that she would be saved by them. Rahab teaches us that it is not the amount of truth one has that saves, but it is the obeying of the truth one has that saves. From God's perspective, Christ magnified His grace when He came from such as Judah and Tamar, their son Pharez, Rahab and others. Simple people; not perfect people.

During the Age of David, the man after God's own heart yielded to his inner temptations but acknowledged his transgressions against God. Recognizing that he had sinned against God and desiring in his innermost part the forgiveness of God, it was David who so eloquently penned the heartfelt words of Psalm 51: "Be gracious to me, God, according to Your faithful love; according to Your abundant compassion, blot out my rebellion. Wash away my guilt and cleanse me from my sin. . . against You—You alone—I have sinned and done this evil in Your sight."[211] Ultimately, through the line of this great king, God continued to implement His redemptive plan.

During the Age of Ezra, this scholar of the Scriptures led the second wave of Israelites from Babylonian Captivity back to Jerusalem. He knew the commandments and the Law and was, in fact, an instructor in the Law. Ezra 7:10 states: "Now Ezra had determined in his heart to study the law of the Lord, obey it, and teach its statutes and ordinances in Israel." The people's lack of faithfulness to God concerned Ezra, and he sought to bring about a sense of repentance and obedience in their religious life. God inspired Ezra to motivate change in the people and rekindle their religious zeal, once more instituting facets of the law so long neglected.

During the Christian Age, God sent his own Son to replace the old sacrificial system of forgiveness. Jesus Christ came in the flesh, born of a virgin, and ministered to a world that was dreadfully in need of a Saviour. In the end, He was destined, as God had planned from before eternity began, to become that "once-and-for-all" blood sacrifice. After His resurrection, He ascended to the Father where He sits on the heavenly throne until the day of His return.

It is my sincere belief that the God who ordered the world in creation would also order the end of the world and equally offer us His plan on how it will end. How else could we be prepared? It is for this reason that I believe the Book of Revelation to be a forth-telling of the end times and the Second Coming. God would not wish for us to be uninformed about His coming, and that belief underlies my own interpretation of The Revelation.

On that day Jesus will come down from His heavenly throne, stand on the Mount of Olives and announce His return, just as He promised. He will reign as King of Kings and Lord of Lords, and all who know Him and have been obedient to Him will shout praise to the glory of God the Father.

THE MESSAGE OF THE REVELATION TO A POST-CHRISTIAN WORLD

We live in an upside-down world. For centuries man has lived in accordance with the facts as he perceived them or could prove them. Today, not so much. We have a world, the majority of which believes, that the universe was the result of some distant primordial explosion, and by a twist of fate, molecules haphazardly bonded to form the "stuff" out of which life emerged. Ask such a person one question: If I place all the ingredients for a cake on the counter of my kitchen, what are the chances that they will result in an edible cake? You will receive a resounding "No chance." Yet that same person is willing to accept an unproven theory that the world, and ultimately mankind, is the result of some prehistoric cataclysmic event which conjoined in a random, unsystematic manner all the ingredients necessary for the universe to exist and man ultimately to form. Do you see any inconsistency in such an idea?

That same person refuses to acknowledge, perhaps, that God even exists and denies the validity of God's Word. But let's take a look at only a select number of facts, real facts, not theory, in the form of fulfilled prophecies.

- Babylon will rule over Judah for 70 years, Jeremiah 25:11-12.
- Babylon's kingdom will be permanently overthrown, Isaiah 13:19.
- The Jews will survive Babylonian rule and return home, Jeremiah 32:36-37.
- Messiah will be born of a virgin, Isaiah 7:14.
- Messiah will be a descendant of Abraham, Genesis 22:18.

- Messiah will be born in Bethlehem, Micah 5:2.
- Messiah will enter Jerusalem riding on a donkey, Zechariah 9:9.
- Messiah will be betrayed for 30 pieces of silver, Zechariah 11:12-13.
- Messiah will die by crucifixion, Psalm 22:14-16.
- Messiah will be raised from the dead, Psalm 16:10; 30:3.

This list reflects prophecies that were proclaimed hundreds of years before their fulfilment. One cannot argue with the certainty of their completion. History does not lie. So, what can be said for the person who declares that the universe is the result of a cataclysmic game of chance yet denies the validity of the Scripture?

God has possessed a plan for His creation from the moment He spoke it into being. While He did not bring sin into the world, He created man with a free will, allowing mankind to decide for himself whether he would live for God or evil. Man chose evil; God knew that He would. But God had a Plan B. He planned for man to have an "out." That plan included the death of His Son, Jesus Christ, whose death provided the necessary blood sacrifice to cover the sins of all mankind. Man has but to accept that sacrifice in faith.

The changing world in which we live distracts us from our singular focus. When we face the trials of everyday living, we must be humble, courageously and faithfully dedicated to living our lives with purpose. God has revealed in The Revelation His supreme reward for such fidelity, a crown of life. Yes, heaven is real; yes, the end times will happen. Whether John is writing in images or describing reality as it will actually occur, the events of the Great Tribulation will be of such severity as to make one cringe with fear. But the choice is always left to the individual. I cannot make that decision for you. God is calling you NOW to turn to Him in repentance and faith. TODAY IS THE DAY OF SALVATION!

CONCLUSION

I close this treatise on Revelation by sharing words from one of my favorite authors, James Weldon Johnson. The words of this prominent black poet of the 19th and 20th centuries in his "Judgment Day" message from *God's Trombones*, not only ring true to the Scripture but also paint a picture of the dread and suffering that shall befall all those who reject Jesus Christ until the end.

In that great day,
People, in that great day,
God's a-going to rain down fire.
God's a-going to sit in the middle of the air
To judge the quick and the dead.
Early one of these morning's,
God's a-going to call for Gabriel,
That tall, bright angel, Gabriel;
And God's a going to say to him: Gabriel,
Blow your silver trumpet,
And wake the living nations.

And Gabriel's going to ask him: Lord,
How loud must I blow?
And God's a-going to tell him: Gabriel,
Blow it calm and easy.
Then putting one foot on the mountain top,
And the other in the middle of the sea,
Gabriel's going to stand and blow his horn,
To wake the living nations.

Then God's a-going to say to him: Gabriel,
Once more blow your silver trumpet,
And wake the nations underground.

And Gabriel's going to ask him: Lord,
How loud must I blow?
And God's a-going to tell him: Gabriel,
Like seven peals of thunder.
Then the tall, bright angel, Gabriel,
Will put one foot on the battlements of Heaven

And the other on the steps of hell,
And blow that silver trumpet
Till he shakes old hell's foundations.

And I feel Old earth a-shuddering–
And I see the graves a-bursting–
And I hear a sound,
A blood-chilling sound.
What sound is that I hear?
It's the clicking together of the dry bones,
Bone to bone–the dry bones.
And I see coming out of the bursting graves,
And marching up from the valley of death,
The army of the dead.
And the living and the dead in the twinkling of an eye
Are caught up in the middle of the air,
Before God's judgment bar.

Oh-o-oh, sinner,
Where will you stand,
In that day when God's a-going to rain down fire?
Oh, you gambling man–where will you stand?
You whore-mongering man–where will you stand?
Liars and backsliders–where will you stand?
In that great day when God's a-going to rain down fire?

And God will divide the sheep from the goats,
The one on the right hand and the other on the left.
And to them on the right God's a-going to say:
Enter into my kingdom.
And those who've come through great tribulations,
And been washed in the blood of the Lamb,
They will enter in–
Clothed in spotless white,
With starry crowns on their heads,
And silver slippers on their feet,
And harps in their hands;--

And two by two they'll walk

Up and down the golden street,
Feasting on the milk and honey
Singing new songs to Zion,
Chattering with the angels
All around the Great White Throne.

And to them on the left God's a-going to say:
Depart from me into everlasting darkness,
Down into the bottomless pit.
And the wicked, like lumps of lead will start to fall,
Headlong for seven days and nights they'll fall,
Plumb into the big, black, red-hot mouth of hell,
Belching out fire and brimestone.
And their cries like howling, yelping dogs,
Will go up with the fire and smoke from hell,
But God will stop his ears.

Too late sinner! Too late!
Good-bye sinner! Good-bye!
In hell, sinner! In hell!
Beyond the reach of the love of God.

And I hear a voice, crying, crying:
Time shall be no more!
Time shall be no more!
Time shall be no more!
And the sun will go out like a candle in the wind,
The stars will fall like cinders,
The moon will turn to dripping blood,
And the sea will burn like tar;
And the earth will melt away and be dissolved,
And the sky will roll up like a scroll.
With a wave of his hand God will blot out time,
And start the wheel of eternity.[212]

AMEN! COME, LORD JESUS!

APPENDIX A
GLOSSARY OF TERMS

AD.—Anno Domini, refers to the period of the Christian era from the time of Christ to the present day.

A-Millennialism.—A system of eschatology (doctrine of the last things) espousing no literal earthly millennium or thousand-year reign of Jesus Christ on the earth. The millennium is entirely spiritual in nature.

Apocalypse.—A word describing the last book of the Bible, Revelation. It is derived from the Greek word, ἀποκάλυψις (*apokalupsis*), "to reveal." Literally meaning to "lay bare," it refers to a revelation or uncovering, making known what has been hidden.

Apocalyptic.—The adjectival form of "apocalypse." It describes literature of a specific nature and includes not only the Book of Revelation but also the book of Daniel. It can also be applied to sections of the writings in Joel, Amos and Zechariah. Even the Psalms, specifically Psalm 17 and 18, contain writings concerning the glories of the Messianic era, and therefore, could be described as apocalyptic.

Balaamites.—Based upon the account in the book of Numbers, these people were Jewish descendants of those Jews tricked by Balak to participate in immoral acts during a festival which he declared. These acts resulted in the execution of 24,000 Jewish men. The reference regarding the church at Pergamos speaks of the immorality that the church was tolerating among its congregation.

BCE.—Before the Christian Era. This period includes all historical periods prior to the appearance of Christ.

Eschatology.—Derived from ἔσχατος (*eschatos*), "last" and λόγος (*logos*), "study of." So this is the discipline of studying last things or the end of the world.

Free City.—A city granted self-governance by a king or emperor. Some cities were even authorized to issued coinage which would bear the name of the city.

Gematria.—A system of alphanumeric codes designed to assign a numerical value to a name, word or phrase based on its letters. Although this book refers to the Hebrew Gematria, it has also been applied in numerous other languages.

Gnostics.—Derived from the Greek γνῶσις (*gnōsis*) meaning "to know," it is a complex miasma of religious thought based mostly upon illusion and enlightenment. With respect to the historical Jesus, Gnostics can be divided into two classes. (1) Cerinthian Gnostics who taught that the Christ and Jesus are separate beings. Begun by Cerinthus who was educated in Egyptian matters declared that "the Christ" came upon Jesus at his baptism and left him just prior to his crucifixion. (2) Docetic Gnostics who taught that Jesus only appeared to have a body; his human form was actually an illusion.
Judaizers.—Christians, both Jew and non-Jew, who support the idea that it is necessary for one to adopt the customs and laws contained in the Law of Moses in order to become a Christian. This concept was the central focus of the Council of Jerusalem in AD 50.
Millennium.—A period of 1,000 years mentioned in Revelation 20. It refers to a time after the return of Christ when Satan will be bound in chains and during which the saints of God will reign with the Messiah King.
Nicolaitans.—Prominently extant in Ephesus and Pergamos, they are believers in a kind of spiritual hedonism. They held that man can freely partake in sin because the Law of God is no longer binding, therefore, it was lawful to engage in certain acts like eating things sacrificed to idols, and to commit fornication, in opposition to the decree of the Church rendered in Acts 15:20, 29. Followers of Nicolas of Antioch, they believed that a person's spirit is saved by faith in Jesus Christ. But because humans live in the flesh where evil is ceaselessly present, one will always be a sinner and continue in sin.
Post-Millennialism.—A system of eschatology that believes that man will become progressively good, and Christ will reward that goodness by the Second Coming. They consider that we are actually living in the millennial period now and hold that, during this indefinitely long period of time, Christians are responsible for expanding the Kingdom of God in the world.
Pre-Millennialism.—A system of eschatology that espouses the belief that man will become progressively and sufficiently evil that God's nostrils cannot tolerate the stench from such sin. God will summon His saints at the Rapture, and the Tribulation will begin. After seven years, Christ will return and reign on earth for 1,000 years with His saints.

APPENDIX B
BEATITUDES OF THE REVELATION

1:5 -- "The one who reads this is blessed."

14:13 -- "The dead who die in the Lord from now on are blessed."

16:15 -- "The one who is alert and remains clothed . . . sees his shamc is blcsscd."

19:9 -- "Those invited to the marriage feast of the Lamb are fortunate (blessed)."

20:6 -- "Blessed and holy is the one who shares in the first resurrection."

22:7 -- "The one who keeps the prophetic words of this book is blessed."

22:14 -- "Blessed are those who wash their robes."

FOOTNOTES

1 Ray Summers, *Worthy is the Lamb*, 20.
END OF CHAPTER 1
2 I am indebted to the late Dr. John Bisagno, former pastor of the First Baptist Church of
Houston, Texas, for the inspiration of these keys.
3 Video Sermon, Mike Glenn, December 15, 2019 "The Last Battle."
4 See references to Jesus as the "first-born" or "first-fruit" in Romans 8:29, Colossians 1:18,
Hebrews 1:6, Acts 26:23, 1 Corinthians 15:20 and Revelation 1:4.
5 John Pratt,
http://www.johnpratt.com/items/docs/lds/meridian/2014/mary.html
6 Arthur Weigall, *Nero* (New York: G. P. Putnam Sons, 1930), p. 3f.
7 "The Latter Rain," http://www.latter-rain.com/eccle/domit.htm
8 https://biblearchaeology.org/research/new-testament-era/3080-the-king-and-i-the-apostle-john-and-emperor-domitian-part-1
9 Irenaeus, Ante-Nicene Fathers, vol. I, p. 416.
10 Lance Ralston, Sermon, November 20, 2014, Calvary Chapel, Oxnard, California, https://calvaryoxnard.org/four-ways-to-interpret-the-book-of-revelation
11 Merrill Tenney, *Interpreting Revelation*, (Grand Rapids: William Eerdmans Publishing
Company, 1957), 146.
12 Patrick Zukeran, https://probe.org/four-views-of-revelation
END OF CHAPTER 2
13 See Appendix A for a listing of the Beatitudes of Revelation.
14 See chapter 2, subhead "The Resource" for an explanation of the Holy Spirit.
15 McDowell, *The Meaning and Message of the Book of Revelation*, p. 27.
16 Summers, *Worthy is the Lamb*, p. 103.
17 See Joel 2:31, 1 Thessalonians 5:2, Revelation 6:12-17 or Matthew 24:19-31.
18 Justin Martyr, *First Apology*, chapter 67.
19 Compare this account to a description of the garments of the high priest in Exodus 28, or the
clothing that adorned an ancient king.

20 See Exodus 15:6.
21 Recall the words of 1:8.
END OF CHAPTER 3
22 T*he Epistles of Ignatius*, "The Epistle to the Ephesians," XII.
23 Ray Summers, *Worthy is the Lamb*, chapter 4, p. 6
24 Audio Sermon, Dr. John Bisagno, September 30, 1979.
25 See Revelation 1:8, 17-18.
26 Audio Sermon, Dr. John Bisagno, October 21, 1979.
27 1 Kings 18:20-29
28 Summers, p. 116.
29 McDowell, p. 53.
30 See chapter 2, subhead "The Resource" for an explanation of the Holy Spirit.
31 Summers, p. 121.
32 Summers, p. 122.
33 McDowell, p. 57.
34 McDowell, p. 60.
35 A form of this quotation has been attributed to Alexis DeTocqueville in *Democracy in America*. The actual quote is, "America is great because America is good, and if America ever ceases to be good America will cease to be great." There is some controversy as to whether he actually spoke this statement. Nevertheless, its truth cannot be questioned.
36 *Interpreter's Dictionary of the Bible*, Vol. 3, p. 71.
37 Summers, *Worthy is the Lamb*, p. 124.
38 Summers, *Worthy is the Lamb*, p. 114.
END OF CHAPTER 4
39 Ken Cayce, www.discoverrevelation.com, "Rapture."
40 Gervan Spinney, Sermon, July 8, 2018.
41 H. E. Dana, *The Epistles and the Apocalypse of John*, p. 115.
42 See also 1 John 4:18, Revelation 1:17; 2:10.
43 For a complete explanation of this theological tenet, I refer you to Archibald M. Hunter,
Interpreting Paul's Gospel (Philadelphia: The Westminster Press), 1954, pp.17-63.
44 Audio Sermon, Dr. John Bisagno, January 13, 1980.
45 John's skill as a dramatist is aptly described in *The Signs of the Christ* by J. Rodney Taylor,
published by Innovo Publishing, 2018, especially pp. 144f.

46 John Henry Thayer, *Greek-English Lexicon of the New Testament* (Grand Rapids: Zondervan
Publishing House, 1966), p. 347.
47 See Colossians 1:16-17.
48 See Luke 21:28.
END OF CHAPTER 5
49 See also Exodus 19:19; 1 Samuel 2:10.
50 See chapter 5 of this book.
51 The number four is important to this part of the Revelation narrative. The number 4 derives its meaning from creation. On the fourth day of what is called "creation week" God completed the material universe. We see the use of the number throughout the Bible. For example, there are four seasons in the year; the fourth of the Ten Commandments has to do with keeping the Sabbath holy, a day directly related to creation week; the Garden of Eden divided into four rivers; Roman soldiers divided Jesus' clothing into four parts; and there are four Gospels which tell the story of Jesus' life on earth.
52 See also Matthew 24:15 and Daniel 11:31.
53 See also Joel 1:15-2:11.
54 *God's Trombones*, "The Great Judgment Day."
55 Summers, p. 142.
56 See also Revelation 7:9, 13-15; Matthew 24:9-14; Mark 13:9-13; and Luke 21:12-19.
57 See Revelation 9:21 and 16:17f.
58 Herbert Morrison is best known for his reporting of the Hindenburg disaster of May 6, 1937. This is a quote from that radio broadcast.
59 James Weldon Johnson, "Judgment Day," *God's Trombones*.
60 See Romans 11:25-27.
61 Summers, p. 153.
62 Joshua 6
63 Audio Sermon, Dr. John Bisagno, March 2, 1980.
64 "What Will You Do with Jesus?" by Albert B. Simpson, 1905.
END OF CHAPTER 6
65 McDowell, p. 103.
66 Tim LaHaye
67 Hal Lindsey, *There's A New World Coming*, p. 116.

68 R. P. Turco, O. B. Toon, T. P. Ackerman, J. B. Pollack and Carl Sagan, "Nuclear Winter: Global Consequences of Multiple Nuclear Explosions," *Science*, December 23, 1983.
69 See also Deuteronomy 28:49; Hosea 8:1; Habakkuk 1:8.
70 See also Luke 10:18.
71 Audio Sermon, Dr. John Bisagno, March 16, 1980.
72 See John 5:17.
73 See Genesis 15:18.
74 See Numbers 21:6-9.
75 Nikki Haley: https://www.youtube.com/watch?v=nN51HBGvUFo
76 https://billygraham.org/story/billy-graham-my-heart-aches-for-america.
77 Wallace, Foy E. "Commentary on Revelation 10:1". "Foy E. Wallace's Commentary on the Book of Revelation". https:https://www.studylight.org/commentaries/foy/revelation-10.html. 1966.
78 See Luke 1:32-33.
79 Echoed in Matthew 24:15-16.
80 Much of the following information can be found in a May 25, 2019, interview of Chris Katulka by the host Steve Conover of "Friends of Israel Today." For more information on the history of efforts to rebuild the Temple, see Randall Price, Rose Guide to the Temple (Peabody, MA: Rose Publishing), 2012. See also William L. Krewson, Jerome and the Jews (Eugene, OR: Wipf & Stock), 2017.
81 McDowell, p. 122.
82 Refer to Revelation 19:11-21; Daniel 2:34-35.
83 1 Thessalonians 3:13.
84 See Daniel 7:13-14, 27.
85 Cross-reference with Revelation 3:12; 7:15; 14:15, 17; 15:5-8; 16:1, 17.
86 See Exodus 25:11-22.
87 William Hendriksen, *More than Conquerors*, Grand Rapids: Baker Books, 1967, p. 133.
END OF CHAPTER 7
88 See Revelation 12:1, 3; 13:13-14; 15:1; 16:14; and 19:20.
89 Refer to Isaiah 54:5-6; Jeremiah 3:6-8; Ezekiel 16:32; Hosea 2:16.
90 In the Old Testament, New Moons were often associated with worship. See 1 Chronicles 23:31; 2 Chronicles 2:4; 8:13; Psalm 81:3.
91 See a similar dream story of Joseph in Genesis 37:9-11.

92 See Matthew 24:15-21.
93 See Isaiah 14:12-15.
94 See 2 Peter 2:4; Jude 6.
95 See Matthew 2:13-18.
96 "Christianity in the UK," Faith Survey, 08 May 2020.
97 "Dramatic Drop in Church Attendance in Scotland," *BBC News*, 16 April 2017.
98 Susan Jones, "Gallup: 89% of Americans Say They Believe in God, Down From Past Decades," https://www.cnsnews.com/news/article/susan-jones/gallup-89-americans-say-they-believe-god-down-past-decades.
99 Dalia Fahmy, "Key Findings about Americans' Belief in God," https://www.pewresearch.org/fact-tank/2018/04/25/key-findings-about-americans-belief-in-god.
100 Cross-reference Revelation 19:15.
101 Verse 5. See also John 10.
102 See Acts 1:9.
103 https://www.lifenews.com/2019/12/31/abortion-was-the-leading-cause-of-death-worldwide-in-2019-killing-42-million-people/
104 https://www.lifenews.com/2019/12/31/abortion-was-the-leading-cause-of-death-worldwide-in-2019-killing-42-million-people/
105 Ken Cayce, www.discoverrevelation.com
106 Compare Exodus 19:4 and Deuteronomy 32:11.
107 See Romans 9:27.
108 Hendriksen, *More Than Conquerors*, p. 144.
109 See Isaiah 57:20-21.
110 See Revelation 15:2.
111 See 2 Thessalonians 2:3-5.
112 Ken Cayce, www.discoverrevelation.com
113 This conclusion is drawn by using Hebrew number equivalents to the Greek letters for Nero Caesar.
114 Hal Lindsey, *There's a New World Coming*, p. 183.
115 https://www.oikoumene.org/en/about-us
END OF CHAPTER 8
116 See Jeremiah 2:3 where they were called "firstfruits" when Jehovah brought them out of Egypt.
117 See 1 Peter 1:12.
118 Ken Cayce, www.discoverrevelation.com
119 More detailed commentary will be offered at chapter 18.

120 See Luke 16:23-24.
121 See Matthew 3:12; 25:41; Mark 9:48.
122 Audio Sermon, Dr. John Bisagno, June 15, 1980.
123 Ray Summers, p. 182.
124 See Matthew 24:30.
125 See Matthew 13:39-43.
126 Hal Lindsey, *There's a New World Coming*, p. 193.
127 Reference 6:9-11 and 8:3-5.
128 Audio Sermon, Dr. John Bisagno, June 15, 1980.
END OF CHAPTER 9
129 David Smith, *The Disciple's Commentary on the New Testament*, p. 672 quoted in Ray Summers, Worthy is the Lamb, p. 184.
130 William Milligan, The Book of Revelation, p. 260 quoted in Ray Summers, *Worthy is the Lamb*, p. 184.
131 The use of the Greek word ἐπί, *epi* with a verb in the accusative tense means "on" or "upon." Here it is used with ἑστῶτας, *hestōtas*, the accusative form of the word ἵστημι, *histēmi*, "to stand."
132 Kevin Halloran, https://www.kevinhalloran.net/jim-elliot-quote-he-is-no-fool/
133 Audio Sermon, Dr. John Bisagno, June 22, 1980.
134 Audio Sermon, Dr. John Bisagno, June 22, 1980.
135 Hebrews 2:3
136 See also Exodus 9:9-11, Deuteronomy 28:27; Job 2:7.
137 Recall the horror of seeing victims of the bombings of Hiroshima and Nagasaki who experienced hideous lesions.
138 See Exodus 7:20-25.
139 See Romans 1:20-23.
140 Recall Revelation 6:9-10.
141 Be aware of the difference between "revenge," to get even, and "avenge," to set things straight. Here God is avenging the saints.
142 See references to darkness in Amos 5:18; Nahum 1:8; Zephaniah 1:15.
143 https://www.theguardian.com/world/2015/jun/03/isis-closes-ramadi-dam-gates-cutting-off-water-to-pro-government-towns
144 https://samsontours.com/stop/the-list-of-battles-fought-at-megiddo-176
145 See Leviticus 11:10-11, 41.
146 Ken Cayce, www.discoverrevelation.com, chapter 16.

147 Stephen M. Miller Blog, “Valley of Armageddon,” January 4, 2013, https://stephenmillerbooks.com/2013/01/valley-of-armageddon.
148 For references to the “time of trouble,” see Jeremiah 30:4-7; Daniel 12:1; Matthew 24:15-22.
149 Lindsey, *There's a New World Coming*, p. 214.
150 See Isaiah 13:6-13.
151 Sermon by C. Bouwman, https://yarrow.canrc.org/a-bit-to-read/280/wrath-of-god-in-todays-world, March 25, 2011.
END OF CHAPTER 10
152 Audio Sermon, Dr. John Bisagno, July 13, 1980.
153 Chuck Missler, https://www.youtube.com/watch?v=3d-bFfzLcTE, September 4, 2013.
154 See Daniel 2:42; 7:7; 7:23; and 7:24.
155 See 1 John 2:18, 22; 4:3; 2 John 7.
156 See Matthew 24:15 and Revelation 19:20.
157 Chuck Missler, https://www.youtube.com/watch?v=3d-bFfzLcTE, September 4, 2013.
158 Compare Jeremiah 51:6-9, 45 and 2 Corinthians 6:17.
159 Compare Isaiah 47:7-8.
160 Recall another time when Babylon fell so swiftly, in one evening, in Daniel 5:30.
161 Audio Sermon, Dr. John Bisagno, July 20, 1980.
162 Ella Lee, “Fact Check: A Cashless Society isn't imminent and wouldn't mean total end of cash,” https://www.usatoday.com/story/news/factcheck/2020/07/27/fact-check-cashless-society-isnt-imminent-wouldnt-eliminate-cash/5415027002/
END OF CHAPTER 11
163 See 1 Corinthians 13:12f.
164 Ken Cayce, www.discoverrevelation.com, chapter 19.
165 Lindsey, There's a New World Coming, p. 246.
166 Audio Sermon, Dr. John Bisagno, July 27, 1980.
167 Paraphrase of “Go Down, Death,” from James Weldon Johnson, *God's Trombones*.
168 Audio Sermon, Dr. John Bisagno, July 27, 1980.
169 See Revelation 14:20; also a reminder of Isaiah 63:1-4.
170 See Isaiah 63:3 and Joel 3:13).
171 See the fulfilment of the angels' prophecy in Luke 1:33.
END OF CHAPTER 12

172 William Hendriksen, *More Than Conquerors*, p. 187.
173 Hal Lindsey, *There's A New World Coming*, p. 264.
174 William Hendriksen, *More Than Conquerors*, pp. 191-192.
175 William F. Arndt and F. Wilbur Gingrich, A Greek-English Lexicon of the New Testament (Cambridge: University Press, 1957), p. 336.
176 Audio Sermon, Dr. John Bisagno, August 10, 1980.
177 See Acts 17:31 and 2 Timothy 4:1.
178 See Psalm 139:16.
179 Edward A. McDowell, *The Meaning and Message of the Book of Revelation*, p. 206.
180 See 1 Corinthians 15:26.
181 Hal Lindsey, *There's a New World Coming*, p. 273-274.
END OF CHAPTER 13
182 See Isaiah 65:17 and Isaiah 66:22.
183 See 2 Peter 3:10. See also Psalm 105:25-26; Luke 21:33; Hebrews 1:10-12.
184 Consider the works of H. B. Swete, *The Apocalypse of St. John*, Isbon Beckwith, *The Apocalypse of John*, David Smith, *The Disciple's Commentary on the New Testament*, Donald W. Richardson, *The Revelation of Jesus Christ*.
185 Recall the words of the great hymn, "In the Garden."
186 See 1 Corinthians 15:54-57.
187 See 1 Peter 1:4; Romans 8:16-17.
188 A quotation from William Marcy, a senator from New York, 1832.
189 See Revelation 2:7; 2:11; 2:17; 2:26; 3:5; 3:12; and 3:21.
190 Edward A. McDowell, *The Meaning and Message of the Book of Revelation*, p. 210.
191 Recall 1 Corinthians 13:12.
192 See 2 Corinthians 5:1.
193 A stadia is approximately 600 feet.
194 William Hendriksen, *More Than Conquerors*, p. 202.
195 A cubit is 18 inches or a foot and a half.
196 Lyrics from the final verse of "Amazing Grace," by John Newton.
197 See Isaiah 2:4.
198 Ray Summers, *Worthy is the Lamb*, p. 214.
199 Hal Lindsey. *There's A New World Coming*, p. 287.

200 See also John 1:18 and 1 Timothy 6:16.
201 https://hymnary.org/text/the_sands_of_time_are_sinking
END OF CHAPTER 14
202 See Daniel 9:24; 12:4; 12:9.
203 From "There Is a Fountain Filled with Blood," words by William Cowper, 1731-1800.
204 St. Augustine of Hippo, Confessions, *(Lib 1,1-2,2.5,5: CSEL 33, 1-5)*.
205 David Russel Schilling, "Knowledge Doubling Every 12 Months, Soon to be Every 12 Hours," April 19, 2013; https://industrytap.com/knowledge-doubling-every-12-months-soon-to-be-every-12-hours/3950
206 See 1 Timothy 3:1-5.
END OF CHAPTER 15
207 Hal Lindsey, *There's a New World Coming*, p. 265.
208 See verses 22-23.
209 See Psalm 16:8-11.
210 See Genesis 12:1-3.
211 See verses 1-4.
212 James Weldon Johnson, "Judgment Day," *God's Trombones*, New York: The Viking Press, 1954, 53-56.

Made in the USA
Columbia, SC
09 May 2023